POLITICAL SOCIOLOGY

OPPRESSION, RESISTANCE, AND THE STATE

Davita Silfen Glasberg
University of Connecticut

Deric Shannon
University of Connecticut

Los Angeles | London | New Delhi
Singapore | Washington DC

For information:

Pine Forge Press
An Imprint of SAGE
  Publications, Inc.
2455 Teller Road
Thousand Oaks,
  California 91320
E-mail: order@sagepub.com

SAGE Publications India Pvt. Ltd.
B 1/I 1 Mohan Cooperative
  Industrial Area
Mathura Road, New Delhi 110 044
India

SAGE Publications Ltd.
1 Oliver's Yard
55 City Road
London EC1Y 1SP
United Kingdom

SAGE Publications
  Asia-Pacific Pte. Ltd.
33 Pekin Street #02-01
Far East Square
Singapore 048763

Printed in the United States of America

Library of Congress Cataloging-in-Publication Data

Glasberg, Davita Silfen.
Political sociology : oppression, resistance, and the state / Davita Glasberg,
Deric Shannon.
      p. cm.
Includes bibliographical references and index.
ISBN 978-1-4129-8040-1 (pbk.)
    1. Political sociology. 2. Oppression (Psychology). 3. Social movements.
I. Shannon, Deric. II. Title.

JA76.G54 2011
306.2—dc22   2010040661

This book is printed on acid-free paper.

10   11   12   13   14   10   9   8   7   6   5   4   3   2   1

Acquisitions Editor:	David Repetto
Associate Editor:	Julie Nemer
Editorial Assistant:	Maggie Stanley
Production Editor:	Karen Wiley
Copy Editor:	Megan Markanich
Proofreader:	Penelope Sippel
Typesetter:	C&M Digitals (P) Ltd.
Indexer:	Maria Sosnowski
Cover Designer:	Gail Buschman
Marketing Manager:	Erica DeLuca
Permissions Editor:	Karen Ehrmann

POLITICAL SOCIOLOGY

Contents

Preface

Interest in political sociology has ebbed and flowed with the intensity of political events. Keen interest piqued during the Vietnam War and its aftermath, waned somewhat during the Reagan years, and now appears to be resurging once again in the wake of the terrorist attacks of September 11, 2001, and the subsequent wars in Iraq and Afghanistan and the presidential election process of 2008. The severe global recession of 2008 through 2010 has also grabbed the attention of many people eager to understand how and why such a significant economic and political quake could happen and arguably galvanized the likes of the Tea Party movement in the United States. Indeed, the current wave of interest began well before the September 11 attacks: *The American Sociological Association's Guide to Graduate Departments of Sociology* lists 52 graduate-degree-granting institutions as offering political sociology as one of their specialties. Political sociology has one of the largest section memberships of the American Sociological Association. And student interest, at both the graduate and undergraduate levels, appears to be increasing. Political sociology is identified by many of the top graduate programs in sociology as one area of graduate qualifying examination taken by a significant number, if not a majority, of students. These suggest a rising demand for materials to teach political sociology.

Oddly enough, there is a frustrating limitation of political sociology textbooks available, and those that are currently in print do a variable job of covering the main theoretical currents and empirical research issues one would need to cover when teaching such a course. Further, while the study of the intersections of race, class, gender, and sexualities is increasingly a focus in sociology, none of the existing textbooks deals with these as important relative to a study of political sociology. In addition, questions of compliance and resistance are not satisfactorily covered. The question of how we may come to accept and comply with the interests of dominants in society, even when this may contradict our own interests, is at least partially explained by exploring issues and processes of political socialization. However, this is often left unexplored. And while social movements are often understood among sociologists to be an important organizational mechanism used by those with relatively little power to resist and challenge power structures, existing textbooks devote variable attention to its analysis. Without a focused examination of social movements, students may be left with an overriding belief that power structures are inexorable and unchangeable, a conclusion many sociologists would be loathe to encourage in our students.

Finally, theoretical perspectives in political sociology largely frame their analyses on class-based concepts and issues of power and the state. None of them explore the question of multiple oppressions. But how do we understand oppression beyond class-based oppression? Are the prevalent models of class-based theories of power and the state sufficient, such that we simply need to "add and stir" concepts of gender, racialization, and heteronormativity for insight? Or is there a need to reconceptualize our framework and develop a more flexible view of the relationship among the state, society, and oppression that enables us to understand multiple oppressions? This book explores possible ways to respond to these questions.

The book is intended for use in political sociology courses as well as sociology courses in race, class, and gender and theories of the state. It may serve as a comprehensive text for the courses or as a core text to be supplemented with other readings and materials (such as videos, for example). It can also be used as a monograph in addition to other monographs. Students who take most of these courses are commonly juniors and seniors (students in Sociology of Race, Class, and Gender commonly are also first-year students and sophomores) majoring in sociology, political science, history, anthropology, peace studies, women's studies, African American studies, Asian American studies, Latino studies, labor studies, and philosophy. They have usually taken an introductory sociology, social problems, or political science course as preparation. This book is intended to help students develop a wide array of concepts and theoretical perspectives so that they may analyze and understand new developments in the world around them after they leave the course. It also intends to propose a multidimensional view of the relationship among the state, society, and oppression and inequality that blends elements of the prevalent theories of power and the state. That proposed view allows for greater analytical flexibility to better understand gendered, racialized, and heteronormative relationships as well as the more commonly explored class-based relationships among the state, society, and multiple oppressions.

Unique Features

The central theme of the book is the interplay among power, inequality and multiple oppressions, and the state. That is, the book takes critical issue with the idea that power is random, dispersed, and shared by all so that any one interest at any point in time may rise to have its interests met. Instead, the book focuses on the structure of power and inequality to examine the *patterns* of who gains, who loses, and why. In general, then, the book takes a critical perspective.

Moreover, we introduce commonly ignored theoretical perspectives on the question of power, the state, and oppression: anarchist theory, queer theory, and poststructuralism. We discuss what anarchist theory, queer theory, and poststructuralist theory is (and is not) and engage in a comparative analysis of these perspectives with the more commonly acknowledged frameworks.

In addition, since sociology increasingly is moving toward the recognition that the main organizing principles in society are race, class, gender, and sexualities, it is imperative to talk about the dynamic tension between the intersection of racialization, class, gendering, and heteronormativity and political economy. Political sociology, then, should be able to provide some tools for understanding how these affect and are affected by power inequalities. As such, the book will appeal to examples of these and will devote several chapters to exploring gendering, racialization, class, and heteronormative dynamics.

That said, the book does not adopt a conspiracy position or assume that power is absolute so that elites or dominants always get their interests met while subordinates remain powerless. Instead, the book also explores paths of resistance, challenge, and subversion, particularly social movements. While there may be patterns defining who wins and who does not, this does not mean that those at the bottom of the power structures never manage to develop strategies to alter these patterns at least occasionally.

Finally, the book explores avenues to developing a view that incorporates the elements of different perspectives on the question of the relationship between the state and society and that enables us to examine multiple oppressions. We offer a conceptual framework for addressing this challenge.

Pedagogical Aids

Each chapter concludes with a set of critical thinking and discussion questions as a pedagogical aid for classroom analysis or writing assignment exercises. These are designed to facilitate application of the frameworks and concepts introduced in the chapter to major contemporary issues or current events.

Several chapters offer charts and diagrams to help students process conceptual ideas, data, and a wide range of perspectives. Chapter 1 provides diagrams to illustrate the institutionalized power of oppression. Chapter 2 offers a comparative chart of power structure theories and a chart of dimensions of power. Chapter 4 provides graphs and tables of data to aid students in their understanding of patterns of participation in the electoral process. Chapter 5 includes a comparative chart of theories of the state. Chapter 6 offers diagrams of three possible scenarios of relative deprivation. Chapter 7 includes diagrams of our reconceptualized framework for analyzing the relationship between the state and society and a chart of the dimensions of each of the main concepts in that framework.

Acknowledgments

This book has been a huge undertaking and has involved countless others' collective efforts in helping us think and talk through our ideas, brainstorm issues, and identify resources. We thank Daniel Skidmore who helped sort out Bob Jessop's main concepts; Sandra Bender Fromson, who, as a graduate student, helped to diagram our reconceptualization of the relationship between the state and society; and William T. Armaline, who read countless versions of our ideas. We also want to thank Noel Cazenave for his generosity in allowing us to use his wonderful classroom diagram of the institutionalized power that is white racism and adapt it to our analysis here. And we thank the many graduate students who have listened to and commented on the reconceptualized model we present here through several political sociology seminars. We are indebted to the reviewers Kathy Tucci Edwards (Ashland Community and Technical College), P. Rafael Hernandez-Arias (University of New Mexico), Yvonne A. Braun (University of Oregon), and Katja M. Guenther (University of California, Riverside) for their incredible attention to detail, their invigorating challenge to us for clarity and precision, and their invaluable suggestions, all of which helped us develop a better manuscript. And we are grateful for the wonderful editorial work and stewardship of our work from David Repetto, editorial assistant Maggie Stanley, and copy editor Megan Markanich. It was a great pleasure to work with all of them!

Deric Shannon would like to thank Davita Silfen Glasberg (for letting me in on such a wonderful project and being a brilliant teacher and mentor), Nancy Naples, Gaye Tuchman, and Clinton Sanders (for their mentorship and help), and the memberships of the Anarchist Studies Network in Europe and the North American Anarchist Studies Network (for recognizing and acting on the fact that knowledge construction is explicitly political).

Davita would like to thank Deric for a delightful coauthoring adventure. I learned a great deal, and I expect I'll learn a great deal more as we collaborate in the future. And I'd like to thank my children Gillian and Morgan for their kind indulgence and patience while I was engrossed in my thoughts, and my conversation became dominated with these ideas. They constantly remind me what is most important in this life. I wish for them the freedom and the right to explore and live what is most important to them and the power to fully access their human rights.

1

Oppression, Resistance, and the State

An Introduction

Pick up any newspaper or tune in to any newscast on television and you will undoubtedly see or hear at least a few items concerning the advantages of some and the oppression of many in the United States: tax policy reform that enriches the powerful and affluent while not benefiting the working class or the poor significantly (or at all); the disproportionate representation of the poor and working class in the military deployed to war in Iraq and Afghanistan, in contrast to the absence in these troops of the wealthy; the disenfranchisement of thousands of voters of color in the 2000 and 2004 presidential elections; and the struggle of women to preserve their reproductive rights. Clearly, relatively few people are advantaged by policy and practice, while the great majority is not. Sociologists often refer to this imbalance as an issue of *oppression*.

When sociologists use the term *oppression*, they are referring to "those attitudes, behaviors, and pervasive and systematic social arrangements by which members of one group are exploited and subordinated while members of another group are granted privileges" (Bohmer & Briggs, 1991, p. 155). Oppression is not simply about one or more groups' deprivation or exploitation; it is a relationship. To speak of some people's disadvantage is to imply others' privilege. The relationship, then, is one of a power imbalance in which one group has the ability to secure and maintain its advantages relative to those of others. To speak of the economic, political, and social disadvantages of women means to speak of the prerogatives of being male in a patriarchal society. To talk of the exploitation of the poor and the working class implies the relative privilege of the affluent. To discuss the oppression of people of color in a racialized society is to also discuss the advantaged position of whiteness. The power imbalances of oppression also mean that one group enjoys unearned privileges or undeserved enrichment and others unjust impoverishment and deprivation. Undeserved enrichment is "the unjust theft of labor or resources by one group . . . from another group . . ." (Feagin, 2001, p. 18). Unjust impoverishment is the inequitable deprivation suffered by the oppressed. The dominance of the affluent, whites, and men derives from their unjust enrichment over centuries of the exploitation of the labor of workers, people of color, and women.

The notion of oppression does not necessarily mean that those who are among the privileged are individually to blame for their advantage or that they themselves oppressed the disadvantaged for their own gain any more than the exploited are themselves to blame for their oppression. Rather, the point here is that the accidents of birth accorded each of us our various positions, which means that the advantages enjoyed by the privileged are not necessarily the result of their own hard work. Likewise, the disadvantages of the oppressed are not necessarily their own doing. Instead, it is important to understand the structure of power inequalities as a fundamental feature of oppression and to explore how society may be structured so as to privilege one group over the other, regardless of individual efforts. That said, we are not arguing that such structures are written in stone, forever inexorable and unchangeable. Rather, organized collective struggles in systems of oppression may affect those relationships in significant ways.

Systems of oppression are not isolated from one another. Systems of oppression intersect in significant ways, forming a complex *matrix of domination* (Collins, 1990). People do not experience, for example, their gendered oppression one moment, their racialized oppression at another, and their class oppression at yet another. Rather, people live in their respective statuses of oppression simultaneously. So, for example, an individual is not a woman at one time during the day, white at another, and later middle class; that individual lives as a white, middle-class woman every moment of every day. As such, the intersectionality of multiple systems of oppression forms status inconsistencies so that an individual may be advantaged on some dimensions of this complex matrix of domination but disadvantaged on others. In the case of the hypothetical person here, she is advantaged in the dimensions of her class and her racialized group membership but disadvantaged in the dimension of her gender.

The question of what shapes these systems of oppression, singly and as intersecting multiple oppressions, and the positions individuals occupy in them implies the concept of power: What is power? Where does it come from? Who has it? Who doesn't? What are the processes and structures that affect power? Is power absolute? What are the dimensions of power? We will explore these questions in Chapter 2.

Discussions of power and oppression often suggest avenues through which people may seek to affect power structures. In what we commonly refer to as "democratic" systems, one oft-cited characteristic mechanism is the right to vote. Indeed, pluralists emphasize the power of voting as the key to nonelite participation and the means by which people may hold elites accountable. If voting is such a crucial element of power to the people, how widespread is electoral participation? Is there a pattern to who votes and who doesn't? How effective is voting for nonelites' ability to hold leaders accountable or to confront and challenge systems of oppression? Chapter 3 examines these questions about voting.

Moreover, since it would seem that those who are among the oppressed would be resistant to embracing a system that clearly disadvantages them, how is it that mass rebellions are so rare? What makes people accept, often without question, such a system? We will pursue this issue in Chapter 4.

Systems of Oppression and the State

As political sociologists, we stress the changing nature of power and politics; we therefore often see the polity and other institutions of power as arenas of conflict, not necessarily structures of cooperation and consensus. Since the state makes and enforces laws and budgetary decisions affecting the distribution of rewards, resources, and opportunities, the question of power also implies the relationship between the state and society: When the state makes policy, is there a pattern to whose interests get met and whose ignored? If there is, what is that pattern? What factors affect which interests get addressed and which get ignored? Is the state a neutral actor? Chapter 5 will examine these questions.

Structures of Oppression: Power, Politics, and the State

Structures of oppression are patterned and formidable. This raises the questions of what those patterns look like and what might affect those patterns.

What is the role of the state in generating and reproducing or resisting and changing structured systems of oppression and inequality? Since oppression generates contrasts of privilege and power for some and the subordination of many, questions of how these imbalances are replicated bear examination. Structures of oppression may imply unfairness and thus invite rebellion; they therefore require ideological justifications to elicit widespread support for or at least tacit acceptance of them. Structures of oppression are thus institutionalized and appear as unchangeable, natural, or objective rather than ideological. Of interest to political sociologists is the identification of the dominant structures of oppression and the relationship of these to political processes. Political sociologists also pursue the question of how the state might participate in the reproduction of these structures of oppression.

Political Economy

That economics appears to be a central feature to the patterns of inequality signals the need to examine that institution. However, the economy is not isolated from other institutions; there are important intersections between the economy and the state, which political sociologists call *political economy*. The institutions of the state and economy intersect and overlap, generating economic power differentials and systems of structured class inequality. These power differentials and systems of structured class inequality are in turn reinforced by the state. For example, *capitalism* is a political economy in which workers cooperate to produce wealth that is then privately appropriated by whoever hired the workers. Workers do not own the means of production; they only own their labor power, which they sell as a commodity to an employer who pays them a wage for the use of their labor. Capitalists own or control the means of production and therefore own the wealth that workers produce using these means (Marx, 1954).

The state in a capitalist political economy operates on the ideological assumption that it is the legitimate right of employers to own the wealth produced by workers. Inequality becomes based in part on whether one is an owner of the means of production or an owner only of labor power. This is the political economy that dominates the United States and most, if not all, of the industrialized Western nations.

Typically, sociologists suggest that capitalism stands in contrast to the political economy of *socialism*. In Marxist variants of socialism, the leading theory of socialism in most academic disciplines, production of goods and services in a socialist political economy may involve the social cooperation between workers to create wealth, as it does in capitalism. And workers may be paid a wage in exchange for their labor, just as they are in a capitalist economy. But where the means of production in a capitalist political economy are privately owned, these are more likely to be owned or controlled by the state in a socialist political economy according to the Marxist model. In such models, the state becomes the owner and controller of the wealth produced and therefore has the power to determine its distribution. This does not mean there is no economic inequality or oppression in a socialist political economy. However, the state's role in the political economy becomes more apparent in a socialist system because it is more likely to actively moderate economic inequality by providing or subsidizing basic goods and services for all. In such a system, for example, the state often becomes a provider of health care, housing, food, and income support when employment is unavailable. Variations of the socialist political economy can be found in Cuba and in Sweden and Norway, where elements of both capitalism and socialism structure the political economy as "social democracies" or "mixed economies."

Worker cooperation in the production of goods and services is also a key feature in *communist* political economies; but here the means of production are collectively owned by the workers themselves. In this case, ownership of the means of production positions the workers to determine the distribution of the wealth they produce. This does not necessarily mean everyone is guaranteed an equal share of the wealth. The decision-making process of the distribution of wealth may stimulate the creation of structured systems of inequality as workers strive to develop criteria to determine who gets what. Karl Marx and many other radical social theorists envisioned a system in which individuals' wealth production and share of that wealth would not be directly linked. Instead, wealth would be created from each according to one's ability to produce for the group as a whole and distributed to each according to one's need regardless of ability to produce (although Marx was not specific about how to evaluate either ability or need). Israeli kibbutzim are small-scale examples of a communist political economy (though not internationalist in scope), where the distribution of the wealth produced by the kibbutz as a whole is determined in part by the amount of time commitment made by individual members to the collective: Those who have been living on the kibbutz longest receive the greatest benefits. Structured inequality in this instance becomes a function of longevity and loyalty to the collective. Likewise, experiments in communist political economies can historically be found in revolutionary Spain in the early 1900s, particularly in areas largely controlled by the Spanish anarchists.

These political economy types are ideal types rather than distinctively different types. Most political economies are more a hybrid of these types so that differences between political economies are more likely to be ones of degree than of actual type. The United States, for example, is often cited as the prototype of the capitalist political economy; but the state has at various points in time taken an active role in subsidizing some basic needs for some people. Moreover, there are many worker-owned production facilities (such as Joseph Industries, Inc., a forklift parts manufacturer in Streetsboro, Ohio, that is entirely worker owned) and worker cooperatives (like Moosewood Inn in Ithaca, New York) in the United States. The former Soviet Union was also more of a hybrid than a pure communist political economy. The workers there did not own the means of production nor did they own or control the wealth they produced. Instead, the state owned the means of production, and workers were paid wages in exchange for their labor. The former Soviet Union's political economy was thus more one of "state capitalism" than pure communism.

The notion of political economy emphasizes that the economy is not necessarily a neutral institution. The interplay between the state and economic interests increases the likelihood that other factors will come into play in the functioning of the economy as well as in the production of state and economic policy. Think, for example, about market-based notions like supply and demand as the equation that affects wages and prices: The more demand there is for a product, and the scarcer its availability, the higher its price will be; similarly, the more demand there is for labor—and the fewer workers available—the higher wages will be. But is the equation this simple? What might affect the equation? Can the equation be manipulated?

Power and resource imbalances can alter how causal the connection between supply and demand is on one side and prices and wages on the other. It is possible to falsely create shortages or demand to boost prices, like spilling milk into the ocean or destroying cattle or crops; withholding supplies like oil to falsely create scarcity; or using advertising and credit cards to create demand that otherwise would not exist. Similarly, the equation of supply and demand can be manipulated to affect wages. It is possible to train too many workers for limited jobs to create a glut of workers and therefore depress wages, or, on the other hand, some (relatively powerful) workers may in fact *limit* the number of trained professionals so as to keep wages high (e.g., the American Medical Association [AMA] limits the number of medical school slots even though there is a severe shortage of physicians and health care workers in rural areas and in inner cities); organized workers can use collective bargaining and the fact that they are organized to force employers to boost wages and benefits in order to avert costly strikes and work slowdowns.

Note that policy making by legislators facilitates, enables, hinders, or makes illegal many of these activities to alter how straightforward the "law" of supply and demand is. Examples may include the right to collective bargaining, closed-shop policies, recognition of professionalization standards (such as those used by the AMA) to facilitate higher wages; price supports and subsidies to keep prices of products like agricultural products high enough to satisfy farmers; and antitrust and industrial deregulation legislation to limit prices (on the assumption that competition will keep prices down).

The political economic view of power and politics thus examines the relative roles of political and economic leaders in the power structure of society and in the production and reproduction of structured oppression. The intersection of the institutions of state and economy raise important questions about the distribution of rights, privileges, and opportunities. The ability of the state to collect revenues and to budget these for specific expenditures places state managers in a unique position to affect existing systems of inequality. Chapter 7 will pursue the question of how the state may shape the historical struggle between labor and capital as well as the struggle for gender and racial/ethnic rights.

Patriarchy

In addition to systems of class inequality and oppression, most states, including the United States, also maintain systems of gendered inequality and oppression, most commonly organized as a *patriarchy* in which males are more valued and generally more privileged than women. In a patriarchy, male dominance is ideologically justified as a natural, inalienable right, thereby enforcing the inferiority and subordination of women. Such is the case in arguments emphasizing that "anatomy is destiny": women's childbearing role and their hormones arguably make them biologically unsuited for a wide range of activities requiring intellect, reason, authority, physical strength, and speed. This produces women's restricted opportunities in education and labor force participation; lower wages for work; and relative economic, social, and political deprivation (Cubbins, 2001).

The significance of patriarchy lies less in sexist attitudes and discriminatory decisions individuals might make and more about social structures of institutionalized gendered power. As Figure 1.1 shows, both men and women are perfectly capable of being sexist individuals, engaging in discriminatory and hateful behavior based on others' sex. At the primary group level of social structures, both men and women have exhibited a capacity to engage in peer group violence, as witnessed in gang behavior and fraternity and sorority hazing. And at the formal organization level,

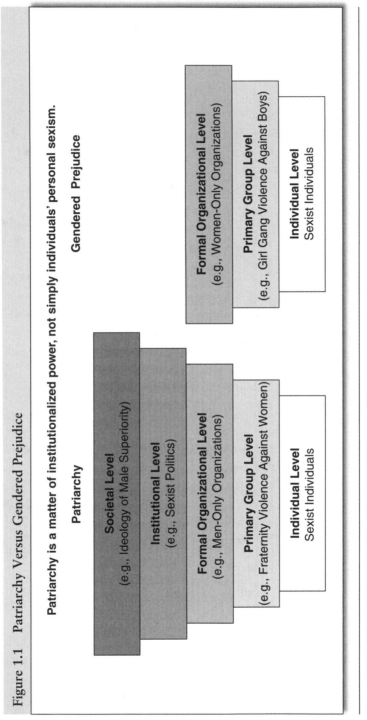

Figure 1.1 Patriarchy Versus Gendered Prejudice

Patriarchy is a matter of institutionalized power, not simply individuals' personal sexism.

Patriarchy

Gendered Prejudice

Societal Level
(e.g., Ideology of Male Superiority)

Institutional Level
(e.g., Sexist Politics)

Formal Organizational Level
(e.g., Men-Only Organizations)

Primary Group Level
(e.g., Fraternity Violence Against Women)

Individual Level
Sexist Individuals

Formal Organizational Level
(e.g., Women-Only Organizations)

Primary Group Level
(e.g., Girl Gang Violence Against Boys)

Individual Level
Sexist Individuals

Source: Adapted from the lectures of Noel Cazenave, University of Connecticut.

there have historically been no shortages of men-only and women-only organizations. Examples of gender-exclusive clubs include the Augusta Country Club and Veterans of Foreign Wars for men and Daughters of the American Revolution and any number of ladies auxiliaries of men's clubs. Thus, individuals, primary groups, and formal organizations might certainly be sexist and discriminatory, but they do not have the power to make their prejudices matter to others in fundamental ways. Only when sexist prejudices and discriminatory behaviors become embedded in the institutions of society do they have the ability to affect the life chances and empowerment of women simply on the basis of their sex. And that is an element of power not structurally available to women in the United States.

At the institutional and societal levels of social structure, there cease to be comparative counterparts for both men and women: Sexist politics privilege males at the institutional level as holders of power and have historically excluded women until the passage of the Nineteenth Amendment giving women the right to vote. Any empowerment of women at this level has required the endorsement of men in order to be included on the public agenda and to be given enough support to become policy. The same cannot be said of women, who have never controlled the political agenda or political structures and institutions in the United States. Such an arrangement has ensured that male privilege becomes embedded in the institutions so that it no longer requires individuals to be sexist in order to continue male privilege and dominance in the institutions. This gendered inequality and oppression are ideologically justified at the society level of social structure in which male superiority is buttressed by assertions that inequality based on sex is rooted in biological differences rather than by social constructions of difference and advantage.

Patriarchal systems of inequality and oppression thus historically institutionalized male privilege by denying women the right to political participation, thereby minimizing if not eliminating their opportunities to participate in the laws that circumscribe their existence. In extreme cases, the intersection of patriarchy as power and privilege and ideological conceptualizations of women as objects and possessions can often become institutionalized into a "rape culture" in which rape and other forms of violence against women are accepted as a common feature of society (Cuklanz, 2000; Feltey, 2001). For example, in the 1990s and into 2000, Serbs in Bosnia, Croatia, and Kosovo used systematic rape of women as a standard strategy of war to punish and terrorize populations viewed as inferior. So, too, has rape been used as a common tactic of terror and warfare in Darfur, Sudan.

Since the state legislates rights and responsibilities, it raises the question of the role of the state in gendering processes.

Racism

Some observers argue that what appears to be racialized oppression or inequality is a reflection of individual effort that is determined by biology. They argue that whites are genetically superior to people of color (particularly African Americans) (see, e.g., Herrnstein & Murray, 1994). However, these analyses have been severely criticized for lack of irrefutable scientific support. Instead, critics argue that these arguments represent social constructions of the meaning of race, which are then ideologically justified and reinforced. Racism is a power structure of oppression.

Similar to structures of patriarchy, the significance of racism does not depend upon individuals' racist discriminatory decisions and actions; it derives from social structures of institutionalized racialized power. As Figure 1.2 shows, in the United States both whites and people of color can be racist as individuals who may discriminate against others and behave in hateful ways based on others' perceived race. At the primary group level of social structures, both whites and people of color may participate in peer group violence. As in patriarchy, one can see this occur in conflicts between racialized youth gangs and in fraternities and sororities that remain exclusively of one racialized group. At the formal organization level, there are many examples of racially exclusive organizations, such as whites-only country clubs and white-power neo-Nazi organizations, and black churches and black separatist organizations. While individuals, primary groups, and formal organizations might certainly be discriminatory, they do not have the power to make their prejudices matter to others in fundamental ways. It is only when prejudices and discriminatory behaviors become fully embedded in the institutions of society that they have the power to affect the life chances and privileges of whole groups of people based on their racial categories. And that is not structurally available to people of color in the United States.

Notice that there are no comparative counterparts for whites and people of color at the institutional and societal levels of social structure: Racist politics have and continue to privilege whites at the institutional level as the incumbents of power and have historically excluded people of color until African Americans were extended the right to vote. To address the interests of people of color in policy requires support of white voters who still outnumber people of color and of white legislators who continue to strongly dominate all branches of government. The same cannot be said of people of color, who have never controlled the political agenda or political structures

Figure 1.2 White Racism Versus Minority Racial Bigotry

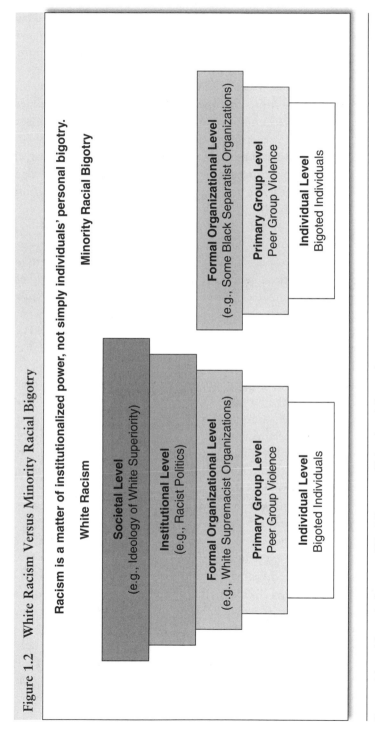

Racism is a matter of institutionalized power, not simply individuals' personal bigotry.

White Racism

Minority Racial Bigotry

Societal Level
(e.g., Ideology of White Superiority)

Institutional Level
(e.g., Racist Politics)

Formal Organizational Level
(e.g., White Supremacist Organizations)

Primary Group Level
Peer Group Violence

Individual Level
Bigoted Individuals

Formal Organizational Level
(e.g., Some Black Separatist Organizations)

Primary Group Level
Peer Group Violence

Individual Level
Bigoted Individuals

Source: Adapted from the lectures of Noel Cazenave, University of Connecticut.

and institutions in the United States. This structural arrangement ensures that white-skin privilege is embedded in the institutions; as such, whites' dominance does not require individuals to be racist in order to reproduce white privilege and dominance. This racist inequality and oppression are ideologically justified at the societal level of social structure: White superiority is bolstered by assertions that inequality based on race is biologically determined and therefore immutable and unchangeable rather than socially constructed.

Since the state is in a unique position to legislate, it may affect the opportunity structures built on these social constructions. What, then, is the role of the state in racial formation processes and in gendering processes?

Heteronormativity

As well as the advantages accrued to people because of their class, gender, and racial composition, people are likewise accorded privileges because of their sexual and/or gender *practices*. Indeed, since the 1800s, when scientists declared the existence of "the homosexual," people have been split into various *sexual identities* (Foucault, 1978). As trans activists and people from the intersex movement have shown, this has also had deep effects on gender identity as well (Wilchins, 2004).

This has structured our social life in a number of ways, through the strict enforcement of *heteronormativity*—or the ways that society has built up normative expectations governing our sexual and gender practices. Some, for example, have pointed out that our society has enforced a system of compulsory heterosexuality and monogamy, both through cultural norms and mores, as well as through the institutionalization of relationships in monogamous, heterosexual forms in marriage (Emens, 2004; Rich, 1980). Likewise, people who are gay, bisexual, lesbian, or transgender can suffer violent attacks, employment discrimination, and social ostracism.

This historical legacy has split people into three distinct identities or *sexual orientations*: homo, hetero, and bi. This split limits possibilities for organizing sexuality and invisibilizes people who do not fit neatly into these categories either because of desire (there is a range of sexual attractions sometimes not organized around gender at all and sometimes that does not fit neatly into those three premade boxes) or because of gender performance (this selection ignores that there are gender performances that defy our binary). Therefore, part of the task for creating a free society with a viable social existence for all includes the project of troubling and destabilizing these categories.

Again, the state has a place in institutionalizing the ways that we "do" gender and relationships. In what ways does the state limit and confine the possibilities for a viable social existence for all?

Structures of Oppression and Resistance

This book assumes that people are both shaped by and in turn may shape social structures, relationships, and processes. That assumption leads us to ask in Chapter 6 how people resist, challenge, and perhaps alter the social structures, relationships, and processes that affect individuals' access to opportunities and thus their life chances. This is commonly an important piece missing from most state theories.

The intention here is to develop a framework for integrating the important elements in the relationship between the state, society, and oppression identified by the various state theories, power structure theories, and social movement theories. Each of these emphasizes a useful dimension of the state but commonly suggests that this one dimension is the focal point of the relationship. We argue, instead, that each dimension is like a single piece of a large and complicated jigsaw puzzle, and our challenge is to develop a framework to put those pieces together. Moreover, much of state theory focuses on the relationship between the state and the economy and explores economic and labor policy as indicative of that relationship. We argue instead that the state is also a patriarchal and racialized state and that existing theories of the state are limited as tools to analyze those policies that are indicative of these relationships. We explore a framework in Chapter 7 that integrates multiple dimensions of the state as identified in the literature and that can offer more flexibility to include the various relationships of oppression and the intersections of multiple oppressions.

References

Bohmer, S., & Briggs, J. L. (1991, April). Teaching privileged students about gender, race, and class oppression. *Teaching Sociology, 19*, 154–163.

Collins, P. H. (1990). *Black feminist thought: Knowledge, consciousness, and the politics of empowerment*. Boston: Unwin Hyman.

Cubbins, L. A. (2001). The legacy of patriarchy in today's Russia. In D. Vannoy (Ed.), *Gender mosaics: Social perspectives* (pp. 174–183). Los Angeles: Roxbury.

Cuklanz, L. M. (2000). *Rape on prime time: Television, masculinity, and sexual violence*. Philadelphia: University of Pennsylvania Press.

Emens, E. F. (2004). Monogamy's law: Compulsory monogamy and polyamorous existence. *New York University Review of Law and Social Change*, 29(2), 277.

Feagin, J. R. (2001). *Racist America: Roots, current realities, and future reparations.* New York: Routledge.

Feltey, K. M. (2001). Gender violence: Rape and sexual assault. In D. Vannoy (Ed.), *Gender mosaics: Social perspectives* (pp. 363–373). Los Angeles: Roxbury.

Foucault, M. (1978). *History of sexuality*. New York: Pantheon Books.

Herrnstein, R. J., & Murray, C. (1994). *The bell curve: Intelligence and class structure in American life*. New York: Free Press.

Marx, K. (1954). *The Communist manifesto*. Chicago: Henry Regnery Company.

Rich, A. (1980). Compulsory heterosexuality and lesbian existence. *Signs: Journal of Women in Culture and Society*, 5, 631–660.

Wilchins, R. A. (2004). *Queer theory, gender theory: An instant primer*. Los Angeles: Alyson Books.

2

From the Top Down?

Power Structure Theories

Understanding oppression begins with an exploration of the notion of power. In this chapter, we will examine power structure theories of pluralism, power elite theory, and class dialectic theory. We will differentiate group and elite pluralism and explore how analysts using this perspective pursue the question of who has power and how it is exercised. We will then introduce power elite theory and discuss its conversation and debate with pluralism. The discussion here will examine how analysts using the power elite perspective define and explain its structure, exploring questions such as the following: Who are the power elite? How do we know this? How do individuals become members of the power elite? How diverse is the power elite? How permeable is it? Next, we will contrast pluralism and power elite theory with class dialectic theory. Finally, we will briefly discuss poststructuralist theories of power, which criticize locating power narrowly within institutions such as capitalism and the state. The discussion will engage in a critical analysis of the relative strengths and weaknesses of these perspectives.

Pluralism

One look at the Declaration of Independence and the Constitution quickly establishes the principles that people readily identify as the democratic ideals of the United States: "government of the people, by the people, for the people," "equality before the law," and "separation of powers." These ideals are perhaps part of the reason that pluralist theory has so dominated political science and political sociology as well as popular culture. They portray an ideal type of the society people in the United States would like it to be. These ideals suggest that no one is an absolute, permanent ruler, that "the people" govern and receive the government and the leadership they want, and that everyone is equal. Such is the point of pluralist theory. There are actually two strands of pluralist thought: group pluralism and elite pluralism. The differences between these two strands are relatively small but significant in how they conceptualize the operation and distribution of power in democracies.

Group Pluralism

The central theme of *group pluralism* (Drache, 2008; Fung, 2004; Schwartz, 2005; Truman, 1951) is the ongoing swirl of the vast variety of interests and pressure groups jockeying for position to get their interests met—at least temporarily—and thus providing stability to the social and political order. Political behavior is a group activity rather than one engaged in by isolated individuals: It occurs within and between groups. Indeed, one of the most striking features of the 19th-century United States observed by Alexis de Tocqueville (1966) was that it was a "nation of joiners" in which individuals belonged to many and varied *voluntary associations* and groups, with each group satisfying a particular interest or need of the individual members. These groups may combine the time, energy, and resources of their individual members to collectively exert pressure on existing governmental leaders to address issues that matter to them. Voluntary associations and *interest groups*, then, become the organizational mechanisms through which individuals may exert political power and get their interests met.

That political behavior of such group activity reduces the difficulty of governmental leaders to hear the needs of their constituents through a potential cacophony of millions of individuals demanding to be heard and of individuals to get heard above the din. But with the multitude of voluntary groups and interest groups all struggling for position, is there not a strong potential for chaos as well? Group pluralists did not think so: The interplay between these groups, they argued, provided stability to the social and political system for several reasons.

First, there is a *balance of group power* in that no one interest group is in power all the time: Today's power "in-group" is tomorrow's power "out-group"; today's powerless interests are tomorrow's leading interest groups. This is, in part, because the job of the state is to legislate in the common good so that no one single interest prevails all the time to the permanent disadvantage of all others. The state is a neutral arbiter, standing above the fray of competing interests. It must weigh and evaluate all the competing interests calling for attention and ultimately determine which are in the public interest and must be addressed and which are more narrow or perhaps even damaging to that public interest. Groups are therefore discouraged from pursuing narrow or selfish interests to the detriment of all others but instead must somehow modify their interest to appeal to those of a wider array of interests or to conform to what is best for the public good. They are motivated to negotiate with other interest groups to find common ground. In that sense, power is dispersed among the unlimited number of varied interest groups, all of whom have the same chance of getting their needs met on any given day.

Furthermore, individual governmental leaders are prevented from consistently favoring one interest group over another because there is a *separation of governmental powers* between the legislature, the judiciary, and the executive branches. These act as a system of checks and balances one against the others. For example, the U.S. Congress makes laws, but these can be vetoed by the president or declared unconstitutional by the Supreme Court. The president can declare by executive fiat some policies, but these can be overridden by legislative action or declared unconstitutional by the Supreme Court; in extreme cases, the president may be impeached by Congress. Members of the Supreme Court may remain on the bench for life, so they may adjudicate cases before the Court without fear of antagonizing existing or changing political leaders, but they must first be nominated for their seats on the Court by the president and approved by the Senate in rigorous and often grueling public confirmation hearings. The separation of powers provides stability to the system by preventing members of any one branch from unfairly advantaging some interests as opposed to others and thereby damaging the common good: Any attempts to do so would presumably be checked and balanced by members of the other two branches.

Political and social stability is further ensured by the fact that individuals belong to a wide and diverse array of voluntary associations and interest groups, creating *crosscutting group memberships*. Individuals join groups because these address particular needs or interests. No one group or voluntary association is likely to address every interest of an individual. Therefore, individuals will be likely to join many different groups, each of which may address one or more of their interests or needs. The more groups to which an individual belongs, the more likely it is that these groups will pose countervailing pressures.

For example, a worker in an aircraft manufacturing plant may belong to the machinists' union and thus have strong interests in such things as protection of workers' jobs in the United States and seniority rules protecting the jobs of workers who have been on the job the longest. But suppose that worker is also an African American who belongs to the National Association for the Advancement of Colored People (NAACP). That organization frequently struggles against seniority rules because these reproduce racial inequality by using a rule of "last hired, first fired" to govern layoffs. Since African Americans are often the more recent hires in many job categories, they are likely to be the first to lose their jobs during corporate efforts to downsize. Many members of the machinists' union are also people of color and perhaps members of the NAACP, and many members of the NAACP may be union members. In addition, suppose this hypothetical worker is also a participant through the pension fund in a mutual fund investment group, with significant interests in a strong stock market performance. Corporate stocks commonly rise when corporations announce massive worker layoffs ("downsizing") and exportation of jobs to developing countries. While workers may surely have an interest in supporting policies favorable to the stock market, this hypothetical union member also has a substantial interest in preventing job loss. For pluralists, these crosscutting interest group memberships mean that both organizations will be pressured to modify how aggressively each pursues their respective agendas and thus reinforces stability to the political and social system.

Stability is also reinforced by the presumed existence of a *consensus of values*. Group pluralists argue there is cultural agreement about the need of the state to legislate in the "common good" rather than to favor the narrow interests of a few. Moreover, there exist norms governing the "rules of the game" in participation in democratic processes. Everyone understands and agrees that the leaders in the state must be the final arbiters in deciding among the competing interests, that the state must be neutral in its governance of the common good, and that the three separated branches of government will ensure members of society against tyranny. Since everyone knows and agrees with the rules of the game, people will accept the outcomes of state decisions even when their own interests may not have won the day in a particular instance. The consensus of values for pluralists prevents not only tyranny but also open rebellion and therefore contributes to the stability of the system.

Finally, group pluralists see stability of the system reinforced by *potential groups*. Not all interests are represented at all times by interest or pressure groups. But if particular interests are routinely ignored, people who share these interests will gather together and form a new group, or even a loose collective, to enter the political process. Take, for example, the emergence of third parties, particularly in national elections for president of the

United States. Ross Perot was an independent candidate in 1992 and Reform Party candidate in 1996, attempting to represent the interests of moderates and independents who felt neglected. Ralph Nader ran on the Green Party ticket in 2000 because the two major parties were slighting the substantial interests of the poor, workers, and environmentalists in favor of corporate interests. Joseph Lieberman ran as an independent candidate for the Senate in 2006 in Connecticut after losing the Democratic primary because he believed he represented an ignored bipartisan interest. Each candidate hoped, at the very least, to mobilize a significant enough number of supporters to threaten the main parties and force them to address their respective issues. In the case of Lieberman, the effort succeeded: He won his reelection bid. The threat of this *mobilization of latent interests* is sufficient, pluralists suggest, to motivate the state to bear them in mind when legislating in the common good; to only pay attention to those groups actively articulating their needs is to galvanize ignored interests into pressure groups. Thus, interests do not necessarily have to be formally organized into groups to have a stabilizing effect on the system: The mere threat that at any time these can be mobilized into new groups is sufficient to modify the state's decision making.

Elite Pluralism

In the years since the introduction of group pluralism, many have realized that the focus on interest groups essentially ignored the critical role that political elites play in decision making—even in democracies. While the Declaration of Independence may emphasize "government of the people, for the people, and by the people," the fact is that political leaders are the ultimate decision makers. Elite pluralists expanded the group pluralist model to include this insight, while maintaining the broad outlines of pluralism (Higley, & Burton, 2006; Lipset, 1981; Rose, 1967). They argued that in democracies, "the people" (the masses as some called them) did not make policy in the common good but rather participated in choosing the elites who would. Citizen participation still occurs in a democratic process but indirectly, through elections; the elites they elect more directly participate in policy making on their behalf.

Pluralists argued that political elites are not a monolithic, unified interest group representing their own narrow group interests but rather are diverse, competitive elites representing a wide range of interests. They compete in the political marketplace for support from voters, all of whom are equal regardless of their economic resources, education, race or ethnicity, religion, gender, or age because all have one and only one vote to spend in that marketplace. What group pluralists saw as a stable political system balanced by the competition of interest and pressure groups was now redeployed by elite pluralists as a stable system balanced by competition between elites. The masses would be able to hold elected officials accountable with the threat of voting them out of office if these elites did not adequately pay attention to their interests. Indeed, political analysts often appeal to this notion of the potential for "voter rebellion" when they report on elections in the United States: Voters are said to be "fed up" with elected leaders who remain insensitive, politically out of step, or unresponsive to the common good or to voters' interests. For pluralists, then, power is dispersed among the millions of individual voters, all of whom have an equal amount of power in their single votes.

Furthermore, the political interplay between elected elites themselves contributes to stability in the system, because policy-making procedures typically require a majority of them to agree to pass a bill. This is because all elected elites are equal: Each has one vote in the legislative process, and none of them has enough power to unilaterally push an agenda against the will of the others. Therefore, all elites must negotiate with the others to form coalitions in decision making, thus modifying their points of view and their level of aggression in pursuing a single-minded agenda. Such an arrangement ensures that all interests will eventually get addressed, as elites make deals with each other, as in "you support my issue, and I'll support yours."

In this incarnation of pluralism, political stability and balance continue to be assured by a consensus of values: Here, everyone knows and accepts the rules of the game to include electing leaders from among a slate of candidates who usually run for office with a political party, with the presumption that once elected these elites will dispatch their duties fairly and in the common good. Political participation thus is defined as voting, not violent insurrection, mass rebellion, or revolution. Assassinating leaders who displease the electorate is unacceptable; impeaching such elites, recalling their elections, or waiting until the next election to vote them out of office are. Even when individual voters' preferred candidates do not get elected, the winner of the election is accepted by all as legitimate because all eligible citizens had a chance to participate in the process. Perhaps next time those whose candidate lost the election will have greater success. In the meantime, the masses are expected to rally behind the winner unless and until such time as that leader proves unworthy.

Here, potential interests remain important elements of political stability: The threat of the mobilization of latent interests against incumbent elites with whom voters are displeased is seen as sufficient for ensuring that they do not ignore voters' interests or the common good. Elites will not trample on the interests of the oppressed if there is the real possibility that the oppressed will become galvanized to oppose them and vote them out of office.

Critique of Pluralism

Pluralist analyses of power in democracies have chiefly evolved in examinations of the United States and Great Britain, and this makes them vulnerable to criticisms of ethnocentric or parochial bias. This is a criticism that could just as easily be leveled against power elite theorists as well, as we'll see next. However, even as a model of power in the United States, it remains problematic. While the pluralist model of power structure may be consistent with the basic principles and ideals of the United States, it does not necessarily describe what actually occurs. There are several important analytical points to be considered.

One key element of the pluralist argument of system stability is the threat of "potential interest groups" emerging to pressure the state for attention. While this concept is appealing, it is quite imprecise and unmeasurable: How do we know when there is a sufficient threat as to alter the behavior of existing groups or of political elites? How much of a threat is necessary to capture the attention of existing groups and political leaders? How do we measure these? For example, the tobacco industry in the United States maintains a highly active and well-funded lobby to help them maintain their economic position with as few restrictions on their activities as they can manage. How do we evaluate the effect that "potential interest groups" might have on how aggressively they pursue their interests? Can we reasonably say that they refrain from seeking exclusion from Drug Enforcement Administration (DEA) regulations and legal restrictions against its commodities and that elected leaders refrain from supporting tobacco interests because of the concern that their actions *might* antagonize a growing number of people (how many would be sufficient to provoke this response?); that leaders of these aggrieved parties *might* emerge; that they *might* locate funds to support their own lobbying and resistance; and, *if* enough people have enough time and energy and willingness to devote these to the resistance, that a potential group *might* coalesce, oppose the current advantaged status of the industry, and *might* even seek to reduce the industry's advantage in the United States and abroad? Political leaders and economic interests like the tobacco industry may indeed harbor some apprehension that such groups might develop (and some certainly have), but how much? Enough to say that potential power was exercised? How do we know that this potential actually affected the behavior of the tobacco industry and of political leaders? Moreover, how can we predict such potential effects?

As you will soon notice, this problem of conceptual and empirical imprecision plagues many theoretical models of power, particularly because covert or implicit power is not easily observable. Notice, too, that the mobilization of latent interests in the presidential elections previously noted did not succeed in getting their candidates elected and barely succeeded in altering the main positions of either the Democratic or Republican Parties.

In addition, the very concept of stability or equilibrium presented by pluralists is questionable. Equilibrium may in fact exist in the political and social systems without providing for all substantial interests. And can we necessarily assume that even if substantial interests are not being met it is because to do so is in the best interests of the "common good"? For example, it is possible to achieve "racial balance" in schools and in jobs by pursuing racial diversity among the student bodies and employees that are reflective of the proportions of different racially defined groups in the population. At the same time, however, there may still be a high degree of inequality and discrimination in the programmatic tracks students are enrolled in, the differential wages personnel receive, the mentoring they may or may not receive, and the informal differential treatment people receive in these settings. Can this still be construed as equilibrium in the system? Is this persistent inequality in the "common good"? For that matter, what exactly is the "common good," and who decides? Do all interests and all constituents have a say in formulating that definition? Whose definitions prevail? Is there a pattern to whose definitions are given greater legitimacy, and whose are ignored? These are important empirical questions to explore, as they suggest a critical evaluation of pluralism.

Furthermore, the pluralist model of power implies that all interest groups and all voters are equal: No one enjoys absolute power all the time. At any given time, everyone has a chance to be heard and to have their interests addressed. We might for the moment agree that a principle of "one person, one vote" provides some basis for assuming that perhaps voters have equal ability to affect the outcome of elections (we'll return to this issue in Chapter 3). But this does not address the question of which people are perhaps not "eligible" to vote (and why, and who decides?) and are therefore less able to have their interests met because they do not have even this one ballot to cast. Such is the case, for example, for the homeless, children, and convicted felons in many states.

Moreover, are all interest groups of equal ability to affect decision making in the state to their advantage? Pluralists do not rank groups' relative power or identify the elements that might make some more able than others to have such an effect. In particular, pluralists do not examine the differential resources to which various interest groups might have access and that might therefore affect how much influence they may have. One would be hard pressed, for example, to say that the War Resisters League (WRL) has the same ability to affect the state's decision making about military buildup and going to war against other nations as the major corporations among the Department of Defense's contractors. After all, there is a rather large differential in resources and power between grassroots organizations like the WRL and military contractors.

The presumption of the equality of all interests and groups further ignores how extensively economic institutions—particularly corporations—permeate all facets of society. The economy, and most people, relies substantially on the wealth and health of corporations to provide good-paying jobs (or any jobs at all), goods and services, and tax revenues to enable the state to provide for many of the services corporations do not provide (such as military defense, police protection, fire protection, sanitation removal, education, streets and highways, etc.). This is a position that is not enjoyed by noneconomic actors. The dominance of corporate actors is thus likely to make their interests loom more significantly than many others and to render some interests invisible or unimportant by contrast. The pluralist model does not take this into account.

Similarly, this presumption of equality between interest groups does not take into account how strongly structures of oppression such as patriarchy, racism, and heteronormativity frame and pervade society. Maleness, whiteness, and heterosexuality have historically implied "normal" in the United States, rendering oppressed groups as "the other" and thus symbolically annihilating them (Tuchman, Daniels, & Benet, 1978). To the extent that males, whites, and heterosexuals have historically dominated society and the political agenda of issues to be publicly debated, their interests are likely to be framed as "the common good," while interests of women, people of color, and the LGBTQ (lesbian, gay, bisexual, transgender, and queer) community are more likely to be framed as "special interests." Schattschneider (1975) once observed that "The flaw in the pluralist heaven is that the heavenly chorus sings with a strong upper-class accent. Probably about 90 percent of the people cannot get into the pressure system" (pp. 34–35). One could also note that the chorus also sings with a decidedly male, white, and heterosexual voice as well.

The question of the likelihood of all interests getting addressed sooner or later is further based on the assumption of the neutrality of the state. But "the state" is composed of elite individuals who make decisions affecting everyone's lives in fundamental ways. These individuals, as human beings, have previous status positions in society that shape their personal sets of interests based on such things as class, race, gender, religion, age, and so forth. They are unlikely to eschew these completely as they step into public office; to expect that they could do so is unrealistic. They carry their personal histories and relationships with them, such that their prior interests and connections may certainly affect how they view issues or even recognize various interests at all. Moreover, state managers may have their own interests in maintaining their privileged power positions, and this may be likely to affect their decision making in ways that certainly address their own interests but not necessarily the interests of the "common good."

Pluralists argue that it may very well be that some interests are not getting addressed at this point in time, but that the masses accept this because they share in the consensus of political values and rules of the game and goals. However, this mitigates the notion that the rules of the game have previously been set by those already in power and are therefore likely to reinforce their ability to maintain that power to the detriment of others. If there does appear to be some consensus of the rules of the game, how is it that most people come to accept these even when the outcome may be inconsistent with their own interests? How do people perhaps come to view the interests of the privileged in society as deserving their advantage and they themselves are undeserving? We will explore this carefully in Chapter 4.

In addition, pluralists largely emphasize electoral politics as the arena of political behavior and power and the means by which the masses may hold accountable the elites whose decisions fundamentally affect individuals' lives. Setting aside for now the question of how much power electoral participation may offer individuals to hold even elected elites accountable, there are substantial nonelected elites who also make important decisions that fundamentally affect our daily existence. For example, there are many among political elites who are not elected and whom it would be difficult if not impossible to hold accountable by voting, such as members of the Supreme Court, Pentagon officials, and cabinet officers. To be fair, pluralists would argue that such individuals are appointed by leaders that the masses do get to elect; but the critical point here is that once appointed these individuals may not be held directly accountable through voting, and some, like Supreme Court justices who are appointed for life, cannot be held accountable at all.

Even more to the point, there are many economic actors and groups whose decisions affect people's daily lives in the most basic and significant ways and yet are completely untouchable by voting. For example, corporate CEOs and their boards decide when to downsize, when to close productive facilities in the United States, how much to pay people who work for them, where to operate, and what products to make and services to offer. Financial institutions decide who gets access to money and investment capital and who does not. These decisions substantially affect people's life chances; but the decision makers are not held accountable by voting whatsoever. How are they controlled? How might we hold them accountable? How might their power be restrained? What are the mechanisms which the citizenry can use to influence them? Pluralism does not address these questions.

Finally, pluralism assumes, rather than critically questions, state organization. The state itself, as the sole societal institution that has the legitimated use of violence at its disposal (i.e., the police and the military), has interests of its own, regardless of the background and character of those that control its use. Even if members of historically oppressed and exploited groups were able to routinely elect officials to state positions, they would then enter into an institution that itself represents the systematization of dominance, coercion, and control. Rather than begin with questions like, Are institutions like the state necessary for human social organization? Or, perhaps better yet, under what conditions might the state become unnecessary? Pluralists begin with the assumption of the state as a necessary and, more importantly, "natural" institution (despite the fact that the vast majority of human existence was spent organizing without it). This further problematizes electoral strategies for influencing the political process—particularly if what is sought is structural change or an alternative to the existing system.

These critiques of pluralism do not mean that voting behavior is irrelevant in the study of power, but they do suggest that the pluralist vision by itself is limited. Indeed, by the late 1950s and early 1960s, many observers found the pluralist ideal type to be an unsatisfactory model and began looking for a different model. Enter power elite theory.

Power Elite Theory

Where pluralists see the masses or nonelites in society as power holders in their ability to hold leaders accountable through participation in the electoral system, power elite theorists see the masses as powerless to do so effectively. This is because elites who rule do so in their own interests rather than those of the larger society or the "common good" and set the rules of the game to reinforce and perpetuate their domination. How do elites do this?

Charles Wright Mills (1956) argued that power is concentrated in relatively few hands in the key institutions of society: the *state*, the *corporate economy*, and the *military*. Those who occupy the strategic command positions in these institutions are powerful. What Mills offered is a positional theory of the power elite: Power inures to *positions*, not to individuals. That is, he argued, if the most powerful, the most wealthy, and the most famous individuals in the United States were to be separated from their institutional positions, and were thereby deprived of the resources those positions dispose, they would become politically powerless, poor, and unknown. Power is thus not a trait of individuals; to be powerful requires access to the strategic command positions of the key institutions of power.

Elite rule results from cohesion of the elites: In many significant ways, Mills (1956) argued, the elite are of one mind and of a single interest. The elite who fill these positions come from a single group and share a single worldview because of three related processes: *co-optation*, *class identity*, and the *interchangeability* of the institutional elites.

Co-optation involves the socialization of prospective and new members of the elite so that they come to share the worldview of the power elite. Those who aspire to elite positions must be willing to adopt the prevailing worldview and ideologies espoused by the existing elite who will select the new members of their circle of privilege. Only those who share that prevailing ideology will be selected. Once they are selected, new members of the elite become surrounded by that ideology, which reinforces a single-minded point of view and provides fewer and fewer opportunities for new elites to confront challenging ones. The acceptance into the exclusive club of elites and the subsequent increased isolation from other interest groups contributes to the internalization of elite values and norms by new elite recruits.

Cohesion of elites is further solidified by class identity resulting from the common life experiences of members of the elite, such that they develop a sense of being members of an exclusive group. Members of the power elite have usually attended prestigious private prep schools and Ivy League colleges, belong to the same exclusive social clubs, live in the select communities around the country, and travel in cliques. Their children tend to marry one another, thereby sealing wealth and power between families. As such, it is unlikely for them to confront views held by members of other classes that challenge those they share. They are unified in their beliefs about what is best for society and how the world works because these are constantly reaffirmed by their experiences and their contacts (Domhoff, 2002).

In addition to these "circumstantial" factors of class cohesion are the more conscious, explicit mechanisms of elite unity and class identity. For example, Domhoff (1974) described how the Bohemian Grove functioned as a summer camp retreat of the power elite, where the list of campers attending for the 2 weeks each summer was a who's who of the most powerful corporate CEOs, governmental leaders (including cabinet members, well-placed congressional leaders, and the president and vice president of the United States), and military elites (including the Joint Chiefs of Staff, assorted generals and admirals, and other high-level Pentagon officials). The guest list was exclusively men-only, ostensibly to ensure their comfort after a year of demanding and challenging decision making. But Domhoff emphasized that the Bohemian Grove was hardly a simple vacation respite for men who worked extremely hard all year. It was, rather, the place where the elites of the most important institutions not only rubbed shoulders and played but also discussed critical policy and developed common viewpoints about issues; it was where, together, they formulated agendas for the coming year and strategies for successfully translating those agendas into policy (Clogher, 1981).

The power elite are also unified by their *interchangeability* among the three main institutions. The people who fill the top positions in the state, the corporate economy, and the military are drawn from a common pool of exclusive personnel, and they circulate easily from the leadership positions of one institutional realm to another. This mingling of personnel blurs any sharp distinctions in experience, perspective, ideology, or worldview such leaders may have. Look, for example, at the administration of President George W. Bush beginning in 2000. President Bush himself had been a board member of Harken Energy, an oil company, between 1986 and 1993 (Lardner & Romano, 1999); his Vice President Richard Cheney was an executive with Halliburton (a major Department of Defense contractor) and the Secretary of Defense from 1989 to 1993. Both men had substantial corporate ties and stockholdings with Enron Corporation, Philip Morris, AT&T, and Microsoft. Secretary of State Colin Powell was a U.S. Army general and a corporate board member and stockholder of AOL Time Warner, Gulfstream Aerospace, and General Dynamics. Secretary of Defense Donald Rumsfeld was an executive with G. D. Searle and Company and sat on the boards and held stock of the Tribune Company; Motorola; Gulfstream Aerospace; General Dynamics; Sears, Roebuck, and Co.; Allstate; and the Kellogg Company (Dye, 2002). Considering the major corporate interests these leaders had, including several chief Department of Defense contractors, it is difficult to imagine that these ties and previous sets of experiences would not have any effect whatsoever on their thinking as they sought to make policy.

Mills (1956) argued that the interchangeability of elites among the three most powerful institutions results in a fusion of views among leaders whose institutional position at a given moment would seem to indicate viewpoints and interests specific only to that institution. When the power elite switch hats from one institutional realm to another, they bring with them their prejudices, their beliefs, and their interests. There are no competing viewpoints expressed among leaders who challenge each other; there is only one viewpoint expressed by one group of people: the power elite. The interests of dominant corporations, the Pentagon, and the United States hence become fused into one set of common interests.

The state, according to power elite theorists, is not neutral or autonomous, as suggested by pluralists; it is instead heavily influenced by capital accumulation and corporate interests. Voting processes simply make the existing state appear legitimate and channel nonelites' energies into relatively safe and innocuous activities that appear to empower them. Electoral politics also distract nonelites' attention from an understanding of the relationship between the state and the economy and therefore give them the false security of believing that the state legislates in the common good.

Given the combined processes of co-optation and class identity, it is not surprising to find evidence of an overwhelmingly white, male, relatively affluent network mentoring, supporting, and promoting new elites much like themselves. Yet there is also evidence that this network is not entirely closed or so powerful as to render it impossible for anyone outside that network to break into elite ranks. It is noteworthy, however, that despite evidence of some increasing diversity among the power elite as a group they remain largely white, male, and college educated at the nation's most prestigious institutions. Thomas R. Dye's (2002) analysis of the George W. Bush administration era since 2000, for example, found that of the top 7,314 institutional positions in the power elite, less than 10% were filled by women, and only 0.3% were filled by African Americans. Almost all the occupants of these institutional leadership positions were college educated; 54% of the corporate elite and 42% of the state elites graduated from 1 of the 12 most prestigious private universities. And more than two thirds of the institutional elites belonged to social clubs; more than one third belonged to 1 or more of 37 exclusive clubs.

Zweigenhaft and Domhoff (2006) found some evidence of increased presence of women and people of color in the power elite over the past half century, but their numbers remain very small relative to their overall proportions in the national population. More importantly, Zweigenhaft and Domhoff found that women and people of color tended to remain drawn from the same class background, regardless of their sex or race. Most were college educated at Ivy League or highly exclusive and prestigious private colleges and universities. They took this as evidence that although the sex and race profile of the power elite indeed showed progressive change that progress was actually quite small and relatively insignificant. Moreover, it is noteworthy how little evidence there is that many individuals from the working class rise to the top positional elite ranks. The power elite remain solidified in its common class background characteristics. Together, the findings of Dye (2002) and Zweigenhaft and Domhoff suggest a substantial race, class, and gender bias to the power elite. Power is not dispersed among millions of equal voters but rather consistently concentrated in the hands of a relatively small group of largely white, male, and especially upper-class elites.

Given the concentration of power they enjoy, the power elite may set the rules of the game so as to make it difficult, if not impossible, for nonelites to hold them accountable—even with their votes. Voters may decide between two or more candidates in an election, but the likelihood that all possible candidates are drawn from the narrow ranks of the elites themselves is quite strong. Even if voting were a viable way for nonelites to hold elected leaders accountable, it is unclear what mechanism might be available to the masses to control the economic and military elites, whose positions are not dependent upon voter support.

Critical Assessment of Power Elite Theory

When Mills (1956) first introduced his notion of the power elite it was greeted as a breath of fresh air by observers dissatisfied with the limitations of pluralism. While it certainly challenges many of the weaknesses of pluralism, power elite theory itself is not without its own limitations. There are several critical issues to be considered. For example, power elite theory shares the limitation of pluralists in its failure to weight or rank resources of power. Ironically, it makes the pluralist assumption that money, prestige, and status are all available to those in positions of power in equal amounts, regardless of the institutional realm in which they are situated: That is, all institutional elites are equally powerful and have access to similar kinds and amounts of power resources, regardless of whether they are corporate elites, political elites, or military elites. However, it could be that different elites access different resources; different resources may offer different power bases in kind and magnitude and importance. For example, financial leaders access finance capital flow resources, which are more crucial to the state and to nonfinancial corporations than any other resources. And the largest commercial banks control far greater capital resources than small, local credit unions. Is the power derived from the prestige and status of being president of the United States the same as that derived from being in a position to control the money needed to run the country or to maintain production of a major corporation? Power elite theory makes little room for such questions.

A key conceptual element of power elite theory is based on Mills's (1956) assertion that power is derived from individuals' occupation of the strategic command positions of the key institutions. This may well be, but it is offered as an assertion of fact rather than empirically demonstrated. Instead, much of the empirical evidence offered to link positions to actual decisions and behaviors is illustrative rather than analytical. Researchers first define the presumably key positions and then work to identify who fills them and their background characteristics. While the patterns of common background characteristics are certainly strong, and there is good reason for observers to expect that to produce substantial consistence of worldviews among the power elite, it is important to demonstrate empirically that this is indeed the case.

Even if one were to accept the basic assumptions and assertions of power elite theory and the existence of such an entrenched concentration of power in so few and unvaried hands, there remains a problem of a historical analysis: How did it get that way? How did elites ascend to such power and control in the first place? Power elite theory thus ignores the significance of racism, for example, in the historical development of elite power: Institutional racism (including legal support of slavery, legal denial of blacks' voting rights, and strictures against education of blacks) historically hindered the ability of some to counter the concentration of elite power. It also ignores the significance of imperialism in facilitating the privileged access by multinational corporations—and political and military elites—to essential power resources internationally.

Finally, power elite theory ironically shares pluralists' tendency to focus on the structure of power primarily in Western nations in general and in the United States in particular, while implying a more universal power structure. Do all power structures throughout the world look like the power elite? Even if one were to agree that power elite theory is describing power structure in capitalist political economies, do all capitalist nations' power structures look like this? They may very well, but that is an empirical question that must be demonstrated in a comparative analysis.

Power elite theory draws a picture of an entrenched, almost untouchable, and relatively small group of leaders who enjoy a significant concentration of power. This implies that the power elite should be found to prevail in all struggles to get their interests met above those of nonelites. However, that raises an empirical question: If the power elite are so powerful, how do they *not* get everything they want all the time? For example, the right to collective bargaining for workers and the existence of affirmative action policies would appear to be anathema to the interests of the power elite. The right to collective bargaining allows workers to organize into unions to more effectively challenge the prerogatives of management and capital accumulation interests in the power elite to gain such worker interests as better wages, health and pension benefits, safer work environments, and job security. Affirmative action policy challenges the ability of the power elite to remain white and male, if not upper class. If the power elite are presumably all-powerful, how was it possible in the first place for the oppressed to prevail in securing both of these policies which confront the privileges of the power elite?

Part of the difficulty results from power elite theory's derogation of the masses. Here, not only are elites omnipotent but nonelites are helpless to challenge them. This is because the power elite largely controls the flow of information, important resources, and rewards so that they are in a position to manipulate and exploit nonelites to believe that elites' interests are in fact the "common good": What's good for General Motors really is what's good for the United States. This analysis overlooks the dynamics of organized struggle as well as conflict in challenging and perhaps redefining the balance of power. In the examples just used, it would be difficult to understand affirmative action policy and collective bargaining rights without discussing the role of the American labor movement, civil rights movement, and the women's movement.

Class Dialectic Theory

Karl Marx (1954) viewed power as rooted in the structure of production relations. He saw society as divided into two basic classes based on these production relations. In a capitalist political economy, *capitalists* (or *bourgeoisie*) own the means of production, and they are concerned with producing those commodities that will generate the greatest profit for them. They are relatively few in number compared to the great masses: the *proletariat* (or *working class*). The proletariat do not own the means of production; they are actually commodities themselves, selling their labor to capitalists in exchange for wages. They do not own the commodities they produce; nor do they own or control the wealth generated by their labor. They are laboring for the bourgeoisie, who will sell the commodities for their own profit. For their part, the bourgeoisie exploit the proletarians by paying them the lowest wages possible. Since the bourgeoisie own the means of production, they have far greater power over the proletariat. Marx implored the proletariat to organize and resist the bourgeoisie as a unified group instead of as competing individuals.

The bourgeoisie and the proletariat are thus in constant conflict with one another over the distribution of the fruits of the proletariat's collective labor. The bourgeoisie are normally competitive with one another for greater and greater market share and profit, but what binds them together is their common conflict with workers. Workers, on the other hand, may compete against each other over increasingly scarce jobs paying lower and lower wages, but what binds them together is a common struggle against the power of the bourgeoisie to exploit and oppress them. Marx (1954) emphasized the importance of workers to organize, to rise above what differentiates them one from the other, and to join forces to resist and challenge the structure of power that disadvantages them. He urged workers of the world to unite, because they "have nothing to lose but their chains" (p. 82).

Marx (1954) thus viewed power to be structured as a fluid, ongoing process marked by conflict and struggle in which the proletariat engages in organized strategies to challenge the ability of the bourgeoisie to expropriate the wealth workers produce, to control their life chances, and to force them to toil in unacceptable work conditions. As such, although the bourgeoisie may own the means of production, they must negotiate with workers who may go on strike en masse if the bourgeoisie do not negotiate with them. Or they may engage in direct action tactics, such as sabotaging or slowing down production to interfere with the bourgeoisie's capital accumulation. The bourgeoisie may be the elites, and they may own and control the crucial means of production, but they are not all-powerful, and the power they may enjoy at one moment is not necessarily guaranteed forever: The proletariat also has power but only if they are organized and unified in their struggles against the bourgeoisie (see Clawson, 2003; Gordon, 2005; Kumar, 2007; Levine, 1988; Whitt, 1982).

Critical Assessment of Class Dialectic Theory

Class dialectic theory widens the focus of analyses of power structure to examine not only elites but nonelites as well. Its contribution is the recognition that power is not only a behavior or a position; it may also be understood to be a relationship and a process of struggle between elites and nonelites. Less clear, however, is what might stimulate greater or lesser organization among workers at any particular point in time. Neither is it clear what might affect the salience of worker organization. Indeed, there are times when one might expect workers to exhibit greater agitation toward organized resistance, yet none occurs. Such was the case in the 1980s in the United States, when a severe recession and aggressive antilabor sentiment prevailed. Although wages had stagnated or declined—and workers were increasingly losing their jobs—workers showed decreasing interest in striking or in unionization. Why did workers not show greater willingness to organize at a time when they were losing ground previously won? We may be able in retrospect to reconstruct events and relationships at the time to divine some explanation, but the point here is that class dialectic theory itself does not identify the conditions under which proletarian activism is more or less likely to emerge— nor under which that activism might be significant and efficacious.

In addition, class dialectic theory is limited in that it specifically pursues analyses of the structure of power as a *class* phenomenon. However, how do we explain struggles over power such as women's rights, the rights of people of color, the rights of the LGBTQ community, and so on, that might intersect with our class system but are not reducible to it? We may certainly borrow insights from class dialectic theory here, but one must be cautious not to assume that the structure of the capitalist political economy in and of itself produces all struggles over power.

Poststructuralist Theories of Power

One thing that pluralism, power elite theory, and class dialectic theory share in common is their tendency to locate power within specific institutions like the economy or the state. Pluralism, for example, assumes that competing interests leverage for power within the state apparatus. Power elite theory locates power within the intersecting institutions of the economy, the state, and the military—particularly in rotating positions held by those people in power within those institutions. Class dialectic theory sees power as emanating from the economy, as workers struggle against capitalists for power.

Poststructuralist theory, particularly as developed by the French social theorist Michel Foucault, however, posits power as behaving quite differently. Rather, poststructuralists suggest that power is not located within specific institutions such as the state and capitalism but is dispersed throughout social life. Rather than the Marxist idea that social change would come from replacing the existing state with a worker's state, for example, poststructuralists look at how power operates at the everyday level. This prompted Foucault (1980) to note that "nothing in society will be changed if the mechanisms of power that function outside, below and alongside the State apparatuses, on a much more minute and everyday level, are not also changed" (p. 60).

Charting histories of punishment, sexuality, and madness, Foucault found that the bodies of knowledge that we created over time had productive power. That is, those discourses had the power to create specific identities and social relationships. For example, Foucault (1969) noted the historical development of factories, prisons, and schools and the disciplinary techniques each used to create certain types of people. Further, these institutions borrowed from one another so that similar disciplinary techniques were used in each of them. This created a highly disciplined and managed social body, accustomed to control. Likewise, his work on sexuality (Foucault, 1985) showed how the development of sexual identities actually had the power to manage and discipline desire.

Poststructuralists thus were left with needing new ways to conceptualize power and how it operates in our social world. Deleuze and Guattari (1987), for example, developed the concept of the "rhizome" to describe power operating as a rootlike structure throughout our social world, with multiple points of connection. In this conceptualization, power has no "base" (as in Marxist theory) but is complex and multidimensional. This model for analysis describes quite well the Foucauldian conception of power as diffuse and not centrally located within specific institutions.

Critical Assessment of Poststructuralist Theories of Power

While poststructuralism is often credited with giving us new ways to understand power and how it operates in society, it doesn't give us many tools for changing society. While many social movements with which people are familiar, such as the women's movement and gay and lesbian movement, are based on mobilizing around specific identities, poststructuralism has the tendency to destabilize those identities. Perhaps this means new political models are necessary, but many people involved in identity-based organizing are suspicious that poststructuralist critiques of identity actually have the effect of erasing social oppression based on identity categories.

Likewise, poststructuralism is often criticized as emerging from the French intelligentsia and being distanced from the material experiences of everyday people. Indeed, much of it is written in a highly obtuse language, difficult to digest, and even more difficult to put to use in analyzing (not to mention changing) society. Critics often suggest that poststructuralism is obfuscatory instead of illuminating and can create real barriers to effective political organizing and the creation and maintenance of mass movements capable of influencing, or overthrowing, state power.

Nevertheless, people who do wish to alter society have put these perspectives to use in their work. And this leaves students with the task of comparing and evaluating these competing theories of power. We turn to this project in our next section.

Comparing Power Structure Theories

Pluralism, power elite theory, and class dialectic theory provide strongly contrasting models of how power structures work in democracies (see Table 2.1). Pluralists, for example, insist that power is dispersed among millions of equally powerful voters and thousands of diverse, competing interest groups (and potential interest groups) and political elites. In contrast, power elite theorists contend that power is concentrated in the hands of a relatively few privileged individuals who share a coherent vision and unified interests.

Class dialectic theorists see power as concentrated in the hands of those who own the means of production, but, in contrast to power elite theorists, they see elites' power as subject to challenge from below and as rooted not in their institutional positions but in their relationship to the structure and process of production. Pluralists see voting as the key to power with everyone having an equal chance of affecting the outcome (and presumably of getting their interests met) because each has exactly one—and only one—vote. Power elite theorists see institutional position as the key to power, with only a small elite monopolizing these positions and therefore gaining a significant advantage to consistently secure their interests over and above everyone else. Class dialectic theorists see organized struggle as the key to power.

Table 2.1   Power Structure Theories

	Pluralism	Power Elite Theory	Class Dialectic Theory	Poststructuralist Theory
1. Power is:	dispersed.	concentrated.	concentrated but fluid.	diffused throughout social life.
2. Elites are:	competitive and divided.	unified.	usually competitive.	diffuse but powerful insofar as they may dominate the production of knowledge.
3. Nonelites are:	diverse and divided.	diverse and powerless.	relatively powerful but only if organized.	powerless insofar as their interests are managed by the social body.
4. Elite interests are:	diverse and crosscutting.	unified due to common backgrounds and positions.	competitive against each other but unified against labor.	diffuse.
5. The defining characteristic of power is:	behavior.	institutional position.	relationship and process of institutionalized struggle.	process of everyday interaction and production of knowledge and discourse.

Pluralists, power elite theorists, and class dialectic theorists agree that whoever controls the government controls policy. But they strongly disagree about how entrenched, inexorable, or responsive that control is. Pluralists argue that the people control government, primarily through voting power: If the elected elites fail to pay attention to important needs and interests or to lead effectively, the people can hold them accountable and vote them out of office. Power elite theorists instead argue that the elites in the corporate economy, the military, and the state control the government and are responsive only to their own unified interests. Their overwhelming power derives from their monopoly of the strategic command positions of the key institutions and cannot effectively be challenged by the masses. That enables the power elite to deny the interests of the masses with little concern for their resistance. In contrast, class dialectic theorists suggest that while elites in government make policy, real power resides elsewhere: Whoever can most affect the production process to their advantage is more powerful. Concerns to keep the economy healthy may prompt the government to implement policy that reinforces the production and accumulation process, but organized efforts by workers can gain the government's attention—or, in some cases, overthrow the existing governing structures.

The Meaning and Dimensions of Power

The power structure debate is essentially a debate about the definition and nature of *power*: What is power? Who has power? How do we know where power resides? How is power attained and preserved over time? How is power challenged over time?

Bachrach and Baratz (1962) noted that power is not of one dimension. They argued that there are two "faces" of power: the explicit or overt exercise of power in decision making and the implicit or covert exercise of power in non-decision making. When we look at electoral or voting behavior—or at any other decision-making process—we are looking at *one* face of power. This is the face that pluralists see in voting. For pluralists, power is dispersed among competing groups or among elites competing for voters' support, with no one dominating all the time. This is because power is limited for pluralists by shifting and crosscutting loyalties. Power is therefore the ability of X to *temporarily* address his/her interests over and above others. In this regard, pluralists concentrate on the exercise of power: Power is a *behavior*.

But Bachrach and Baratz (1962) argued that the pluralist, single-faced conception of power neglects non-decision making, or agenda setting. The scope of decision making, they argued, can be confined to relatively safe or non-challenging issues by setting the agenda so that particular articulated interests or issues can be prevented from reaching the point of decision making. This restrictive, non-decision-making aspect of power is the second face of power. We can see the ability of those who set the agenda to control discussion and determination of even the very issues to be discussed in the use of Robert's Rules of Order. Public and organizational meetings commonly use Robert's Rules of Order to keep meetings focused and on task, which can be enormously helpful in preventing the gatherings from veering off into unproductive or time-wasting directions. But these rules can also be highly effective in confining the meeting to only those items on a predetermined agenda, leaving "new business" for the very end of the meeting. That means that "new business," or the issues that challengers may wish to introduce, frequently do not get heard because time runs out. Robert's Rules may also be used to squash serious challenges if dominant forces at the meeting "call the question" and rule out further discussion.

Indeed, Schattschneider (1975) criticized pluralists by arguing that they failed to consider the notion of *mobilization of bias* in decision-making and non-decision-making processes. He noted that some issues are commonly organized *into* politics by dominants and therefore brought into the center of decision making; other issues are organized *out* of politics and therefore are silenced. Such is the case when the leaders of political parties set the planks in their party platforms during elections. Party platforms set the agenda identifying the issues of importance upon which the campaign will focus, effectively ruling "out of order" any other issues. So, for example, when both the Democratic and Republican Parties struggle to keep abortion rights off their respective national platforms, they are attempting to silence a highly divisive issue as they battle for the center. Schattschneider argued that one must consider the processes by which this political process of mobilizing bias occurs.

Note that neither pluralists nor power elite theorists see this second, non-decision-making face of power. In fact, Bachrach and Baratz (1962) pointed out that power elite theorists do not see either behavioral face of power (i.e., they do not see decision making or non-decision making). They do not look at behavior at all but rather *assume* that certain positions are stable and powerful and then examine who fills these presumably powerful positions. Power for power elite theorists is concentrated in relatively few hands rather than dispersed as pluralists contend. There are no identifiable limits to elite domination in this conception: The power elite are portrayed as almost omnipotent, with the masses unable to challenge their domination successfully. In this conception, power is a *position* enjoyed by institutional elites to assert their class interests over and above everyone else. This conception of power neglects the problem of those times that the power elite seem to fail to get all their interests addressed or times that decisions are made that contradict their interests. It also equates the reputation for power with actual power, concentrating on the sources of power and ignoring the exercise of power.

While Bachrach and Baratz (1962) introduced a critical analysis of the notion of power, they did not necessarily go far enough: they were still assuming power to be a behavior. But Lukes (1974) argued that there is a third face to power that Bachrach and Baratz did not see: the preemptive face. *Potential* issues and interests (not just actual, articulated issues) can be preempted before people even recognize that they have such interests. That is, challenging issues may be silenced when dissenters attempt to articulate and publicly debate them; in the preemptive face of power, the mobilization of bias has functioned so effectively as to shape how people see the world and thus prevent them from even recognizing their interests. This third face of power is the ability to prevent people from even having grievances in the first place,

> by shaping their perceptions, cognitions and preferences in such a way that they accept without question their role in the existing order of things, either because they can see no alternative to it, or because they see it as natural and unchangeable, or because they value it as divinely ordained and beneficial. (Lukes, 1974, p. 24)

Here, power is both a position *and* a *relationship*. Those whose positions enable them to control information access and shape perceptions can do so because others do not have such access. This implies political or oppression socialization as an important element to power: Those who function as agents of political socialization may preempt subordinates from even realizing that their own interests may not be one and the same as those of dominants. (We will examine the notion of political and oppression socialization more fully in Chapter 4.)

For example, arguments that women's position in society as subordinate or inferior is natural or that people of color are genetically inferior are effectively preempting challenges to sexism and racism by using "science" to shape people's perceptions that such challenges would be futile. Similarly, arguments that capitalism may have problems, including economic inequality, but state-run socialism has been no better, are framing the discussion in a false dichotomy that may preempt consideration of perhaps a third possibility. Since there is no viable alternative to capitalism, we must accept it, warts and all. The result may be that women, people of color, the poor, and the working class will be less likely to struggle against oppression and inequality if they believe it is unchangeable or biologically natural. When people's perceptions have thus been so successfully shaped, we may not observe conflict. Does the absence of observable conflict necessarily mean there is no issue or no grievance? No: It may simply mean that grievances have been either silenced or preempted.

Moreover, power involves an element of domination, coercion, and oppression. These can be explicit, deliberate, and overt as well as implicit, or even covert, and unconscious (Airaksinen, 1992; Young, 1992). Domination and preemptive oppression is particularly operative when unequal power becomes embedded in institutions. As such, coercive power can be paternalistic, apparent, real, preventive, or inductive (Airaksinen, 1992); oppression can involve exploitation, marginalization, powerlessness, cultural imperialism, or violence (Young, 1992). All of these forms of coercion and oppression can be overt and obvious as well as institutionalized and implicit.

The notion of power as a relationship implies that power is situated in a social setting (Wartenberg, 1992): Forces coordinated along dominant as well as oppressed interests affect the magnitude and salience of dominants' power over subordinates. That is, power is not a trait that dominants possess; it can be mitigated by resistance of subordinates.

Foucault (1969, 1979) viewed power as a social relation that is expressed both in institutions and in bodies of knowledge called *discourses* and that it can be mobilized to shape and define social realities. However, although he recognized the central role of the mode of production in shaping power relations, Foucault did not agree that it necessarily ensured elites would be unified to produce a common preemptive strategy or viewpoint or that capitalist class domination is inevitable. Rather, he argued that there may be conflicts and rifts within the capitalist class (e.g., between large monopoly capitalists and small competitive businesses) that could interfere with the development of a unified preemptive message and thus with asserting their agenda. Further, Foucault's view of power as a social relationship with no inevitable outcome favoring specific class domination suggested that power could also be a *process* as well as a social relationship. It also suggested a need to consider the role of resistance in power relations, which is embedded in the social relations rather than marginalized outside these. Further, if power is a relationship and a process, it implies that resistance is likely to provoke counterresistance. The examination of power must explore not only elites but those at the bottom as well. To do so, the analysis of power must pursue the strategies used rather than some assumed structure of class domination. These strategies involve the use of discourse that shapes and frames power relations and processes.

Queer theorists (see, e.g., Butler, 2004; Halperin, 1995; Sedgwick, 1990; Warner, 1999), for example, have put Foucault's insights into the productive nature of power, particularly with discourse, to rigorous use. Foucault (1985) looked at how the discourses surrounding sexuality medicalized homosexuality. In this process, some time in the 1800s, same-sex sexual practices became more than just a practice—it became an identity. Thus, "the homosexual" became a species of a being. Therefore, out of all of the variety of ways that people enjoy sex, including preferred positions, number of partners, preference for certain acts, etc., it was the sex of one's partners that came to determine this thing we now call "sexual orientation" or "identity." Through this process, a type of person was created—the homosexual. Discourse has productive power. It has the power to create docile bodies and a sense of identity and self.

While Foucault's analysis of power suggested the need to explore discourses that might affect the potential for preemptive shaping of people's perceptions and preferences, critics took issue with his focus on the role of discourse. For example, Smith (1990) argued that power "is always a mobilization of people's concerted activities" (p. 80). Knowledge as a form of power involves a process of coordinated effort to disconnect people's experience from discourse so that some people's lived experiences and perspectives are marginalized or otherwise treated as illegitimate. In this way, then, power is not simply *shaped* by discourse; power is *embedded* in discourse. Therefore, any analysis of power must be infused with an assessment of the way knowledge is framed from the standpoint of those whose experiences and lives are routinely discounted and ignored.

Power thus involves more than simply a behavior, a position, or a relationship; it also involves processes of connecting and disconnecting people's experiences and discourses. But while discourse has the real potential to shape people's perceptions and preferences so as to preempt their recognition of grievances, power processes also involve struggles between parties over discretion and constraint or how much room they might have to maneuver to position their interests. In a simple model, X is attempting to expand his or her range of discretion while simultaneously constraining or restricting the discretion of Y. Meanwhile, Y may be attempting to do the same to X. Here, power is the ability of X to access the resources of discretion of Y and therefore constrain Y's range of discretion by denying those resources to Y or minimizing the significance of these resources. This is an ongoing process of struggle in which both X and Y bring resources to bear on the struggle to try to increase each one's range of discretion while constraining that of the other participants. The scarcer and more valuable the resources actors control, the greater their respective power in the process. Moreover, that power is further enhanced if there are few or no alternatives to the scarce and valuable resources controlled.

Bank hegemony theory argues that those who collectively control finance capital may expand their own range of power and discretion and limit these for all other actors by deciding who gains access to that resource and who is denied access (Glasberg, 1989a). Their collective control of finance capital enables banks and other financial institutions a greater ability than other actors to shape agendas and perceptions, as well as the structure of resource access. This is because finance capital is a unique resource: Unlike all other resources, there are no alternatives. Individuals, political parties, major corporations, the military, and governments alike need money or other sources of investment to carry out their activities and address their interests. All other resources have alternatives. For example, if major corporations find human labor too expensive or too contentious, they may close operations in the United States and seek cheaper, more docile or desperate labor abroad or they may automate. If an auto producer finds steel too costly, management may shift from steel to aluminum or other materials. But everyone needs money.

Finance capital is also unique among resources because it is the only resource used to purchase all other resources necessary for production and for operating the state. And unlike other resources, it's also a relationship: Once forged, it's quite difficult to break those ties without long-range and fundamental consequences. This is because unlike other resources finance capital is typically extended to its users by a coalition or consortium of providers rather than by single, competitive providers. This means there is essentially no competition among providers.

While collusion among banks to harm other parties is expressly illegal, one provision of the Glass-Steagall Act of 1934 regulating banking stipulates that no single bank can legally lend more than 10% of its lending assets to a single borrower. However, the borrowing needs of large corporations and most governments far exceed the legal lending limit of individual banks. Hence, in order to meet these huge borrowing needs, financial institutions commonly pool their lending resources in a package of loans, creating *lending consortia*. This creates bank hegemony. Bank hegemony is structural coordination such that financial institutions may access the discretionary powers of other actors in the political economy and alter the options available to those other actors.

Processes and relationships of bank hegemony increase the likelihood that the banking community will have its interests addressed over other groups' interests, such as stockholders, workers, the state, industrial and commercial corporations, communities, and so on. In effect, it is the power of *collective* purse strings: Individual banks alone do not have the ability or the resources to shape the options available to other actors, but many banks structurally unified to control access to finance capital do (Glasberg, 1989b). These structures of pooled lenders are typically very large. For example, when the Chrysler Corporation nearly went bankrupt in 1979, there were 325 banks in its lending consortium. When Mexico faced bankruptcy in 1982, it struggled with more than 1,600 banks in its lending consortium for relief. Lending consortia mean that these become the "only banks in town" with which to do business, giving them the upper hand in dictating terms of loans like interest rates, maturities, corporate and state policy, and so on.

The notion of power as a process of oppression and struggle over discretion and constraint widens our conceptualization of power from something only elites possess. Power is not something that comes only from the top down: It can, in fact, come from the bottom up in a process of struggle with elites. This is a focal point of class dialectic theory. However, while class dialectic theory explores the dynamics specifically of *class* struggles, the notion of a dialectical process of struggle between elites and subordinates lends itself as well to analyses of such struggles along a wide range of dimensions (such as gender or race). Social movements, in which those who are oppressed pool their efforts and resources, may in similar ways structurally empower the oppressed well beyond the ability of individuals acting alone to effectively challenge the power of oppressors above them. (We will explore this in Chapter 6.) This suggests that part of power may be a *claiming process*, involving struggles over the contested terrain between oppressors and the oppressed of social constructions of what is "natural" and therefore unchangeable politically and what is "artificial" or socially constructed—and therefore subject to change.

Peattie and Rein (1983), for example, argued that the line between the conception of sex as "anatomy is destiny" and the artificial social constructions of gender is constantly being moved as a result of this claims process. Arguments that women were biologically unsuited for the physical, intellectual, and emotional demands of work outside the home were challenged and undermined when millions of women in the United States took the place of men deployed abroad in combat during World War II. Women worked in munitions factories, steel mills, coal mines, and foundries. They built battleships, tanks, aircraft carriers, and other heavy equipment in support of the war effort. When the war was over, it became politically difficult to return to the position that biology precluded women from working outside the home and in demanding jobs: The line between biology and social constructions of gender had been permanently shifted and the claims process begun anew.

Hegemonic relationships and processes can, indeed, be accessible to those with relatively little power. For example, when workers collectively deny producers the use of their labor, it can broaden their range of discretion in negotiating better wages, benefits, and work conditions from employers. This is especially the case when there are few or no alternatives to human labor. The use of the strike was most effective when manufacturers could not easily mobilize production abroad to exploit cheap and unorganized labor and when automation was extremely costly and time consuming for them. Employers had little choice but to negotiate with workers under such conditions. That does not mean workers got everything they wanted; it does mean, however, that they had greater power to constrain employers' power to thoroughly deny them their rights. Similarly, core world powers like the United States found their range of global discretion somewhat constrained by the collective control of oil and petroleum by the Organization of Petroleum Exporting Countries (OPEC) in the 1970s. The United States' heavy reliance on imported oil and petroleum for fuel and its failure to develop alternative, renewable sources of energy meant that OPEC was in a greater position to determine prices and supplies. Notice that in both of these examples the combination of scarcity; lack of alternatives; and organized, collective control of a necessary resource greatly enhances the position of those who possess it to increase their range of discretion while denying others access to it and thus constraining the range of discretion of these others.

Summing Up

Our discussion of the various conceptualizations of power and its structure identifies five dimensions of power (summarized in Table 2.2). It is important to recognize that we are not suggesting that one of these conceptualizations

Table 2.2   Dimensions of Power

Dimension	Example
1. Position	power elite theory; military-industrial complex
2. Behavior:	
Decision making	pluralism; voting
Non-decision making (agenda setting)	political party platforms; Robert's Rules of Order
3. Relationship:	
Preemption of interests; mobilization of bias	class dialectic theory; political socialization
4. Process:	class dialectic theory; bank hegemony theory; social movements
5. Everyday interaction	poststructuralist theory

is correct and the others are incorrect. Nor are we suggesting that these are necessarily mutually exclusive. Rather, different dimensions of power may be at play at different points in time or in different situations. So, for example, while bank hegemony theory and social movement theory may emphasize power as a process, these processes also frequently involve power as a relationship, as a structural position (particularly one affecting access to important resources), and as a behavior (whether decision making or non-decision making). Gaventa (1980) argued that the dimensions of power are, in fact, interdependent, and often reinforce each other. This is in part because power is often cumulative so that when a person or interest group has access to one dimension of power they often also gain access to other dimensions of power. And the power of one actor in struggles is neither absolute nor occurs in a vacuum irrespective of the relative power of other actors. In his analysis of resistance and quiescence in Appalachia, for example, Gaventa found that rebellion occurred only when the structure of power of the oppressors became weakened. Power, thus, is multidimensional and frequently cumulative, as well as relational. It is rarely absolute or isolated. And it is dynamic.

Discussion

1. Consider recall elections (such as the 2003 election recall of California Governor Gray Davis that ultimately brought Arnold Schwarzenegger to the governor's office) or electoral challenges (such as the challenge to U.S. Senator Al Franken's election in 2008). How might a pluralist analyze such electoral challenges? What role did interest groups play? What role did a plurality of elites play? What role did the electorate play in holding the incumbent accountable? Was the state a neutral arbiter? What was the common interest?

2. Both the federal government and state legislatures have often struggled to balance their respective budgets, a struggle that challenges many interests. What are some of the interests that are likely to be affected by how leaders balance the budget? How? Are these interest groups of equal strength? Why or why not? Consider the different ways that this issue might be resolved. Whose interests are served, and whose are hurt by each possible outcome? What potential interest groups might arise out of this debate?

3. What is the meaning of "common good"? Select an issue from the newspaper, and try to identify how each interest or elites define the common good. Is there consensus about the meaning of this concept? Whose interests may not be addressed in that definition?

4. Does the existence of power elite mean that nonelites are powerless? Why or why not? What can you point to as evidence of nonelite power or powerlessness?

5. Is it true that what is best for major corporations is also what is best for the United States as a whole? Are the interests of major corporations necessarily one and the same as the interests of the nation? Why or why not?

6. Are nonelites powerless to challenge the power of elites? Why or why not?

7. If power is diffuse, as Foucault and postmodernist theorists suggest, how might we explain the repeated patterns of privileged interests in society?

References

Airaksinen, T. (1992). The rhetoric of domination. In T. E. Wartenberg (Ed.), *Rethinking power* (pp. 102–121). Albany, NY: SUNY Press.

Bachrach, P., & Baratz, M. S. (1962). Two faces of power. *American Political Science Review, 56*(4), 947–952.

Butler, J. (2004). *Undoing gender.* New York: Routledge.

Clawson, D. (2003). *The next upsurge: Labor and the new social movements.* Ithaca, NY: ILR Press.

Clogher, R. (1981, August). Weaving spiders come not here: Bohemian Grove: Inside the secret retreat of the power elite. *Mother Jones,* pp. 28–35.

Deleuze, G., & Guattari, F. (1987). *A thousand plateaus: Capitalism and schizophrenia.* Minneapolis: University of Minnesota Press.

Domhoff, G. W. (1974). *The Bohemian Grove and other retreats: A study in ruling-class cohesiveness.* New York: Harper & Row.

Domhoff, G. W. (2002). *Who rules America?* (4th ed.). New York: McGraw-Hill.

Drache, D. (with Froese, M. D.). (2008). *Defiant publics: The unprecedented reach of the global citizen.* Cambridge, UK: Polity Press.

Dye, T. (2002). *Who's running America: The Bush reconstruction.* Englewood Cliffs, NJ: Prentice Hall.

Foucault, M. (1969). *Discipline and punish.* London: Tavistock.

Foucault, M. (1979). *Power, truth, strategy.* Brisbane: Feral.

Foucault, M. (1980). *Power/Knowledge: Selected interviews and other writings 1972–1977.* New York: Pantheon.

Foucault, M. (1985). *The history of sexuality.* New York: Vintage.

Fung, A. (2004). *Empowered participation: Reinventing urban democracy.* Princeton, NJ: Princeton University Press.

Gaventa, J. (1980). *Power and powerlessness: Quiescence and rebellion in an Appalachian valley.* Urbana: University of Illinois Press.

Glasberg, D. S. (1989a). Bank hegemony research and its implications for power structure theory. *Critical Sociology, 16*(2–3), 27–50.

Glasberg, D. S. (1989b). *The power of collective purse strings: The effect of bank hegemony on corporations and the state.* Berkeley: University of California Press.

Gordon, J. (2005). *Suburban sweatshops: The fight for immigrant rights.* Cambridge, MA: Harvard University Press.

Halperin, D. (1995). *Saint Foucault: Towards a gay hagiography*. Oxford, UK: Oxford University Press.

Higley, J., & Burton, M. (2006). *Elite foundations of liberal democracy*. Lanham, MD: Rowman & Littlefield.

Kumar, D. (2007). *Outside the box: Corporate media, globalization, and the UPS strike*. Champaign: University of Illinois Press.

Lardner, G., Jr., & Romano, L. (1999, July 30). Bush name helps fuel oil dealings. *The Washington Post*. Retrieved from http://www.washingtonpost.com/wp-srv/politics/campaigns/wh2000/stories/bush073099.htm

Levine, R. F. (1988). *Class struggle and the New Deal: Industrial labor, industrial capital, and the state*. Lawrence: University Press of Kansas.

Lipset, S. M. (1981). *Political man* [Expanded edition]. Baltimore: Johns Hopkins University Press.

Lukes, S. (1974). *Power: A radical view*. London: Macmillan.

Marx, K. (1954). *The Communist manifesto*. Chicago: Henry Regnery Company.

Mills, C. W. (1956). *The power elite*. New York: Oxford University Press.

Peattie, L., & Rein, M. (1983). *Women's claims: A study in political economy*. Oxford, UK: Oxford University Press.

Rose, A. (1967). *The power structure*. New York: Oxford University Press.

Schattschneider, E. E. (1975). *The semi-sovereign people* [Reissued edition]. Hinsdale, IL: Dryden.

Schwartz, M. A. (2005). *Party movements in the United States and Canada: Strategies of persistence*. Lanham, MD: Rowman & Littlefield.

Sedgwick, E. K. (1990). *The epistemology of the closet*. Berkeley: University of California Press.

Smith, D. (1990). *The conceptual practices of power: A feminist sociology of knowledge*. Boston: Northeastern University Press.

Tocqueville, A. de. (1966). *Democracy in America* (J. Mayer & M. Lerner, Eds.). New York: Harper & Row.

Truman, D. B. (1951). *The governmental process*. New York: Random House.

Tuchman, G., Daniels, A. K., & Benet, J. (Eds.). (1978). *Hearth and home: Images of women in the mass media*. New York: Oxford University Press.

Warner, M. (1999). *The trouble with normal: Sex, politics, and the ethics of queer life*. Cambridge, MA: Harvard University Press.

Wartenberg, T. E. (1992). Situated social power. In T. E. Wartenberg (Ed.), *Rethinking power* (pp. 79–102). Albany, NY: SUNY Press.

Whitt, J. A. (1982). *The dialectics of power: Urban elites and mass transportation*. Princeton, NJ: Princeton University Press.

Young, I. M. (1992). Five faces of oppression. In T. E. Wartenberg (Ed.), *Rethinking power* (pp. 174–196). Albany, NY: SUNY Press.

Zweigenhaft, R. L., & Domhoff, G. W. (2006). *Diversity in the power elite: How it happened, why it matters*. Lanham, MD: Rowman & Littlefield.

3

Is This the Best (or Only) Possible World?

Oppression and Socialization

The interests of dominant members of society may often be at odds with those of subordinates. Yet, subordinate members of society commonly "follow the rules" and accept dominants' rule, even if they may grouse about the inequality of power. How is this possible? Part of the answer lies in the process of oppression and political socialization. *Socialization* is the general process by which members of society learn what is expected of them and what they can expect from the world around them: They learn their rights, privileges, responsibilities, and obligations. *Political* and *oppression socialization* are particular forms of the more general socialization process. Political socialization refers to the process by which individuals learn and frequently internalize a political lens framing their perceptions of how power is arranged and how the world around them is (and should be) organized; those perceptions, in turn, shape and define individuals' definitions of who they are and how they should behave in the political and economic institutions in which they live. Oppression socialization, like political socialization, is a process whereby individuals develop understandings of power and political structure, particularly as these inform perceptions of identity, power, and opportunity relative to gender, racialized group membership, and sexuality.

This chapter will include a discussion of agents of oppression and political socialization, including schools, families, media, the state, and work.

What are the various political messages and values we might get from these agents? How do we sort out the gaps between abstract values in oppression and political socialization messages and people's lived realities, such that some messages and themes are likely to be accepted uncritically while others are more likely to be met with resistance, challenge, and defiance? The chapter will thus explore both the power of oppression and political socialization to shape perceptions and preferences, and the limits of socialization and how people may resist conforming to dominant interests and values.

Oppression Values and Ideologies

The way people come to see the world around them is contoured by the basic political values and ideologies they adopt. These values and ideologies, however, are not random, to be chosen by individuals of each generation like a dish from a smorgasbord. They are rooted in power structures that precede specific generations, and they can frame and shape individuals' perceptions and preferences so as to preempt challenges to the status quo. That said, what are the prevailing ideological frames and values that define, for example, the United States?

Individual Rights, Group Interests, and Oppression

In communist and socialist political economies, prevailing ideological systems emphasize ideal values of collective responsibility for all, as embodied in the famous 1875 Karl Marx quote: "from each according to his [sic] ability, to each according to his [sic] needs" (Marx, 1970). The fruits of individuals' collective labor are intended to be shared by all, regardless of any one person's contribution of effort to production. This ideal has certainly varied in practice, as seen in the former Soviet Union where party loyalty afforded some greater advantage and privilege over others regardless of need and on Israeli kibbutz where length of service to the group is a condition of level of privilege. But the ideals of the collective good as disconnected from individual effort stand in contrast to those of the United States.

The political history of the United States is replete with emphases on a promotion of individual rights and responsibilities and self-interest, as well as a contradictory concern for the well-being of communities and the common good, democratic representation and equality of opportunity. Much of the provisions of the U.S. Constitution preserve and protect ownership of private property. Moreover, the "inalienable rights" to life, liberty, and the pursuit of happiness that are extolled in the Declaration of Independence stress individual rights and underscore an ideology of *competitive individualism* (Cummings & del Taebel, 1978; Lipset, 1990): Individuals are responsible for their own personal well-being. Economic success (wealth) or failure (poverty) is thus understood to be the result of individual effort and competitive capabilities. This would seem to be particularly so if one assumes the value of equality of opportunity: Anyone can succeed with an investment of personal effort and hard work, because everyone has an equal chance. As such, those who are wealthy are presumed to have earned their affluence and privilege through their own individual hard work; if they did not deserve it, they would not have it (an analysis that ignores the reality that each generation benefits from the advantages that the wealth of previous generations were able to provide them, having nothing to do with their own individual effort or values). Similarly, those who are poor are widely understood to deserve their poverty because they lack an adequate work ethic: They are lazy, lack motivation or initiative, or have no competitive capabilities. If not for these personal shortcomings or inadequate value choices, they would not be poor.

Poverty, then, is a cultural problem, not a political problem: It is rooted in a culture of poverty that devalues engaging in hard work, earning a living, or gaining an education (Billings & Blee, 2000; Lewis, 1959). The assumption here is that the poor share a value system that markedly differs from the rest of society because of the effect of poverty on their lives: Poor individuals learn to embrace instant gratification, avoid formal education, disrespect law and order, and eschew the importance of hard work and effort because of the adaptive strategies they must adopt as a result of the circumstances of their poverty (Banfield, 1974). The likelihood is that they will share these values with their children, thus condemning multiple generations to poverty. This *culture of poverty* thesis discounts the larger institutional and structural factors contributing to poverty. For example, can individuals' work ethics and strong educational values ensure that they will not be poor if there are not enough jobs paying living wages (with health insurance benefits) for everyone who wants and needs them?

The preeminence of competitive individualism extends to the political economy, where the ideologies of free markets and the pursuit of private profit prevail. Individuals are free to trade and to engage in economic activities as they see fit, to generate private profits. Individuals are also free to sell their labor to whomever they wish. Should individual businesspersons fail to conduct their business efficiently and profitably, they will be punished by the invisible hand of the marketplace: They will go bankrupt. Governments, therefore, must adopt a laissez-faire position in the economy: They must not interfere in the daily operations of individuals but rather stay out of the way of individual economic actors and let the marketplace do its job. Under such a free market environment, those businesses that fail deserve their failure because they were not run efficiently; those that are successful, or grow ever larger, have earned their economic dominance and profitability. This does not take into account that a huge firm can pose a barrier to entry to an industry for small businesses that simply cannot compete with the sheer size and economy of scale of the corporate giant. Like competitive individualism, the free market ideology does not take into account that the players in this great marketplace do not necessarily confront each other on a level playing field or that one team may show up for the game with much better equipment.

Linked to these economic ideologies are ideologies that justify and reinforce patriarchy, white superiority, and heteronormativity. Patriarchal ideologies tend to treat women as property and justify women's second-class position as a "natural" or biologically immutable fact. For example, the ideology of "anatomy as destiny" identifies the different potential reproductive roles of men and women as signifying biological differences in other ways as well: Hormones and biology dictate men's and women's presumed differing intelligence, temperament, strength, agility, ability to assume leadership roles, and the like. Since these are assumed to be rooted in biology, they are immutable—not subject to change. Women are therefore constrained by their hormones and by their biology. Men are thus the superior being and because of their superiority may take possession of women to protect them. That women were not among the original founding "fathers" who framed and signed defining documents like the Constitution is not surprising, given patriarchal beliefs. Women's second-class citizenship was reinforced by the fact that they could not vote or own property and were themselves treated as property to be bought and sold. Social customs like women taking their husband's name after marriage, to be referred to as "Mrs. John Smith" rather than as "Jane Person," subverts or buries her identity under his, clearly identifying her as belonging to him. Ideologies that consider women as biologically inferior justify their treatment as property and thus as less than human and as second-class citizens.

Ideologies of white superiority similarly treat people of color as less than human and as subordinate to whites as a biological fact. Embedded in the very basic principles of the United States, white superiority rises to law. Consider, for example, that the Constitution emphasized the protection of property and affluence, including slaves as material property. The belief that persons of African descent were property rather than independent humans was reflected in several constitutional provisions, including Article I, Section 2, which counted slaves as three-fifths of a human being rather than as fully human; Article I, Sections 2 and 9, which determined states' tax apportion based on this three-fifths measure; and Article 4, Section 2 requiring the return of runaway slaves to their "rightful" owners (Feagin, 2001).

As well, those with nonnormative sexual and/or gender practices are institutionally marginalized and treated as second-class citizens. Basic citizenship rights like marriage (and the many social benefits that come from marriage), for example, are denied to same-sex couples as well as multipartner (polyamorous) relationships. Likewise, certain forms of sex work are illegal, as are some BDSM (bondage and discipline, dominance and submission, and sadism and masochism) sexual practices in some states. Same-sex partnerships face added hardships when trying to adopt children, and transgender and intersex people often suffer humiliating treatment when crossing national borders, being arrested, or even doing something as simple as using the restroom.

It would seem from this discussion so far that the prevailing ideologies of the culture of poverty and competitive individualism, anatomy as destiny, white superiority, and heteronormativity are not consistent with the interests of large numbers of people. And yet so many accept these with little question and adopt them as the political lenses through which their perceptions of the world around them are shaped. How is it possible that most people would readily adopt these lenses, even if these preempt their own interests?

Political Socialization

Individuals learn values, attitudes, and repertoires of political and economic behavior through a process of political socialization. That process contributes to the development of a lens that shapes people's assumptions and expectations about how the world works and what they might consider acceptable or even viable politically and economically. Several agents are especially important in this process: schools, media, and the state.

Media

The media are highly significant agents promoting the acceptance of dominant political and economic values (including the defense of these with individuals' lives in war) (McChesney, 1999; Parenti, 1998). News media cover wars as if they were covering sporting events, adopting the same terminology and metaphors of competitive sports. They frequently present "up close and personal" vignettes of "our" young warriors and broadcast nightly score reports of casualties and destruction. Reporters embedded in deployed U.S. troops provided such close-range coverage in the war against Iraq and in Afghanistan as if they were reporting from locker rooms or sidelines' vantage points. Sometimes the coverage takes on a game quality: for example, television news footage of U.S. Patriot missiles encountering Iraqi Scud missiles in the Middle East in 1991, when the night vision images of ghostly green blips looked very much like an innocuous video game.

Viewers are more likely to accept war as necessary and legitimate when the media demonize the leaders and citizens of other nations as evil or somehow less than human. President Ronald Reagan often referred to the former Soviet Union as "the Evil Empire." Similarly, in 1991, President George H. W. Bush emphasized that the war against Iraq was one of good against evil. The media often portrayed the Iraqis as a people who "don't value human life the way we do." In 2003, President George W. Bush described an "axis of evil" he alleged to be created by Iraq, Iran, and North Korea. Ideological broadcasts like these facilitate viewers' ability to transcend the norms against killing by dehumanizing the "other." Media coverage may stress themes such as "we're all in this together," "we'll all benefit equally from our team effort," and "we all agree that this is right and should occur" (see MacArthur, 1992). Such was the case during the wars against Iraq in 1991 and again more than a decade later, when coverage of the disproportionate representation of working-class members among the U.S. troops and the growing opposition to these wars within the United States was minimal.

This same process of demonizing the "other" in the run-up to war in an effort to socialize the citizens of the United States to accept war can be seen in assimilation and political socialization of immigrants to become citizens. At least one study of Jewish émigrés from Russia and the Ukraine to Israel illustrated the process as one involving several stages. The first of these involves devaluing and demonizing the homeland country while simultaneously idealizing the host country as the best possible place to be. Personal experience and confrontation with discrimination is likely to lead immigrants to be disillusioned of the idealized version of the host country and to strengthen their cultural identities with their homelands, but their contradictory bicultural identities and the continued devaluing of their homelands reinforces a political identity that remains with the host country (Tartakovsky, 2009). While this particular study was not of immigration processes in the United States, it identifies a common political socialization experience of immigrants to the United States, wherein mandatory attendance in (typically) public schools and exposure to media demonization of their homelands continues to reinforce the political lens that elevates the values of the United States above all else.

In addition to promoting the acceptance of war, the media may advance the legitimacy of domination and capitalism by carefully selecting the stories to report and the perspectives they use to frame them. Project Censored publishes an annual list of the top 25 stories mainstream media refused to publish in a given year. In 2009, for example, the top five stories censored from mainstream media included one noting that more than one million Iraqis have violently died as a result of the 2003 U.S. invasion of that country. While it's not surprising that significant numbers of people become casualties of war, what is astonishing here—and notable in the media's lack of attention—is that this body count is similar to that of some of the worst mass killings in recent history: Rwanda's genocide in 1994 and Cambodia's "killing fields" genocide under the Khmer Rouge in the 1970s, both of which received a high degree of media attention. A second story described how the political leaders of the United States, Mexico, and Canada have been quietly meeting to expand the North American Free Trade Agreement (NAFTA) to cover homeland security of the three nations in a militarized force, without public debate or informed consent. A third story detailed how the FBI and the Department of Homeland Security deputized more than 23,000 representatives from private industry in a group called InfraGard to gather private information on U.S. citizens for the agencies. In exchange for providing the agencies with this information, InfraGard receives warnings of terrorist threats prior to notifying the public or even elected officials. Another censored story involved a "resurgence of US-backed militarism" in Latin America, supported by an increase in U.S. aid by 34 times the aid provided prior to 2005. That increased aid for the training of military and police personnel, including techniques of torture and execution of citizens, threatens to subvert peace and democracy in many Latin American countries. And finally, Project Censored pointed to a story of an executive order signed by the then president George W. Bush in 2007 to allow the U.S. Treasury Department to seize the assets of antiwar protestors, a move that was aimed at stifling dissent (Project Censored, 2010).

These stories call into doubt the ideologies that hold that the state legislates and implements policy for the common good in an open and democratic fashion or that corporations are socially conscious and balance their need to be profitable with the social need to protect human rights, health, and safety priorities. Censorship of news contributes to the suppression of challenges and buttresses uncritical faith in dominant institutions and the elites who run them by controlling the availability of critical information necessary in the development of people's perceptions and preferences.

In spite of conservatives' complaints that the media are biased toward liberals, studies show otherwise. One study found that the selection of sources for news stories was heavily biased toward elite interests: "Network news demonstrated a clear tendency to showcase the opinions of the most powerful political and economic actors, while giving limited access to those voices that would be most likely to challenge them" (Howard, 2002). This media bias is not surprising: Mass media are commonly owned and controlled by large capitalist interests (Hackett & Adam, 1999) and are thus themselves corporate entities. The three dominant commercial television networks (ABC, CBS, and NBC) are owned and controlled by major institutional investors (McChesney, 1997): General Electric owns NBC, Disney owns ABC, and Westinghouse owns CBS. In addition, these networks maintain direct ties with some of the largest Fortune 500 corporations through common members of their boards of directors—ties that form interlocking directorates. These interlocks have intensified in the past couple of decades because the largest media firms have merged with ever-larger firms who have their own substantial interlocks (Moore, 2003). That the main broadcasting networks belong to corporate giants with interlocks to other corporations is significant because people in the United States get their news from television more than any other source: A Pew Research survey found that while 35% in the United States read a national newspaper, 70% watch national television for news (Schonfeld, 2008). And although cable networks may pose some competition and the Internet is quickly growing—particularly among younger adults, as a source of news—the three main commercial networks still hold the dominant share of the audience.

Newspapers and magazines are somewhat less concentrated than television broadcast media, but they are owned and controlled by industry conglomerates as are the television networks. A mere 10 newspaper conglomerates maintain half of the total newspaper circulation in the United States (Knee, 2003). Moreover, media conglomerates commonly own several major newspapers, magazines, and local television affiliates, a fact that produces the homogenization of news. People are likely to get a single analysis from one perspective of highly complex news items regardless of how many different media they may use as their sources of news. This is especially likely if all the media sources an individual uses are owned or controlled by the same media conglomerate.

Look, for example, at the holdings of Time Warner, Inc., the world's largest media conglomerate. Among its many interests are Netscape and Legend (an Internet service in China); Time Life books including Book-of-the-Month Club, Inc., and the academic textbook publisher Little, Brown and Company; a large assortment of television and cable subsidiaries, including HBO, CNN, CNN Radio, Court TV, TBS, TNT, and Comedy Central; magazines, such as *Time*, *Time for Kids*, *Fortune*, and *People*; film production companies, including Warner Bros., Castle Rock Entertainment, New Line Cinema, and Turner Original Productions; and media companies specializing in classroom services, such as Turner Learning, CNN Newsroom, and Turner Adventure Learning. In addition to this wide array of companies owned by Time Warner, Inc., are more than a dozen joint ventures with some of the largest corporations. Finally, the firm has ties in interlocking directorates with at least 37 other major corporations.

This structure of media matters for several reasons. When one firm owns or controls such a wide assortment of information sources and maintains joint ventures and interlocking directorates with many of the world's largest corporations, the probability that stories critical of the many companies and industries involved with the firm will be broadcast or published become minimal (Herman & Chomsky, 1988). For example, in 2000 ABC News refused to broadcast a reporter's story about pedophilia at a Disney-owned amusement park; Disney is ABC's parent company. ABC also declined to air a story about the use of sweatshop factories to produce Kathie Lee Gifford's clothing line for Kmart; that department store is a major advertiser for ABC News (FAIR, 2000). And after Disney took over Miramax, it refused to release *Fahrenheit 9/11*, Michael Moore's feature documentary film starkly criticizing President George W. Bush's administration and its policies. The film was ultimately released and distributed independently, but Disney made its political position and its willingness to use its power as a media giant to enforce that position quite clear.

Disney is not alone in its use of media power to shape perceptions and affect political processes: Sinclair Group is a huge media corporation owning 62 television stations nationwide (13 of which, significantly, are in key swing states affecting the outcome of the 2008 presidential election); Sinclair Group's executives have been generous contributors to the Republican Party and many of its causes. The corporation decided to preempt its regular programming to broadcast—commercial free—the film *Stolen Honor*, which assailed Bush opponent John Kerry's military record and accused his subsequent antiwar activism of harming Vietnam-era U.S. prisoners of war. Moreover, the Sinclair Group refused to provide equal air time following the film's broadcast for Kerry or the Democratic Party to respond to the film's charges. The absence of a full array of information in instances such as this robs viewers of the opportunity to sift through the material and draw their own conclusions.

The ability to influence large numbers of people is not readily available to everyone; media corporations are far more likely than anyone else, given their ownership and control of information outlets, to do so and in support of their own interests. When a single media giant owns both news and entertainment outlets, it also empowers the owners and controllers to reinforce notions of "us" and "them" in their portrayals of stereotypes in both the news and entertainment in ways that are consistent with corporate interests and thus to shape public sentiment. For example, stereotypical portrayals of Arabs and Muslims as violent thugs and brutal terrorists abound in animated feature films such as *Aladdin* and *The Prince of Egypt*, in live-action films like *300* and *The Siege*, and on television entertainment shows such as *24, The Agency, JAG, The District,* and *Family Law,* as well as on news broadcasts (Shaheen, 2001). It is no wonder, then, why many people in the United States readily assumed that the 1995 bombing of the federal building in Oklahoma City was the work of Arab terrorists, even though non-Arab U.S. citizens actually carried out the attack. Increasing concentration of ownership and control of media by large corporate interests thus contributes to political socialization because these interests are in a position to define what is news and how it is interpreted and presented for public consumption. And that can influence the outcomes of elections as well as public support for policies such as the war against Iraq and the Patriot Act restricting people's civil liberties in the name of increased national security.

On the other hand, while the ownership and control of traditional print and broadcast media can discourage dissent and shape our political lenses in concert with their own corporate interests over and above our own, there is growing evidence that the rise of the Internet may encourage more independent thought and perhaps resistance. Research suggests that when individuals' views were at odds with those of mainstream media they were more likely to turn to the Internet to seek out information and chat rooms more in line with their perspectives. The more immersed they become in the Internet, the more dissociated they become from mainstream media and therefore, the more likely they were to challenge official political viewpoints and become politically active in resistance (Bennett, Wells, & Rank, 2009; Hwang, Schmierbach, Paek, Gil de Zuniga, & Dhavan, 2006). This suggests a shift in the structure of media that can mitigate the political socialization role of traditional, corporate-controlled media.

Schools

Children spend anywhere from 10 years or more in schools in the United States, most in federally mandated public schools. Educational institutions therefore become important agents teaching and reinforcing a world view that privileges capitalism and ownership, competitive individualism, and democracy. Students are taught principles of the preeminence of private property, individual rights, personal responsibility for one's own existence, civic obligations, and duty to country in their study of the Constitution and Bill of Rights. Students often begin each day with the Pledge of Allegiance, and athletic competitions often begin with the National Anthem. Participation in such group recitations of patriotic loyalty are constant reminders of those basic nationalistic values (Tyack, 2001). By and large, these values may not be problematic, but uncritical acceptance of them may be. This is because these values encourage people to believe that the United States is a completely free and open society in which upward mobility and accomplishment are achieved simply by individuals' hard work and discourage exploration of how institutionalized social arrangements may play a role. The implication is that those who are poor, homeless, illiterate, or powerless are solely responsible for their own plight. Those who may be better off are therefore not responsible for providing help to the less fortunate. An uncritical acceptance of this individualistic ideology sharply reduces the likelihood that one might question the role of political and economic institutions in creating inequality (Euben, 1997).

Textbooks underscore the perspective that power, wealth, and privilege are earned rather than endowed in their portrayals of American history. Commonly, the most violent aspects of slavery, the violence by employers and the state against the labor movement, and the genocide of Native Americans in the westward expansion are downplayed or ignored altogether. The state's extreme measures of repression against dissenters during the McCarthy era as well as during the Vietnam War are typically portrayed as the excesses of individual historical figures, such as McCarthy, former FBI Director J. Edgar Hoover, and former president Richard Nixon, rather than as standard state policy. In the absence of readily available challenging information that might invite a more critical analysis of institutional arrangements and practices, this crisper, sanitized view of American history impels students to accept the power and privilege of the few at the expense of the many as legitimate and repression as rare departures from the free and open society defined and embraced in the Declaration of Independence and the Constitution.

Schools also teach students basic democratic values and the norms of political behavior in democracies. The legitimate means to redress grievances in a democracy is to vote. Organized protest demonstrations that disrupt business as usual are not legitimate and neither is the use of violence: Only the state has the legitimacy to use force and violence. Even if one does not prevail in an election, principles such as "one person, one vote" teach people that having participated in the process in and of itself produces a legitimate outcome. The process of elections thus validates the rule of politically and economically dominant interests because everyone appears to have participated equally in selecting that rule, despite the fact that the candidates they choose from are overwhelmingly drawn from the ranks of dominant groups to begin with. Students begin to assimilate these norms and values early, through elections for class. Class elections teach students their rights and responsibilities of participating in free and open elections, but the process is also likely to teach students to accept as normal the highly competitive nature of electoral processes. They are also likely to convey as normal and desirable notions like "The winner takes all" and "All is fair in love, war, and politics."

Furthermore, schools reinforce the preeminence of capitalism and the norms and values that support it. For example, the constant bombardment of students with commercial messages emphasizes the norms of citizens as consumers. This is because corporations have an increasingly high profile and presence in schools by supplying teachers with free curricular materials and classroom posters, vending machines in cafeterias that sell only certain brand-name products, and sponsorship of athletics and other extracurricular activities in exchange for prominent displays of corporate logos. In addition, Channel One, a seemingly innocuous news program broadcast to thousands of middle school and high school classrooms around the country, bombards its captive audience with several minutes of commercials along with news stories skewed toward corporate interests. Corporations thus increasingly affect the curriculum. Students quickly learn to accept without question the political economy of capitalism and their need to consume mass-produced products and labels (Brint, 1998; Hayta, 2008).

In addition to the corporate and democratic ideals that reinforce inequality as individualistic and fair, schools also socialize students to the norms and values of war. Competitive school sports prepare students to accept political decisions involving the nation in wars. This is particularly so in a culture in which warfare is often seen as just another sporting event characterized by team spirit and "us" against "them." People often accept physical injuries and casualties as normal and justified in both competitive sports and war; concepts like "to the winners go the spoils" become legitimized. Wars and competitive school sports even share a common terminology. Athletic teams typically select warlike or aggressive figures or symbols for their names, mascots, and logos. Aggression thus becomes a normal feature of competition. Competitive team sports may also contribute to political socialization by channeling violence and aggression into a carefully organized competitive setting governed by rules (Dunning, 1993; Wilson, 1992). Organized school athletics teams thus become part of a "civilizing" process that teaches the norms of violence and aggression: It is acceptable to inflict bodily harm on players of the opposing team, but it is not acceptable to do so to neighbors, coworkers, or authority figures. The parallel analytical frames of competitive team sports and war facilitates the transference of the norms of violence to situations of war: "War is hell," but it's a necessary hell, and inflicting death and injury to opposing forces is an unfortunate but necessary part of the conflict in which the winner gains the spoils.

On the other hand, when schools teach students to read and to independently and critically assess information, they also inadvertently encourage the possibility of discussion and dissent. If students can read the assigned material, they are armed with the skills to read other materials as well, increasing the possibility of exposure to subversive ideas and independent challenges to authority. School activities such as student debate teams require the ability to take a position, marshal evidence to support that position, and to challenge the logic and validity of opponents' arguments so as to convince observers. Classroom discussions (as opposed to lectures and rote learning) similarly have the capacity to foster the development of critical thinking skills. These skills are likely to discourage robotic acceptance of official viewpoints and to encourage resistance and dissent in settings outside the classroom as well as within it. Where, then, do we encounter information in this process, and how do these sources affect the shaping of political perceptions and preferences? Let's look at the influence of media as one such powerful source.

The State

A key source of information for newspapers and broadcasters is the state itself. High-level officials in government, including Congress, the White House, and various state-level and municipal leaders and offices, provide information to the press. That gives the state a unique ability to inform, misinform, or disinform the press and thus the public according to the needs and interests of these elites. While that may seem highly conspiratorial, the fact is the state has often used the media for just this purpose and thus has been a significant influence on the development of public perceptions, a strategy often referred to as *propaganda*. For example, Rampton and Stauber (2003) argued that the administration of George W. Bush used "perception management" techniques to generate widespread public support of a war against Iraq on the pretext that Saddam Hussein harbored weapons of mass destruction. That perception management included misrepresentation of investigation findings to bolster the administration's insistence that such weapons existed, placing the United States in imminent danger of being attacked in a replay of the September 11, 2001, attacks that leveled the World Trade Center and therefore required the United States to defend itself in a preemptive attack of Iraq. No such weapons were found, but the information spin and the propaganda clearly worked: Bush's approval ratings were the highest ever of his administration.

To be sure, this was not the first time anyone had used propaganda in service of elites' political or economic agenda; nor was it peculiar to this administration. Propaganda and information spinning is the stock in trade of the state. And when propaganda planted in the media does not accomplish the desired effect, the state may resort to an appeal to patriotism and jingoism in support of elite interests. After September 11, 2001, the National Security Administration adopted images and poster designs similar to those used in World War II in support of the Homeland Security program (Wright, 2003). Posters bearing messages such as "Patriotism Means *No Questions*" suggested that criticism of the administration and its policies was unpatriotic, a theme that was reiterated when some protested the war against Iraq in 2003. Indeed, that position led the administration and its supporters to the odd position of branding Cindy Sheehan, the grieving mother of a soldier slain in Iraq who fiercely opposed the war, as "unpatriotic." Free speech and the right to dissent took a back seat to "national security" as it did during the McCarthy era in an attempt by the state to silence critics and preempt the development of challenging points of view.

But what happens when the state's preemptive political socialization does not work? Although much controversy swirls around the meaning and intent of the Second Amendment to endow individual citizens the right to bear arms, the state remains the sole unquestioned legitimate user of force and violence. As such, it has the physical means and the power to aggressively assert and enforce its own interests and to discourage or squash dissent. Historically, the state in the United States has occasionally used violence to suppress labor unrest by using the National Guard to protect strike-breaking workers, quell unruly picket lines, and break up demonstrations by striking workers by using tear gas and shooting at strikers. (Note: The state has never used violence to quell unruly and exploitative bosses.) The National Guard was also authorized to shoot at and kill demonstrators to silence antiwar protests during the Vietnam era. At other times, local police have jailed civil rights, antinuclear, and anti-abortion demonstrators and have pepper sprayed and arrested protestors against the World Trade Organization from 2000 to 2003. Even an activity as simple as feeding hungry people, as in the case of the activist group Food Not Bombs, has brought down the heavy hand of the state in the form of surveillance, intimidation, and arrests (Food Not Bombs, 2010).

The use of force by the state, often to quell its own citizens' voices, is not restricted to the United States. In China, the state enlisted the army and its tanks to suppress the 1991 student democracy movement. In Israel, the military frequently opens fire upon demonstrating Palestinians seeking political self-determination; in the aftermath of violent clashes between Palestinians and Israelis, the Israeli government often retaliates with ferocious attacks on Palestinian neighborhoods suspected of harboring possible terrorists. In the former Soviet Union, dissenters were often arrested and sent to brutal gulags in Siberia for reprogramming. Argentina, Chile, and the Khmer Rouge of Cambodia staged violent attacks against suspected critics of the state in the 1970s and 1980s; they commonly arrested, kidnapped, tortured, killed, and "disappeared" those who challenged the repressive regimes. And the Afrikaner government in South Africa during the 1980s arrested and often killed black resistors to the regime of white apartheid.

These are only a sample of a common pattern in which the state uses violent oppression to assert its will. When more subtle persuasion and preemptive socialization fail to discourage dissent, the state always has the option of calling out its considerable military with its weaponry to silence the opposition. In the process of demonstrating its typically superior weaponry and legitimacy for the use of force relative to dissenters, the state politically socializes potential future critics to conform to the will of the state, which is itself commonly dominated by elite interests. In the United States, those interests are typically corporate, though the state in any country also has interests of its own.

Schools, the media, and the state contribute to the development of individuals' perspectives on the values and norms governing their participation in political and economic institutions. People often learn to accept and support unquestioningly the existing political and economic structures and relationships and to regard the inequalities of privilege and power produced by these structures as right, inevitable, and legitimate. Processes and relations of political socialization shape and frame individuals' perceptions about how the political and economic world works and affects their views about what is possible and what is not. This is not to say that these institutions necessarily conspire to fool people or that individuals are helpless robots with no ability to resist or change what may seem like "thought control." In a relatively open and democratic society, other sources of countervailing or challenging information are still available so that dissent and resistance are not entirely extinguished. What is important here is that such dissent must struggle to be heard and legitimized in the face of a formidable array of agents that together discourage it. That dissent still does occur at all suggests that political socialization is relatively limited, even if it is robust. (We will discuss how people can become agents for change and resistance in Chapter 6.)

While the dominant interests that shape and frame these perceptions are corporate, as we shall see, heteropatriarchal and white superiority interests dominate as well.

Patriarchal Socialization and Gendered Oppression

Many political sociologists view political socialization as a process by which nonelites learn to accept the political economy as an unchangeable given so that they may be preempted from even considering the viability of challenging it. But individuals are also politically socialized to accept patriarchy and gendered oppression as an unalterable given as well, because of the assumption that sex and gender are one and the same, rooted in biology. Individuals may therefore be preempted from considering resistance to patriarchy as possible or realistic. How does patriarchal socialization occur if its acceptance is oppressive to so many? Several socialization agents play important roles in the process of patriarchal political socialization that ideologically justify the status quo of gendered power imbalances. These agents include media, family, work, schools, and the state. While none of these agents by themselves are sufficient to produce and reproduce patriarchy, the consistent themes they convey together reinforce that ideology and gendered oppression as normal and natural.

Media

As people's main source of information, the media are significant purveyors of gendered ideological filters. Male images dominate in television, as a 2008 Media Matters in America study demonstrated: Only 43% of all characters on television were female, and female characters were far more likely than male characters to be young (i.e., under 40 years old). News shows in particular were overwhelmingly male, as another Media Matters in America study done in 2007 found: Men were four times more likely than women to be guests on Sunday morning news talk shows, and 83% of prime-time cable news anchors and hosts were male (Media Report to Women, 2009). In some media, starkly drawn images depict men as aggressive and dominating actors and women as docile, submissive objects (Dines, 1992). Television and films commonly perpetuate these patriarchal stereotypes by offering very limited roles for women (Hanania, 1999; Hass, 1998; Lont, 2001). Women frequently decry the scarcity of roles for positively drawn, strong leading women; they tend to be cast in secondary roles as insecure, punishing, manipulative, spoiled, prudish, or childish females. And while the depiction of men's work is not related to their marital status, married women are depicted in traditional female jobs if they work outside the home at all (Signorielli & Kahlenberg, 2001). This suggests that when women are married, their main role is one of mother and their occupation secondary; men, whether married or single, are primarily workers outside the home, as if this were a natural division of labor.

Many situation comedies do depict men in buffoonish stereotypes, but there remains enough diversity in the range of images of men to balance these so that they do not become emblematic of maleness. In comparison, the images of women are more likely to be limited to demeaning caricatures; and with few other, more affirmative and independent images of women, the stereotypes become more significant as icons of womanhood. Moreover, when men are portrayed in negative terms, they tend primarily to be poor and working-class men, suggesting that there is something about their class and not their gender that causes them to behave so poorly (Butsch, 1995).

The gender bias in media is not surprising given the industry's power structure. Just as media are dominated by corporate interests, they are also dominated by men. One study of Fortune 1000 media and telecommunications corporations found that women might be increasingly visible on the screen but not in the decision-making and powerful positions behind the camera: One 2001 study found that women held only 3% of "positions of clout" in mainstream media (Jamieson, 2001). Another 2003 study found that fewer than 20% of the editors at the largest newspapers were women (Arnold & Hendrickson, 2003); still another study found that only 27.7% of the radio news directors were women in 2009 (Staniak, 2009). In fact, research shows that the number of women in the top editor and executive positions in U.S. newspapers actually *declined* between 2000 and 2001 (Gibbons, 2003).

In news reporting, media shows a strong tendency to rely on men as the sources of stories and to treat women as objects of stories or as nonexperts. One study found that only 15% of news sources were women; only 9% of the professional and political sources presented were women. In contrast, women constituted 40% of the "ordinary citizens" in the news (Howard, 2002). This suggests a pattern of treating men as the voices of authority and to imply that women are not. Such a gender bias in media is not surprising given the industry's power structure. Regardless of who reads the news to viewers or who writes the stories, those who make the decisions about what to broadcast or to print, whether it is news or entertainment programming, will get to determine what images people see. And when the decision makers are predominantly male, it is likely that male interests, perspectives, and experiences will dominate the programming. That can quite possibly lead to the *symbolic annihilation* of women (Tuchman, Daniels, & Benet, 1978) or "the absence of experience of a group of people in the media" (Lont, 2001, p. 119). When viewers see few women in the media or hear few of their voices talking about their experiences as valid, it suggests that they do not exist or are unimportant. While this can happen in other settings besides media, it is especially important in media, since this is such a significant source of information for many people.

Patriarchal socialization in media begins early and continues throughout the viewers' lives. Research shows that toddlers and preschoolers imitate what they see on television and that this imitative behavior intensifies through adolescence (Comstock & Paik, 1991). Gendered media images can thus be significant socialization agents: Ideological filters adopted at a very young age can begin to skew the intake and analysis of information well before individuals have developed independent critical thinking skills.

Notably, there are encouraging signs of change: Although males continue to dominate as the main characters in children's television programming, shows like *Kim Possible* and *Dora the Explorer* are beginning to feature strong, intelligent female characters. In adult programming, powerful and intelligent images of women are increasing. The long-running and popular 1980s television shows *Murphy Brown* and *Roseanne* and the 1990s series *Ally McBeal, Felicity, West Wing,* and *The Profiler* in the 1990s all showcased independent, powerful women as the main characters. By 2003, these few shows were gone from prime time, but others had taken their place to advance this change: *Alias* and *Buffy the Vampire Slayer* featured strong females as the main characters. Amy Brenneman portrayed a formidable judge and Tyne Daly her intelligent, independent mother on *Judging Amy*. Today they are joined by several articulate, smart, and successful women who are lawyers and district attorneys on the *Law and Order* franchise, and the numerous women who are highly regarded forensic scientists and detectives (even if they do dress provocatively on the job) on the *CSI* franchise.

That such roles are increasing is a good indicator of progress and contributes to a wider array of portrayals to challenge the dominance of patriarchy. But that these characters are notable at all as departures from the norm underscores the persistence and power of the media's gendered stereotypes. Further, even when media provide the public with strong and competent women, they are often hypersexualized and fit a nearly unattainable standard of beauty. Consider, for example, the ridiculous "armors" worn by warrior women in programs like *Hercules: The Legendary Journeys* or *Xena: Warrior Princess*. Not only do the "armors" look more like lingerie but the women, while certainly strong, fit traditional standards of beauty—again, standards that are nearly unattainable. And one study found that while female superheroes are beginning to show up in children's animated programming, their superhero behavior tended to be portrayed in traditionally masculine ways (Baker & Raney, 2007).

Family

The assumption that women are biologically programmed to be the care-takers at home and men are to be the breadwinners (the modern incarnation of hunters and gatherers) and defenders of home and community is commonly played out in family arrangements. Families may reproduce assumptions about men's and women's respective places in the world by the division of labor in the home (Cunningham, 2001). Even when women do work full-time outside the home as breadwinners, evidence indicates that they still perform most of the household and child care chores (Beaujot & Liu, 2005; Demo & Acock, 1993). This means that when women return home after a full day's work for pay in the outside world, their workday is far from over: They now begin their second full-time (albeit unpaid) job at home taking care of house and family, a situation some call the *second shift* (Foner, 1998; Hochschild, 1997; Stohs, 2000). While there is evidence that men are beginning to participate more in household responsibilities, women are still bearing a substantially greater burden even when they work outside the home in the paid labor market (Sullivan, 2000). A household division of labor in which the woman is assumed to be primarily responsible for taking care of the home and family models for children that women's natural role includes cooking, cleaning, and caring for children, regardless of the time spent working outside the home. It also implies that a man's natural role is that of paid worker and that he is ill-suited for household or child care responsibilities.

The adults' gendered division of labor is reproduced in the chores assigned to children in the household: girls babysit, cook, and wash dishes; boys take out garbage and do yard work (Burns & Homel, 1989). In general, "girls are raised to 'keep the home fires burning.' Boys are raised to do battle" (Abbott, 1998, p. 1). These arrangements are common in the United States as well as all over the world (Harkness & Super, 1996), and that ubiquitous pattern could easily be taken as evidence that the gendered division of labor, and the power inequalities this produces, are indeed rooted in genetic predispositions. Such an assumption, if left unexamined, discourages exploration of gendering as a social construction and a social process. It suggests that patriarchy and male dominance are biological and thus inexorable, and acceptance of this position has a strong probability of exercising a preemptive force on individuals' perceptions of oppression. While individuals may certainly determine to adopt different arrangements within their own families, such individual decisions are limited in how successful they are in effectively challenging the political dominance of patriarchy in the face of the structure of work. Let's examine how work may reinforce patriarchy such that individual efforts at resistance alone are unlikely to be sufficient.

Work

Women in the United States now make up at least half the labor force working for pay outside the home—a fact that would seem to challenge the patriarchal assumptions that women are biologically unsuited for such activities. The necessity of having women work in munitions factories, shipyards, steel mills, and the like during World War II dispelled that myth: The success of Rosie the Riveter made it difficult to maintain the ideology that women simply were genetically incapable of withstanding the demands, dangers, long hours, and pressures of paid labor. However, just as the domestic division of labor is gendered so, too, is the paid labor market. Most occupations in industrialized societies are characterized as predominantly male or predominantly female—that is, at least 80% of the people doing them are one sex. Notably, more jobs are male-dominated than female-dominated. In the United States in 2008, more than 40% of the women in the paid labor force were concentrated in only 40 job categories (out of a total of 504 defined by the U.S. Bureau of Labor Statistics) that are predominantly female (U.S. Bureau of Labor Statistics, 2009), and these are primarily in the helping professions. This occupational arrangement means fewer and less varied opportunities for women than for men, underscoring male dominance in the world of work. Not only do female-dominated jobs typically pay less than male-dominated jobs but men are paid more than women even when they perform female-dominated jobs. By 2008, women averaged 80 cents for every dollar men earned, even after education and work experience differences were taken into account. Although this represents an increase of the 62 cents women earned relative to men in 1979, it still indicates a continuation of the devaluation of the work women do (U.S. Bureau of Labor Statistics, 2009). In the absence of policy establishing equal pay for comparable work regardless of sex, patriarchy continues to affect men's and women's earnings differently. Why does this matter?

Many researchers in family studies identify money as a key factor in determining power relationships in the home: Power presumably accrues to whoever brings in and controls the financial assets of the family. Yet, as we already noted, even when women are the primary breadwinners in their families, they are still to be held responsible for domestic chores and are not the dominant power in their families. A simple cash nexus does not appear to be the most salient factor in establishing power arrangements—in the family or in the workplace. Patriarchal assumptions of male dominance appear to be more persuasive.

There is some indication that this may be changing. More men are beginning to take female-dominated jobs, especially as job opportunities in their previous male-dominated jobs dwindle. Although their numbers remain considerably small compared to women in these job categories, an increasing number of men are training and taking jobs as nurses, elementary school teachers, and administrative assistants. As more men do so, they may join the ranks of Rosie the Riveter in undermining the power of patriarchal definitions of male and female ability and place in the world. But until the structure of work is characterized by such things as equal opportunity and training, comparable worth, paid family leave, and flexible scheduling, individual efforts are likely to be limited in substantially altering the power imbalances of patriarchy.

Schools

In some countries, girls are specifically forbidden from attending school or from learning to read, as in, for example, Taliban-controlled Afghanistan. In most industrialized and post-industrialized countries, girls are mandated to attend school, but what happens to them once they are there has strong potential for reproducing patriarchy. Schools in the United States contribute to sustaining patriarchy by providing different learning and training experiences for boys and girls that reinforce a sense of inferiority and lack of initiative among female students and one of superiority and privilege among boys (Sadker & Sadker, 1994; Spade, 2001). Boys are far more likely than girls to be encouraged to set high standards for their work and strive for excellence and to receive detailed instructions to improve their performance (Boggiano & Barrett, 1991). This encouragement is often denied for girls, who instead are more likely to be given responses to their work suggesting that whatever they achieve, however flawed, is "good enough," that it is not necessary for them to try for better.

Girls and boys are often tracked into different paths of study (Kubitschek & Hallinan, 1996). Girls tend to be encouraged to enter into studies in the humanities, social sciences, and secretarial studies rather than math, physical and life sciences, and engineering, a subtle suggestion about the compatibility of these paths of study with their natural abilities and proclivities. They are often guided toward nurturing or helping professions, such as teaching (especially at the preschool and elementary school levels), nursing, social work, and clerical work. Boys tend to be tracked toward math and science, sports, and physically demanding vocations. They are also pushed toward more autonomous professions, such as medicine, science and technology, law, business, engineering, and finance, or physical vocations in fields like auto mechanics and electromechanical technology (Fennema, 1987; Peltz, 1990).

Patriarchal assumptions about men's and women's relative places in the world are replayed even in textbooks. History texts, for example, pay little attention to the significant contributions of women in both American and world history. Sports journalism college textbooks reinforce male hegemony by failing to encourage female journalism students from examining gendered inequalities in sports and athletics (Hardin, Dodd, & Lauffer, 2006). College-level sociology textbooks tend to restrict analyses of women in society to one chapter on gender and included in chapters on the family and socialization, chapters which have traditionally included women (Ferree & Hall, 1996; Hall, 1988). Discussions of the role of women in institutions such as the economy, the state, or religion are rare and thus they are obliterated from analyses of power in society. This implies that males are the consequential actors in the most important institutions, while women's contributions are restricted primarily within the family. More recent research on sociology college textbooks has found some progress in that depictions of women had increased (Clark & Nunes, 2008), many of the stereotypes persisted, particularly the invisibility of women of color.

The presumption that biology makes men the stronger of the species is buttressed by the structure of school athletics. Although Title IX provisions of affirmative action law requires equitable support for both males' and females' sports, women's high school and college athletics still tend to receive less funding for things like equipment, travel, and scholarships. This inequality is reinforced and often justified by the fact that there are far fewer opportunities for women as professional athletes. It reinforces a patriarchal ideology of women as genetically inferior to and weaker than men, justifying the position of male superiority and dominance. It does not invite an analysis of women as having fewer opportunities to develop intellectual and physical capabilities.

On the other hand, although female athletics receive *less* funding than male athletics, Title IX legislation has resulted in a dramatic *increase* in funding and participation opportunities for girls in athletics. By 2000, there was a substantial increase in national participation and spectator interest in women's basketball, as well as in women's soccer and ice hockey, in schools and in the Olympics; that intensified interest spilled over into increased opportunities for women in professional sports. These inroads to patriarchal privilege are, however, under some threat posed by a backlash against affirmative action. The Supreme Court in 2003 reaffirmed the principle of affirmative action, but legal challenges, including those targeting its Title IX provision that has been elemental in stimulating the increase of funding for girls' and women's athletics, remain in the courts. If these cases succeed, they may reverse the progress made by women in sports to reclaim athletics as a male domain. The level of intensity of these struggles, likely to continue for some time, is a measure of the high stakes for patriarchy and an indicator of both the dominating power of patriarchy and the resilience of dissent and challenge in a democratic society.

The State

The state itself becomes an important agent affecting patriarchal socialization by legitimizing some perspectives about gender and denying others through policies and practices. For example, when Congress failed to enact the Equal Rights Amendment, it signaled that the state viewed existing patriarchal power relations as legitimate and thus reinforced gendered power inequalities. Similarly, the legislative battle over the Defense of Marriage Act (DOMA) is a struggle over heteronormativity as a crucial aspect of gendering: Marriage is only legitimate when it occurs between one man and one woman. Any nonnormative relationships, long-term and highly committed though they may be, are not approved as legitimate because they do not conform to the state's definition of appropriate marital relations as gendered between one man and one woman—nor as a dyadic, monogamous "couple." In relationships between partners of the same sex, the gendered power nexus and thus patriarchy are missing. When the state legislates that viewpoint in a policy like DOMA it is doing more than allocating benefits and advantages that accrue to the compliant, including the extension of health care and pension benefits to one's partner, the right to adoption and parenting, and the right to participate in medical care decisions of one's partner; the state is also acting as an agent of patriarchal socialization that reinforces traditional definitions of gender and family.

On the other hand, the state has at times actively entered into a legislative or judicial challenge of patriarchal relations, signaling a shift in perspectives concerning gender. For example, when the federal government shifted gears in World War II to implore women to enter the factories in support of the war, it was denying the erstwhile traditional assumptions about the biological limitations of women's capabilities. That effort required a massive resocialization of both women and men, and the state embarked on a widespread media campaign to make that happen. When the Supreme Court determined in favor of women's rights to reproductive choice in the 1973 landmark *Roe v. Wade* abortion case, it subverted the previous notion that women's reproductive rights were controlled by their husbands, male partners, fathers, or the state itself. It gave women greater power to control their bodies. While that decision has since undergone serious challenges to reduce or eliminate that right, the decision altered an entire generation's perspectives about women's power and their rights; so did affirmative action legislation, as we earlier noted. Indeed, that legislation mandated that prior assumptions about an individual's capability on the job or in the classroom based on their potential reproductive roles as mother or father are not acceptable. That not only opened up previously closed opportunities but it also widened the socialization lens defining gender. And when Congress passed the Family and Medical Leave Act (FMLA) it signaled recognition that women are active participants in the labor force, requiring a redefinition of their roles at home as well.

When the state enacts, or fails to enact, legislation or makes judicial determinations, it becomes part of the patriarchal socialization process in that it is communicating those aspects of gendered oppression that the state considers legitimate. It is not necessarily the case that the state's actions (or inactions) immediately effect a shift in social structures or attitudes. But it does become one of the important filters that shape and define perceptions concerning the possible and the acceptable concerning gender. As such an agent of socialization, the state has the capacity to reinforce and thus reproduce patriarchal power relations or to signal to the population that these are illegitimate and thus worthy of subversion.

Resistance to Patriarchal Oppression and Socialization

Patriarchal socialization appears to be imperfect: Many women and men defy its formidable preemptive force. In the workplace and in educational institutions, for example, more women are charting paths and breaking barriers considered impossible by previous generations. Look at the proportion of female students in your classroom; more women are currently enrolled in colleges than men. Perhaps the professor of your political sociology course is a woman. More women than in previous generations are also currently active in athletics in school and in professional and Olympic sports, including such previously male-only sports as basketball, soccer, football, and ice hockey. An increasing number of women are turning up in corporations as executives and in Congress, the White House, and governor's mansions throughout the United States. Indeed, by 2007 there were more women than ever in Congress, and Representative Nancy Pelosi became the first woman Speaker of the House. And the appointments of Sonia Sotomayor and Elena Kagan to the Supreme Court now establish the unprecedented representation of women as one third of the jurists serving on the highest court in the nation.

Men are also beginning to defy patriarchal socialization. While it is slow to change, some men are becoming more active in household responsibilities, particularly child care if not chores. This is especially the case as more men are finding themselves downsized or laid off from middle management and manufacturing jobs and their wives increasingly becoming the family bread-winners. While most men still consider this arrangement a temporary blip in their career paths, others are making a conscious decision not to unques-tioningly adopt patriarchal assumptions about their roles. Consider the Houston Oilers football player who in 1993 refused to play one Sunday because his wife was giving birth to their first child. He was suspended and given a heavy monetary fine by his angry coach; however, a surprising swell of public outcry supporting the player's defiance of patriarchal demands and condemning his punitive coach caused the team's executive management to rescind the sanction. More recently, Prime Minister Tony Blair took a very brief and public parental leave of absence after the birth of his fourth child in 2000 to help care for the child. While Blair's parental leave was seen by many as a publicity stunt, and cases such as his are still rare rather than common, it signals a limit to the power of patriarchal socialization and therefore to unchallenged patriarchal and gendered oppression. Moreover, while individuals in families may strive to challenge patriarchy in their domestic arrangements, their success may be limited by the structure of work and its intersection with family.

White Superiority Socialization and Racist Oppression

Just as patriarchy and gendered socialization are important aspects of polit-ical socialization and power distribution, so too is white superiority and racist oppression. Where political socialization in general tends to preempt challenges to corporate privilege and power and to economic exploitation in capitalism, white superiority socialization is a significant element in pre-empting challenges to racist oppression and unearned white-skin privilege as unalterable givens because of the assumption that racist inequality is rooted in biology. Patriarchal and white superiority socialization thus reinforce the more general political socialization by acting as triple filters through which the privilege and power of the few becomes legitimized. How does white superiority socialization occur if its acceptance means the oppression and deprivation for so many?

Several agents play crucial roles in the process of white superiority social-ization, including media, family, and schools. Once again, none of these agents in and of themselves is sufficient to produce racism and white-skin privilege. What matters is the replay of consistent themes conveyed by these agents together that reinforces the ideology of white supremacy and racist oppression as normal and natural.

Media

As significant sources of information for the majority of people in the United States, media are powerful transmitters of white superiority socialization, whether that information is provided as serious news or entertainment (Williams, 1996). The images one encounters in entertainment television and film, for example, are limited and stereotypical rather than varied. Many African American and Latino actors continue to lament that the roles available to them are commonly as drug dealers or users, pimps, prostitutes, rapists, murderers, or muggers but rarely are they cast in affirmative leading roles (Dennis & Pease, 1996; Entman & Rojecki, 2000; Rodriguez, 1997). This criticism is supported by the National Association for the Advancement of Colored People (NAACP) and Latino and Asian American critics in the entertainment industry who have condemned this chronic problem (Deo, Lee, Chin, Millman, & Wang Yuen, 2008; Jackson, 2000; Lichter & Amundson, 1997). Their complaints suggest the symbolic annihilation (Tuchman et al., 1978) of people of color in the media: With few countervailing images to challenge the repeated stereotypes, people of color are either absent or delegitimized as valid members of society. Radio broadcasting is not any better. One study of National Public Radio (NPR) found that the voices heard on the airwaves in seven major U.S. urban markets were predominantly white: 88% of the daytime hosts and news anchors were non-Latino white (Rendall & Creeley, 2002).

In addition to this visual and audio symbolic annihilation, people of color are often marginalized in the sourcing and subject matter of news stories. One study found that whites constituted 92% of the total sources quoted for news stories, while African Americans made up 7% of those sources used, Latinos and Arab Americans 0.6% each, and Asian Americans 0.2%; only one source on a single segment on NBC in the study was Native American (Howard, 2002). People of color were far more commonly presented as objects of stories or as nonexperts, signaling to viewers that whites are the authorities to be consulted, the experts, the intelligent people in society. In arguably one of the starkest instances of racialized reporting, victims of Hurricane Katrina were stereotypically portrayed (Shah, 2009): Whites photographed leaving empty stores with armloads of bread and water were identified as resourceful, rational "victims" of the hurricane foraging for desperately needed food, while people of color in similar situations were captioned as irrational and violent "looters." Such racialized stereotyping and symbolic annihilation is not surprising: In 2007, over 89% of the broadcast news directors in television and 88% in radio were white; that same year, almost 94% of the general managers in television and 95% of those in radio were white (Papper, 2007).

Children's programming is no better: One study found that animated cartoons have continued their long tradition of severe underrepresentation and symbolic annihilation of characters of color (although they did find that when animated characters of color do appear they are depicted in similar fashion to that of white characters) (Klein & Shiffman, 2009).

There are signs that this imbalance has begun to improve somewhat: Roles for people of color on television have become more varied. Witness, for example, the characters of David Palmer, president of the United States on *24*, several physicians and surgeons on *Grey's Anatomy*, and the Latino forensic scientists on *CSI*. But such positive roles are still more remarkable than typical. One study of prime-time television from 2000 to 2001 done by Children Now found that people of color remained marginal and that whatever racial diversity occurred tended to be found in nonrecurring characters rather than in central, continuing roles. Furthermore, whites were more likely than people of color to be cast as characters in professional occupations; African Americans were more likely to be cast as characters in law-enforcement-related positions. And only people of color (primarily Latinos) played the roles of domestic workers, nurses/physicians' assistants, and unskilled laborers, with most of these concentrated among Latinos (Children Now, 2000).

The media have not remained consistently attentive to the challenge of expanding and diversifying the positive roles for actors of color. Both television and films continue to rely heavily on racist stereotypes. Whatever diversity has occurred on television was largely on the cable channels of Warner Brothers (WB) and Universal Paramount Network (UPN) rather than on the major networks. By 2006, this concentration became more dense: These channels became the single cable outlet CW when CBS bought UPN and UPN merged with WB. Notable exceptions that do not rely on negative stereotypes include *The Cosby Show*'s (1984–1992) positive portrayal of a successful African American family, a show often cited for its importance in improving both white and African American viewers' perceptions of families of color as respectable, well-educated, and stable—albeit nesting that respectability in the context of a family that was upper-middle class (Havens, 2000; Rhym, 1998). More recently, *The Bernie Mac Show* (2001–2006), *My Wife and Kids* (2001–2005), and *George Lopez* (2002–2007) portrayed middle-class couples struggling successfully with issues confronting many middle-class families as well as families of color. Unfortunately, however, these progressive strides remain more the exception than the rule: The more consistent themes on television resort to reiterating racialized stereotypes, which perpetuate negative racist images.

While media have maintained a pattern of repeating and legitimizing racist stereotypes, several studies evidence the power of media to challenge and alter politically racialized filters shaping viewers' perceptions. Peterson and Thurstone (1933; see also Schaefer, 1990) found that negative attitudes toward African Americans persisted 5 months after respondents viewed *The Birth of a Nation*, a 1915 film that extolled the virtues of the Ku Klux Klan. On the other hand, the 1947 film *Gentleman's Agreement*, which heavily criticized anti-Semitism, reduced viewers' antagonisms and hatred against Jews (Ball-Rokeach, Rokeach, & Grube, 1984). Although these films are quite outdated, the studies of their impact on the audience underscore the power of media to shape viewer perception and thus imply the potential of media to provide information that critically calls into question the racist information generated by other socialization agents. More recently, coverage of the primaries and presidential election in 2008 trended heavily toward racialized (and gendered) stereotypes and did not challenge the hegemonic white, masculinized cultural frames of power and privilege (Walsh, 2009).

Too often, however, media do not capitalize on this potential for challenge and change. Television and print news media are often swift to seize on racist stereotypes in their reporting. Local news crime reports, for example, commonly emphasize the race of perpetrators of crimes (and notice that the crimes typically so reported are street crimes and drug offenses, rather than corporate or white-collar organized crimes). That tendency for racialized crime reporting can lead to a rush to judgment about guilt because of assumptions about linkages between race and propensity for violence. Cases in point occurred in 1989, when Carol Stewart, a young white woman, was murdered in a section of Boston largely populated by African Americans. Both the police and the press uncritically accepted her husband's insistence that she was shot by an African American in a failed robbery attempt. Later it became clear that her own husband had murdered her. But the repeated emphasis in the press on the racial overtones of the case served to reinforce racist stereotypes of the violence of African American males and the danger for whites in such neighborhoods. Similar racially charged coverage marked the 1994 case in South Carolina when Susan Smith claimed an African American carjacker kidnapped and killed her two young sons. She was sentenced to life in prison after a jury found that she herself had drowned her own children by strapping them securely in their car seats and then deliberately sending her car careening into a lake. And in 2006, a woman in Connecticut falsely claimed that she was raped by a black man as she walked in a public park in Hartford. The assumption in these cases that the killers or rapists were people of color was readily accepted by all because viewers and police alike had already been primed that such behavior was a natural characteristic of people of color. And indeed, that attitude is documented in public opinion surveys that continue to indicate the persistence of views that African Americans are inherently more violence-prone than whites (General Social Survey, 2006).

Family

The racially charged information filters conveyed by media are often reproduced by those transmitted by the family as an important source of values and norms. This is because it is within families that stereotypes about groups may take on added significance (O'Connor, Brooks-Gunn, & Graber, 2000). Information regarding superiority or inferiority of some groups of people, the appropriate individuals with whom one is to interact (including friendships, dating, and marriage relationships), whom one can trust and whom not, and how much respect and deference is or is not owed them based on their race, can be formidable in shaping children's perceptions. When families reward conformity with the rules and boundaries of interracial interaction and punish transgressions, they send a clear signal to both white children and children of color about their relative places in the world, about their value, and about racist conceptions of "natural."

That said, families might also be the source of strong racialized identity, resistance, and disregard of racist oppression and the information filters that perpetuate it (Berkel et al., 2009; Hughes, Hagelskamp, Way, & Foust, 2009; Neblett, Smalls, Ford, Nguyen, & Sellers, 2009). African American parents must often teach their children strategies for interacting with a white-dominated law-enforcement system as a means of protecting themselves when they are nonetheless innocent of breaking any laws. Although most families, regardless of racialized categories, are likely to want to teach their children a sense of important social norms, self-respect, and their places in the world, African American families have the additional challenge of doing this in the context of a racist political environment. However, that context may interfere with the development of a positive self-image. The challenge for people of color, then, is to provide their children with the tools to recognize the reality of a racist society and to reinterpret the significance of racism they are likely to experience to preserve a positive sense of self (Hill, 1999; Thornton, 1998).

While most families of color do in fact provide at least some information of the racist context of society, not all African American families actively pursue this: One third of African American parents in one study acknowledged that they do not provide information that challenges the prevailing racist messages other socialization agents are likely to convey (Bowman & Howard, 1985; Thornton, Chatters, Taylor, & Allen, 1990). But among the remaining two thirds of African American families in the study, many reported that they did emphasize for their children the right to actively confront and challenge racism and inequality (Bowman & Howard, 1985; Peters, 1985).

What influences whether and how a family will offer children information to challenge the prevailing racist messages and information? Research suggests that mothers' sense of self-efficacy, in association with their occupational self-direction (more so than that of fathers) affects the racial socialization of adolescents in African American families (Crouter, Baril, Davis, & McHale, 2008). This implies an interaction of gendering and racialization, such that a sense of personal empowerment is linked with one's occupational success, which in turn affects the racial socialization of adolescents (although this research is not clear that there are any gendered effects of racial socialization of adolescents): Mothers who feel empowered are more likely to convey positive racialized socialization messages than messages of racialized limitation. Other research suggests that patriarchal political socialization may interact with white superiority socialization, such that the gender of the child may affect the information parents impart. One study found that African American adolescent males were more likely than females to be cautioned about the racist challenges they are likely to encounter; African American adolescent females were more likely to be given information stressing racial pride (Bowman & Howard, 1985). Fathers were more likely than mothers to provide their sons with strategies for surviving in a racially hostile society (Thornton et al., 1990). Patriarchal notions of natural temperaments may play a role here in the different survival strategies families teach sons and daughters: Militance, defiance, and resistance behaviors are defined culturally as natural traits of males but not of females.

This is not to say that women are never encouraged to resist or defy racism. Consider, for example, such women as civil rights activist Rosa Parks, whose defiance of racism in the early 1960s by refusing to give up her seat on a bus to a white passenger became an icon of resistance to racism. Consider, as well, attorney Anita Hill, whose testimony about sexual harassment by Clarence Thomas before the Senate during confirmation hearings for seating him on the Supreme Court in the 1980s sparked a national debate about racism as well as gendered harassment. Attorney Lani Guinier is an active and talented federal civil rights advocate. And award-winning writers like Maya Angelou, Alice Walker, and Toni Morrison regularly use their literary skills to forthrightly describe, challenge, and defy racism. That such women would mount vocal and forceful challenges to racism at all highlights the role family can play as a proactive agent contradicting racialized themes emphasized by other agents.

Schools

Because children spend so much time in schools, these institutions have strong potential to act as agents of white superiority socialization. The very structure as well as the interactions between teachers and students can contribute to racist oppression.

Institutionalized Structures and Racist Oppression: One of the structural features of educational institutions in the United States that perpetuates racism and racist oppression is how schools are funded. School budgets rely most heavily on property tax revenues and state-matching funds. That means that middle-class (largely white) districts have access to far better funding than do schools in poor and working-class districts where students of color are more likely to be concentrated (Pisko & Stern, 1985; Walters, 2001). The intersections of racism and class inequality occur in part because of patterns of housing discrimination in which communities are likely to be predominantly people of color or largely (if not exclusively) white. Widening economic gaps between whites and people of color suggest that reliance on property tax revenues is likely to contribute to widening racial inequality as well. Moreover, district school boards may allocate different amounts of existing funding to schools *within* districts, providing money unequally from school to school.

One study in New York, for example, found that teachers' pay in predominantly white suburban Scarsdale averaged $81,410 annually, compared with teachers' annual salaries of $47,345 in heavily Latino and African American New York City, a pay gap of 73% (Stern, 1998). Funding and allocation decisions can produce differential educational experiences on the basis of race and class (see Swan, 1995), and these may translate into lower scores on standardized tests used to evaluate students and schools. The resulting differential performance scores of white students and students of color on such standardized tests as the SATs have fueled assumptions that there are genetically generated racial differences in intelligence.

Schools may also contribute to racist oppression by their structured personnel patterns. In 2004 and 2005, only 7.6% of elementary and secondary public school teachers were African American, and 4.4% were Latino (U.S. Census Bureau, 2006). If students enter college, they are likely to find these proportions of faculty of color to decline even further: 5% of college faculty are African American (and half of these work at historically black universities and colleges; at predominantly white institutions, only 2.3% of the faculty are African American) and 3% are Latino (Slaughter, Ehrenberg, & Hanushek, 2004, p. 302). While this does not necessarily indicate that schools deliberately restrict the number of faculty of color, when students encounter so few role models among teachers it suggests that people of color are not as intelligent or qualified to hold positions of authority as whites. This is a powerful racist information filter for all students.

Racist Oppression in School Materials: Students' perceptions of the value of racialized groups can also be affected by the information they encounter (or don't encounter) in the textbooks they use. Texts and curricula often contain a racial and ethnic bias. Textbooks tend to exclude people of color from analyses of U.S. history. One study found that when people of color were mentioned in such textbooks, they tended to be depicted pejoratively (Shaw-Taylor & Benokraitis, 1995; Wills, 1994).

Textbook publishers have been growing more sensitive to this concern, but racist themes and information packaging still remain. For example, photographs of people of color are most likely to appear in textbook chapters dealing with issues of race rather than being integrated throughout the book (which in and of itself implies that race is about people of color, not whites). Textbooks in other disciplines perpetuate racist filters of information by either ignoring race-related themes altogether or segregating images of people of color to specific topics. For example, anthropology and criminal justice textbooks tend to disregard problems of racism (Farrell & Koch, 1995; Shanklin, 2000). Another study noted that introductory sociology textbooks tend to relegate race-related information to chapters such as race and ethnicity, family, and stratification but neglect these in other chapters (Ferree & Hall, 1996). Other studies found that introductory economics and American government textbooks tend to "race code" contemporary poverty as a problem of African Americans, but these same textbooks exclude African Americans in their more compassionate depictions of poverty during the Great Depression of the 1930s (Clawson, 2002; Clawson & Kegler, 2000).

Taken together, these studies of academic textbooks suggest that consistent patterns of obliterating themes of race and racism, or at least of restricting the discussion of these to specific, isolated chapters, contribute to the development of racist filters that can skew information and its interpretation. These, in turn, can contribute to racist oppression.

Racist Patterns of Interaction in Schools: Schools can also reinforce racist oppression through interaction patterns between students and teachers. One study found that African American students' behaviors in the classroom are more likely to be evaluated positively by African American teachers than by white teachers, a pattern that continues from kindergarten through adolescence (Downey & Pribesh, 2004). Another study found that although African American female students are more likely than white female students to ask for help with their work from their teachers, African American students are more likely to be ignored or disregarded (American Association of University Women, 1992). Positive responses teachers do provide to students of color are more likely to contain qualifiers that minimize the praise ("that was good, but . . .") than the praise offered to white students (American Association of University Women, 1992; Freiberg, 1991). Evidence also suggests that teachers' prior expectations of students' abilities and academic performances are likely to be influenced by the race and class of the student (Dei, Mazzuca, McIsaac, & Zine, 1997): Teachers often expect higher academic performance of white and middle-class students than of economically deprived students and of students of color (Allen-Meares, 1990).

These prior expectations of students' academic abilities are often solidified and justified by early tracking of students, in which students of color are commonly placed in slower academic programs or plans of study for students who are not presumed to be college bound. Students in these tracks find it difficult to amass the requisite credits in preparation of college, and they thus have fewer opportunities for educational and occupational advancement. Evidence suggests that early racialized placement in a slower or noncollege preparatory track tends to become permanent and obstructs academic advancement, regardless of early abilities (Jencks & Phillips, 1998; Oakes, 1995). Tracking thus contributes to racist oppression by systematically restricting the opportunity structures of students of color. Another study found that when African American students attended college their majors tended to conform to stereotypical expectations, suggesting a link between racialized bias in expectations and students' academic outcomes (Chavous, Harris, Rivas, Helaire, & Green, 2004). Looked at from the other side of the desk, racialized information and bias in the learning experience affects students' expectations about their teachers' competence as well: One study explored white students' resistance to teachers of color as "the Other," undermining the authority and legitimacy of the teacher in the classroom (Rodriguez, 2009). Taken together, these studies suggest the power of racialized socialization derived from classroom and academic experiences for students as well as for teachers, a socialization process that reinforces racialized bias and outcomes.

Language and Racism in Schools: Language contributes to racist tracking decisions. Schools tend to privilege Standard English usage and to devalue other languages, which enhances perceptions of white superiority. For example, many educators denigrate the use of Black English or *Ebonics*, arguing that it lacks the rules and syntactical organization of Standard English, echoing the hostility to Ebonics as inferior found in mass media (Coleman & Daniel, 2000). Studies have shown, however, that while Black English is certainly different, it is nevertheless governed and organized by syntactical rules just as is Standard English (Baratz & Baratz, 1970). But because of teachers' greater power than students in educational institutions, teachers' perceptions and attitudes of proper language usage carry greater weight. African American students who use Black English are therefore likely to get labeled by teachers as less intelligent or academically capable than white students and thus more likely to be tracked into less rigorous or non-college-bound programs of study (Woodford et al., 1997).

Other studies have found similar biases against many bilingual children, including Latinos (Cobas & Feagin, 2008; Moore & Pachon, 1985) and Native Americans (Ogbu, 1978). Standard English is undeniably the language of high-paying jobs and careers in the United States, so adequate preparation of students of color to successfully compete for these jobs would certainly seem to necessitate assimilation of Standard English usage. But scholars note that assimilation of the English language has ensured limited access to such benefits for immigrants, suggesting that denial of the validity of multiple language acquisition is necessarily a liability (Hartman, 2003). Moreover, even well-intentioned teachers who provide English instruction on the assumption that it is the key to opportunity commonly fail to communicate that knowledge and facility of different languages and linguistic styles may be appropriate for specific settings and audiences and instead denigrate bilingualism and students' everyday language usage. More pointedly, critics argue that insistence on English-only serves to reproduce and sustain white dominance and oppression (Cobas & Feagin, 2008).

The struggle between Ebonics and Standard English signals a potential for resistance to white superiority socialization. Ebonics has been found to provide a vocabulary of resistance to racist conceptions of African American inferiority and thus an empowering mechanism reasserting value and identity (Green & Smart, 1997; Smitherman & Cunningham, 1997). And that hints at the limits of racist preemption of the consideration of the possibility that race is not a matter of biology but rather one of power and oppression.

The State

Legislative and judicial decisions contribute to the legal definitions of race, power, and oppression as well as act as important mechanisms shaping perceptions of citizenship and legitimacy based on race. When the Constitution defined slaves as only three-fifths of a human being, it legitimized and reinforced attitudes and practices of oppression against blacks. It reinforced this racist perception of African Americans as inferior or less than human through a series of laws and social repertoires, including the sanctity of the right of whites to own slaves as property to be bought and sold (and mistreated) and the maintenance of segregated schools. The state continues to frame racist perceptions through such practices as racial profiling and other criminal justice practices, as well as through immigration law that defines groups of people as undesirable based on their racialized group membership or ethnicity.

On the other hand, the state clearly signals significant shifts in racialized perceptions as a socialization agent when it passes laws and makes judicial determinations that subvert white-skin privilege. Such was the case with the Supreme Court's landmark 1954 *Brown v. Topeka Board of Education* determination that the maintenance of separate schools based on race was inherently unequal. Similarly, the passage of civil rights legislation and affirmative action legislation represented the state's subversion of long-standing perceptions and practices that the unequal treatment of people based on race was acceptable and justified and widened the social definition of race and of racist oppression. And, more than other agents of oppression and political socialization, the state has the ultimate power to enforce its decisions to reproduce or to subvert existing oppressions; it can fine, imprison, or execute those who fail to comply. Yet even the state cannot single-handedly impose its point of view without running the risk of insurrection; what it can do is set the definition of acceptable and unacceptable practices, and that ability makes it an important socialization agent.

While none of the agents of white superiority socialization by themselves can be construed as having the power to reproduce racist oppression, together they reinforce and perpetuate racist assumptions about differences between racially defined groups as natural and genetically endowed. If people are convinced that these socially constructed differences are in fact the result of genetic predispositions, they are unlikely to even consider that institutional arrangements may be responsible for artificially creating them and thus can be changed. If that perception is reinforced with a consistent theme from several socialization agents, including the state, it reduces the chances of resistance as anything but futile. But if key agents resist, defy, or otherwise challenge the validity of those perceptions, for whatever reasons, it can broaden power dynamics revolving around dominant racist perceptions by teaching and sanctioning different conceptions of human power and potential relative to race.

Summing Up

Oppression socialization is a form of political socialization in that both are about power and how subordinates and the disadvantaged largely come to comply with their oppression with little overt coercion. This is not to say that the oppressed never challenge the power structures that shape and define their oppression. Although together, the agents of political and oppression socialization are indeed powerful in helping to create ideological information filters and thus to preempt critical thinking and serious defiance of the status quo, they are not inexorably powerful. People are not powerless to critically assess, reject, and resist the oppressive information of political, patriarchal, and white superiority socialization. As we have indicated throughout the discussion in this chapter, there are many indicators of the imperfect ability of political and oppression agents to preempt resistance entirely. That potential for resistance is what allows for the possibility of social and political change.

That said, however, it is remarkable that so many people commonly accept structures of power and privilege inequalities even when these are not in their best interest. While no one socialization agent by itself causes individuals to accept this inequality of power and advantage, the consistency of themes and information from many such agents has the capacity to create the impression that oppression is inevitable or so overwhelming that resistance is without purpose. In that regard, political socialization may preempt challenges to the existing political and economic arrangements of class and power; insofar as oppression socialization similarly has the potential to preempt challenges to existing racialized and gendered arrangements of power, it, too, is a form of political socialization. Importantly, although this socialization is formidable in shaping and co-opting our perceptions of the possible and our preferences, it is imperfect. Many people, even among the most oppressed, do resist compliance. We will explore the mechanisms people commonly use to subvert structures of oppression in Chapter 6.

Discussion

1. Consider the television shows you watch regularly. What are the political socialization messages you see embedded in them? What are the oppression socialization messages you see in them? Is there a consistency to the themes you notice in
   these? Are these themes and messages different from or the same as those you
   notice elsewhere? Do you watch any shows that specifically challenge these?
   How? Are there other agents offering themes and messages that challenge the
   dominant ones? How?

2. If socialization processes are so powerful, how is resistance and change possible? Where do you see such opportunities in your daily existence? If you are
   among the power dominants in oppression relationships, should you be concerned about oppression socialization? Why or why not?

3. How might patriarchal oppression socialization affect sexual orientation socialization? What are some specific examples of socialization agents that might do
   this? How do they do this? Are there any that challenge the dominant theme of
   compulsory heteronormativity? How?

4. Consider the difference between race and ethnicity. Are they the same or different? How? Does it matter? Why or why not? Does racist oppression socialization operate the same way relative to ethnicity? How? How might racist
   oppression socialization affect new immigrants? How might it affect members
   of the dominant majority? What are some possibilities for resistance to racist
   oppression socialization?

References

Abbott, F. (Ed.). (1998). *Boyhood, growing up male: A multicultural anthology.*
   Madison: University of Wisconsin Press.

Allen-Meares, P. (1990). Educating black youths: The unfulfilled promise of equality.
   Social Work, 35(3), 283–286.

American Association of University Women. (1992). *How schools shortchange girls.*
   Washington, DC: AAUW Educational Foundation.

Arnold, M., & Hendrickson, M. L. (2003). Women in newspapers 2003: Challenging
   the status quo. *Northwestern University Media Management Center.* Retrieved
   from http://www.mediamanagementcenter.org/research/win2003.pdf

Baker, K., & Raney, A. A. (2007). Equally super?: Gender-role stereotyping of superheroes in children's animated programs. *Mass Communication & Society, 10*(1),
   25–41.

Ball-Rokeach, S. J., Rokeach, M., & Grube, J. W. (1984). *The great American values
   test: Influencing behavior and belief through television.* New York: Free Press.

Banfield, E. (1974). *The unheavenly city revisited.* Boston: Little, Brown.

Baratz, S. S., & Baratz, J. C. (1970). Early childhood intervention: The social science base of institutional racism. *Harvard Educational Review, 40*, 29–50.

Beaujot, R., & Liu, J. (2005). Models of time use in paid and unpaid work. *Journal of Family Issues, 26*(7), 924–946.

Bennett, W. L., Wells, C., & Rank, A. (2009). Young citizens and civic learning: Two paradigms of citizenship in the digital age. *Citizenship Studies, 13*(2), 105–120.

Berkel, C., Murry, V. M., Hurt, T. R., Chen, Y.-F., Brody, G. H., Simons, R. L., et al. (2009). It takes a village: Protecting rural African American youth in the context of racism. *Journal of Youth and Adolescence, 38*(2), 175–188.

Billings, D. B., & Blee, K. M. (2000). *The road to poverty: The making of wealth and hardship in Appalachia.* New York: Cambridge University Press.

Boggiano, A. K., & Barrett, M. (1991). Strategies to motivate helpless and mastery-oriented children: The effect of gender-based expectancies. *Sex Roles, 25*, 487–510.

Bowman, P., & Howard, C. (1985). Race-related socialization, motivation, and academic achievement: A study of black youth in three-generation families. *Journal of the American Academy of Child Psychiatry, 24*, 134–141.

Brint, S. (1998). *Schools and societies.* Thousand Oaks, CA: Pine Forge Press.

Burns, A., & Homel, R. (1989). Gender division of tasks by parents and their children. *Psychology of Women Quarterly, 13*(1), 113–125.

Butsch, R. (1995). Ralph, Fred, Archie, and Homer: Why television keeps recreating the white male working-class buffoon. In G. Dines & J. M. Humez (Eds.), *Gender, race, and class in media* (pp. 403–412). Thousand Oaks, CA: Sage.

Chavous, T. M., Harris, A., Rivas, D., Helaire, L., & Green, L. (2004). Racial stereotypes and gender in context: African Americans at predominantly black and predominantly white colleges. *Sex Roles: A Journal of Research, 51*(1–2), 1–16.

Children Now. (2000). *Fall colors: How diverse is the 1999–2000 TV season's prime time lineup?* Retrieved from http://www.childrennow.org/uploads/documents/fall_colors_lineup_2000.pdf

Clark, R., & Nunes, A. (2008). The face of society: Gender and race in introductory sociology books revisited. *Teaching Sociology, 36*(3), 227–239.

Clawson, R. A. (2002). Poor people, black faces: The portrayal of poverty in economics textbooks. *Journal of Black Studies, 32*(3), 352–361.

Clawson, R. A., & Kegler, E. R. (2000). The "race-coding" of poverty in American government college textbooks. *Howard Journal of Communications, 11*(3), 179–188.

Cobas, J. A., & Feagin, J. R. (2008). Language oppression and resistance: The case of middle class Latinos in the United States. *Ethnic and Racial Studies, 31*(2), 390–410.

Coleman, R. R. M., & Daniel, J. L. (2000). Mediating Ebonics. *Journal of Black Studies, 31*(1), 74–95.

Comstock, G., & Paik, H. (1991). *Television and the American child.* San Diego, CA: Academic Press.

Crouter, A. C., Baril, M. E., Davis, K. D., & McHale, S. M. (2008). Processes linking social class and racial socialization in African American dual-earner families. *Journal of Marriage and Family, 70*(5), 1311–1325.

Cummings, S., & Taebel, D. (1978, December). The economic socialization of children. *Social Problems, 26*, 198–210.

Cunningham, M. (2001). Parental influences on the gendered division of labor. *American Sociological Review, 66*(2), 184–203.

Dei, G. J., Mazzuca, J., McIsaac, E., & Zine, J. (1997). *Reconstructing "drop-out": A critical ethnography of the dynamics of black students' disengagement from school.* Toronto: University of Toronto Press.

Demo, D. H., & Acock, A. C. (1993). Family diversity and the division of domestic labor: How much have things really changed? *Family Relations, 42*(3), 323–331.

Dennis, E. E., & Pease, E. C. (Eds.). (1996). *The media in black and white.* New Brunswick, NJ: Transaction Publishers.

Deo, M. E., Lee, J. J., Chin, C. B., Millman, N., & Wang Yuen, N. (2008). Missing in action: "Framing" race on prime-time television. *Social Justice, 35*(2), 145–162.

Dines, G. (1992). Pornography and the media: cultural representation of violence against women. *Family Violence and Sexual Assault Bulletin, 8*(3), 17–20.

Downey, D. B., & Pribesh, S. (2004). When race matters: Teachers' evaluations of students' classroom behavior. *Sociology of Education, 77*(4), 267–282.

Dunning, E. (1993). Sport in the civilising process: Aspects of the development of modern sport. In E. G. Dunning, J. A. Maguire, & R. E. Pearton (Eds.), *The sports process: A comparative and developmental approach* (pp. 39–70). Champaign, IL: Human Kinetics Press.

Entman, R. M., & Rojecki, A. (2000). *The black image in the white mind: Media and race in America.* Chicago: University of Chicago Press.

Euben, J. P. (1997). *Corrupting youth: Political education, democratic culture, and political theory.* Princeton, NJ: Princeton University Press.

FAIR (Fairness & Accuracy In Reporting). (2000, November 20). *In the soup at The View: ABC allows corporate sponsor to buy talkshow content.* Retrieved from http://www.fair.org/index.php?page=1708

Farrell, B., & Koch, L. (1995). Criminal justice, sociology, and academia. *American Sociologist, 26*(1), 52–61.

Feagin, J. R. (2001). *Racist America: Roots, current realities, and future reparations.* New York: Routledge.

Fennema, E. (1987). Sex-related differences in education: Myths, realities, and interventions. In V. Richardson-Koehler (Ed.), *Educators' handbook: A research perspective* (pp. 329–347). New York: Longman.

Ferree, M. M., & Hall, E. J. (1996). Gender, race, and class in mainstream textbooks. *American Sociological Review, 61*(6), 929–950.

Foner, N. (1998). Benefits and burdens: Immigrant women and work in New York City. *Gender Issues, 16*(4), 5–24

Food Not Bombs. (2010). *Food not bombs to defy federal court ruling: Good people break bad laws.* Retrieved from http://www.foodnotbombs.net/fnb_resists .html

Freiberg, P. (1991, May). Separate classes for black males? *APA Monitor*, pp. 1, 47.

Gibbons, S. (2003). Newspaper execs clueless about what women want. *Women's eNews*. Retrieved from http://www.womensenews.org

Green, C., & Smart, I. I. (1997). Ebonics as cultural resistance. *Peace Review, 9*(4), 521–526.

Hackett, R., & Adam, M. (1999). Is media democratization a social movement? *Peace Review, 11*(1), 125–131.

Hall, E. J. (1988, October). One week for women: The structure of inclusion of gender issues in introductory textbooks. *Teaching Sociology, 16*, 431–442.

Hanania, J. (1999, March 7). Playing princesses, punishers and prudes. *New York Times*, pp. 35, 38.

Hardin, M., Dodd, J. E., & Lauffer, K. (2006). Passing it on: The reinforcement of male hegemony in sports journalism textbooks. *Mass Communication & Society, 9*(4), 429–446.

Harkness, S. & Super, C. M. (Eds.). (1996). *Parents' cultural belief systems: Their origins, expressions, and consequences.* New York: Guilford Press.

Hartman, A. (2003). Language as oppression: The English-only movement in the United States. *Socialism and Democracy, 17*(1), 187–208.

Hass, N. (1998, September 27). Hard times for strong-minded women. *New York Times*, p. 37.

Havens, T. (2000). "The biggest show in the world": Race and the global popularity of The Cosby Show. *Media Culture and Society, 22*(4), 371–391.

Hayta, A. B. (2008). Socialization of the child as a consumer. *Family and Consumer Sciences Research Journal, 37*(2), 167–184.

Herman, E. S., & Chomsky, N. (1988). *Manufacturing consent: The political economy of the mass media.* New York: Pantheon.

Hill, S. (1999). *African American children: Socialization and development in families.* Thousand Oaks, CA: Sage.

Hochschild, A. (with Machung, A.). (1997). *The second shift: Working parents and the revolution at home.* New York: Avon Books.

Howard, I. (2002, May/June). Power sources: On party, gender, race and class, TV news looks to the most powerful groups. *Extra!* Retrieved from http://www.fair.org/index.php?page=1109

Hughes, D., Hagelskamp, C., Way, N., & Foust, M. D. (2009). The role of mothers' and adolescents' perceptions of ethnic-racial socialization in shaping ethnic-racial identity among early adolescent boys and girls. *Journal of Youth and Adolescence, 38*(5), 605–626.

Hwang, H., Schmierbach, M., Paek, H.-J., Gil de Zuniga, H., & Dhavan, S. (2006). Media dissociation, Internet use, and antiwar political participation: A case study of political dissent and action against the war in Iraq. *Mass Communication and Society, 9*(4), 461–483.

Jackson, J. (2000, January/February). Anything but racism: Media make excuses for "whitewashed" TV lineup. *Extra!* Retrieved from http://www.fair.org/extra/0001/tv-racism.html

Jamieson, K. H. (2001). Progress or no room at the top? The role of women in telecommunications, broadcast, cable and e-companies. *Annenberg Public Policy*

Center. Retrieved from http://www.annenbergpublicpolicycenter.org/Downloads/Information_And_Society/20010314_Progress_and_Women/20010321_Progress_women_report.pdf

Jencks, C., & Phillips, M. (Eds.). (1998). *The black-white test score gap*. Washington, DC: Brookings Institution Press.

Klein, H., & Shiffman, K. S. (2009). Underrepresentation and symbolic annihilation of socially disenfranchised groups ("out groups") in animated cartoons. *The Howard Journal of Communications, 20*(1), 55–72.

Knee, J. A. (2003, May/June). False alarm at the FCC? Ending TV-newspaper cross-ownership rules may have little effect. *Columbia Journalism Review, 42*(1), 65.

Kubitschek, W. N., & Hallinan, M. T. (1996). Race, gender, and inequity in track assignments. *Research in Sociology of Education and Socialization, 11*, 121–146.

Lewis, O. (1959). *Five families: Mexican case studies in the culture of poverty*. New York: Basic Books.

Lichter, S. R., & Amundson, D. R. (1997). Distorted reality: Hispanic characters in TV entertainment. In C. Rodriguez (Ed.), *Latin looks* (pp. 57–72). Boulder, CO: Westview Press.

Lipset, S. M. (1990). *Continental divide: The values and institutions of the United States and Canada*. New York: Routledge.

Lont, C. M. (2001). The influence of the media on gender images. In D. Vannoy (Ed.), *Gender mosaics: Social perspectives* (pp. 114–122). Los Angeles: Roxbury.

MacArthur, J. R. (1992). *Second front: Censorship and propaganda in the Gulf War*. Berkeley: University of California Press.

Marx, K. (1970). Critique of the Gotha Programme. In *Marx/Engels selected works, volume three* (p. 13). Moscow: Progress Publishers.

McChesney, R. (1997, November/December). The global media giants: We are the world. *Extra!* Retrieved from http://www.fair.org/index.php?page=1406

McChesney, R. (1999). *Rich media, poor democracy: Communication politics in dubious times*. Urbana: University of Illinois Press.

Media Report to Women. (2009). Industry statistics. Retrieved from http://www.mediareporttowomen.com/statistics.com

Moore, A. (2003, March/April). Entangling alliances. *Columbia Journalism Review, 41*(6), 64.

Moore, J., & Pachon, H. (1985). *Hispanics in the United States* (2nd ed.). Englewood Cliffs, NJ: Prentice Hall.

Neblett, E. W., Jr., Smalls, C. P., Ford, K. R., Nguyen, H. S., & Sellers, R. M. (2009). Racial socialization and racial identity: African American parents' messages about race as precursors to identity. *Journal of Youth and Adolescence, 38*(2), 189–203.

Oakes, J. (1995). Two cities' tracking and within-school segregation. *Teachers College Record, 96*(4), 681–690.

O'Connor, L. A., Brooks-Gunn, J., & Graber, J. (2000). Black and white girls' racial preferences in media and peer choices and the role of socialization for black girls. *Journal of Family Psychology, 14*(3), 510–521.

Ogbu, J. U. (1978). *Minority education and caste: The American system in cross cultural perspective*. New York: Academic Press.

Papper, B. (2007). *Women and minorities in the newsroom*. Docstoc. Retrieved from http://www.docstoc.com/docs/614777/Women-and-Minorities-in-the-Newsroom

Parenti, M. (1998). *America besieged*. San Francisco: City Lights Books.

Peltz, W. H. (1990). Can girls + science – stereotypes = success? *Science Teacher*, 57(9), 44–49.

Peters, M. (1985). Racial socialization of young black children. In H. McAdoo & J. McAdoo (Eds.), *Black children* (pp. 159–173). Beverly Hills, CA: Sage.

Peterson, R. C., & Thurstone, L. L. (1933). *Motion pictures and the social attitudes of children*. New York: Macmillan.

Pisko, V. W., & Stern, J. D. (1985). *The condition of education, 1985 edition. Statistical report, National Center for Educational Statistics*. Washington, DC: U.S. Government Printing Office.

Project Censored. (2010, April 30). *Top 25 of 2009*. Retrieved from http://www.projectcensored.org/top-stories/articles/category/top-stories/top-25-of-2009/feed

Rampton, S., & Stauber, J. C. (2003). *Weapons of mass deception: The uses of propaganda in Bush's war on Iraq*. New York: Penguin/Putnam.

Rendall, S., & Creeley, W. (2002, September/October). White noise: Voices of color scarce on urban public radio. *Extra!* Retrieved from http://www.fair.org/extra/0209/white-noise.html

Rhym, D. (1998). An analysis of George Jefferson and Heathcliff Huxtable. *Journal of African American Men*, 3(3), 57–67.

Rodriguez, C. E. (Ed.). (1997). *Latin looks: Images of Latinas and Latinos in the U.S. media*. Boulder, CO: Westview Press.

Rodriguez, D. (2009). The usual suspect: Negotiating white student resistance and teacher authority in a predominantly white classroom. *Cultural Studies-Critical Methodologies*, 9(4), 483–508.

Roper Center, University of Connecticut. (2006). *General social survey*. Retrieved from http://roperweb.ropercenter.uconn.edu

Sadker, D., & Sadker, M. (1994). *Failing at fairness: How America's schools cheat girls*. New York: Scribner.

Schaefer, R. T. (1990). *Racial and ethnic groups* (4th ed.). Glenview, IL: Scott, Foresman.

Schonfeld, E. (2008). Pew Survey confirms what we all know: Net beats newspapers as a source for news. *Tech Crunch*. Retrieved from http://www.techcrunch.com/2008/12/25/pew-survey-confirms-what-we-all-know-net-beats-newspapers-as-a-source-for-news

Shah, H. (2009). Legitimizing neglect: Race and rationality in conservative news commentary about Hurricane Katrina. *The Howard Journal of Communication*, 20(1), 1–17.

Shaheen, J. G. (2001). *Reel bad Arabs: How Hollywood vilifies a people*. Northampton, MA: Interlink Publishing Group, Inc.

Shanklin, E. (2000). Representations of race and racism in American anthropology. *Current Anthropology*, 41(1), 99–103.

Shaw-Taylor, Y., & Benokraitis, N. V. (1995). The presentation of minorities in marriage and family textbooks. *Teaching Sociology*, 23(2), 122–135.

Signorielli, N., & Kahlenberg, S. (2001). Television's world of work in the nineties. *Journal of Broadcasting and Electronic Media, 45*(1), 4–22.

Slaughter, J. B., Ehrenberg, R. G., & Hanushek, E. A. (2004). The underrepresentation of minority faculty in higher education: A panel discussion [Special issue]. *The American Economic Review, 94*(2), 302–306.

Smitherman, G., & Cunningham, S. (1997). Moving beyond resistance: Ebonics and African American youth. *Journal of Black Psychology, 23*(3), 227–232.

Spade, J. Z. (2001). Gender education in the United States. In D. Vannoy (Ed.), *Gender mosaics: Social perspectives* (pp. 85–93). Los Angeles: Roxbury.

Staniak, S. (2009, July 28). RTNDA/Hofstra survey: More women leading in local news, journalists of color in local news down from 2008. *RTDNA (Radio Television Digital News Association).* Retrieved from https://www.rtdna.org/pages/posts/rtndahofstra-survey-more-women-leading-in-local-news-journalists-of-color-in-local-news-down-from-2008599.php

Stern, S. (1998). The vanishing teacher and other UFT fictions. *City Journal.* Retrieved from http://www.city-journal.org/html/10_2_the_vanishing_teacher.html

Stohs, J. H. (2000). Multicultural women's experience of household labor, conflicts, and equity. *Sex Roles, 42*(5–6), 339–361.

Sullivan, O. (2000). The division of domestic labour: Twenty years of change? *Sociology, 34*(3), 437–456.

Swan, E. T. (1995). Equitable access to funding. *Contemporary Education, 66*(4), 202–204.

Tartakovsky, E. (2009). Cultural identities of adolescent immigrants: A three-year longitudinal study including the pre-immigration period. *Journal of Youth and Adolescence, 38*(5), 654–671.

Thornton, M. C. (1998). Indigenous resources and strategies of resistance: Informal caregiving and racial socialization in black communities. In H. I. McCubbin, E. A. Thompson, A. I. Thompson, & J. A. Futrell (Eds.), *Resiliency in African-American families* (pp. 49–66). Thousand Oaks, CA: Sage.

Thornton, M. C., Chatters. L. M., Taylor, R. J., & Allen, W. R. (1990). Sociodemographic and environmental influences on racial socialization by black parents. *Child Development, 61*, 401–409.

Tuchman, G., Daniels, A. K., & Benet, J. (Eds.). (1978). *Hearth and home: Images of women in the mass media.* New York: Oxford University Press.

Tyack, D. (2001). School for citizens: The politics of civic education from 1790–1990. In G. Gerstel & J. Mollenkopf (Eds.), *E pluribus unum? Contemporary and historical perspectives on immigrant political incorporation* (pp. 331–370). New York: Russell Sage Foundation.

U.S. Bureau of Labor Statistics. (2009). *Household data annual averages.* Retrieved from http://stats.bls.gov/cps/cpsaat11.pdf

U.S. Census Bureau. (2006). *Statistical abstracts.* Retrieved from http://www.census.gov/prod/www/abs/statab.html

Walsh, E. T. (2009). Representations of race and gender in mainstream media coverage of the 2008 Democratic primary. *Journal of African American Studies, 13*(2), 121–130.

Walters, P. B. (2001). Educational access and the state: Historical continuities and discontinuities in racial inequality in American education [Special issue]. *Sociology of Education*, pp. 35–49.

Williams, G. H. (1996). *Life on the color line: The true story of a white boy who discovered he was black*. New York: Plume.

Wills, J. S. (1994). Popular culture, curriculum, and historical representation: The situation of Native Americans in American history and the perpetuation of stereotypes. *Journal of Narrative and Life History*, 4(4), 277–294.

Wilson, J. (1992). Cleaning up the game: Perspectives on the evolution of professional sports. In E. Dunning & C. Rojek (Eds.), *Sport and leisure in the civilizing process: Critique and counter critique* (pp. 65–95). Toronto: University of Toronto Press.

Woodford, M., California School Board, Baldwin, J., Williams, P. J., McWhorter, J. H., Boyd, H., et al. (1997). The Black Scholar reader's forum: Ebonics. *Black Scholar*, 27(1), 2–37.

Wright, M. I. (2003). *You back the attack, we'll bomb who we want*. New York: Seven Stories Press.

4

Power to the People?

Voting and Electoral Participation

I f you are over 18 years old and a citizen of the United States, you can join in a centuries-old tradition marking the political life of the nation: Every November, most adult citizens in the United States are entitled to participate in choosing their leaders, from local town councils to the president of the nation. Voters typically choose one of two candidates for each office, with each candidate running under the banner of one of the major political parties. On occasion, a third party will field a candidate as well, but in a winner-takes-all system, third-party candidates do not typically draw enough support to play much more than the role of the spoiler, drawing votes from one of the two major parties (although on rare occasions they do manage to win, as Joseph Lieberman did in his 2006 reelection bid as senator from Connecticut). The major party candidates commonly attempt to attract as many votes as possible, so they often try to avoid expressing extreme points of view so as not to alienate too many voters. That means that minority points of view are unlikely to gain representation, no matter how important their views may be. When all is said and done, most elected positions are held by either Republican or Democratic candidates.

In multiparty systems, in contrast, minority parties gain representation in government based on the proportion of votes they can gain. This is the case, for example, in nations like France, Italy, and Germany. In such systems, parties don't have to reach for the broadest appeal possible; they simply must try to draw the most voters they can to increase their proportionate representation in the legislative body. Clear policy choices can be articulated with the understanding that the minority interests they represent have a chance of being included in the policy-making process. Thus, Greens have a presence in the German and French Parliaments, as do far more reactionary or right-wing parties; Fascists can be found in Italy's governing body alongside more progressive parties. Voters in such multiparty systems may thus ignore the major parties without fear of throwing away their votes.

Regardless of these contrasts, both the two-party and the multiparty systems share an important characteristic: They are known as "democracies," a system in which citizens are entitled to participate in choosing their leaders and thus presumably have an effect on decision making. In democracies, then, voting may be seen as a source of citizen or nonelite power. This stands in contrast to dictatorships, in which citizens are denied the right to determine their leadership by the sheer tyrannical power of the existing leader or monarchies, in which national leadership is determined by birthright, even if citizens may still choose representatives in legislative bodies such as parliament. Indeed, the pluralist power structure model specifically analyzes voting as a critical source of citizen power, suggesting that power is dispersed and shared by all, primarily through voting and through group memberships. Voting is thus the key to power, since it is the mechanism by which the masses may hold (elected) elites accountable. If this is so, who votes and who doesn't and why? Can there be power without voting?

Moreover, in the United States, where economic inequality means that some will have greater resources to apply to the voting process than others, it becomes crucial to level the political playing field as much as possible to avoid the domination of the process by monied interests. The funding of political campaigns was reformed in 1973 in an attempt to address this issue. Political action committees (PACs) were instituted as a mechanism for limiting how much money individuals and organizations could contribute to a single candidate. What effect have PACs had on the electoral process? In addition, recent controversies surrounding campaign financing have raised public awareness of the problem of "soft money," a form of campaign financing that falls outside the control of PAC restrictions. What is "soft money," and how does it affect voting processes?

Who Votes?

Did you vote in the last election? Did you vote in the last presidential election? Did your friends or family vote? If you did not, you are not alone. Look at Figure 4.1: While the rate certainly fluctuates some, in national elections for president of the United States, when voting participation rates are typically at

Figure 4.1   Participation Rates in National Elections in the United States, 1932–2008

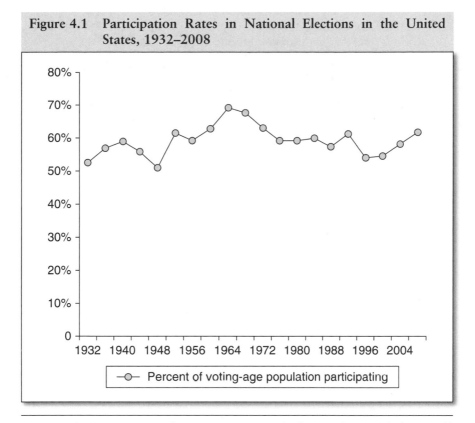

─○─ Percent of voting-age population participating

Source: U.S. Census Bureau, http://www.census.gov/prod/2008pubs/09statab/election.pdf; http://www.census.gov/prod/www/abs/statab1901-1950.htm; http://www.census.gov/prod/www/abs/statab1951-1994.htm.

their highest, little more than half of the eligible electorate actually votes. And these rates go much lower in the years between presidential elections, when voters are selecting local, state, and congressional leaders. This pattern of non-participation in local and state elections is somewhat surprising, considering that these are the elections where individuals' votes are more likely to have an effect on the outcome: They involve fewer eligible voters, and the candidates are more likely to be known personally or nominally by the voters. These are the elections where outcomes are often determined by fairly slim margins, and so every vote would appear to count. In national elections, over one hundred million people may vote, and it is unlikely that the outcome will be decided by one or a few votes.

Further, Table 4.1 shows that the United States has one of the lowest voter participation rates among industrialized democracies. Only Switzerland and Israel had lower rates than the United States in the opening decade of the 21st century, and both of those elections were parliamentary,

Table 4.1   Comparative Voter Participation Rates in Selected Industrialized and Post-Industrialized Democracies, 2002–2009

Country	Year	Percentage of Voting Age Population Participating
Australia	2007	82.0
Austria	2008	75.0
Belgium	2007	85.0
Canada	2006~	64.7
Finland	2007	68.0
Germany	2005+	72.0
Greece	2003^	63.0
India	2009+	62.0
Italy	2008	79.0
Ireland	2002	61.0
Israel	2009	50.3
Japan	2005	67.0
Mexico	2006	62.0
Sweden	2006	80.0
Switzerland	2003	37.0
United States	2008#	58.2

Sources: Table adapted from OECD Family Database. (2009, June 29). Chart CO4.2.A: Voter turnout in latest parliamentary election, around 2005. *OECD—Social Policy Division—Directorate of Employment, Labour and Social Affairs*. Retrieved from http://www.oecd.org/dataoecd/1/20/43200248.pdf.

(~) Parkinson, R. (2001, March 1). Voter turnout in Canada. *Mapleleafweb*. Retrieved from http://www.mapleleafweb.com/features/voter-turnout-canada#historical

(+ and ^) The Hindu Business Line. (2009, May 16). Does India's 62% voter turnout compare favourably? *The Hindu Business Line*. Retrieved from http://www.blonnet.com/2009/05/16/stories/2009051651811700.htm

(#) U.S. Census Bureau. (2009). Statistical abstracts, 2009. Retrieved from http://www.census.gov/compendia/statab/2010/tables/10s0406.pdf

not presidential elections. Pluralists would argue that this indicates a high degree of voter satisfaction with the existing leadership: If people were dissatisfied, they would mobilize their latent interests and vote as they did in 1992 with Ross Perot as an independent, again with Ross Perot's Reform Party in 1996, and in 2000 with Ralph Nader and the Green Party.

Who, then, are the individuals who do vote? Are they among those most likely to be dissatisfied? Or are they more a cross section of the general eligible voting population? Do they look similar to the nonvoters? Do they represent the diversity of interests that are presumably found in the wider population? Let's look at the social correlates of who votes and who doesn't. According to the U.S. Census Bureau, those who are more advantaged are more likely to vote than those who are more deprived or oppressed. People who had jobs, higher incomes, and more education were more likely to vote in 2008, as were women, white non-Hispanics, and older people (U.S. Census Bureau, 2009; see Table 4.2 and see also Wattenberg, 2002). These social correlates represent those with higher relative

Table 4.2 Social Correlates of U.S. Voter Participation, 2008

Social Characteristic		Percentage Voting
Income:		
	Under $10,000	41.3
	$10,000–$14,999	41.2
	$15,000–$19,999	44.3
	$20,000–$29,999	48.0
	$30,000–$39,999	54.4
	$40,000–$49,999	58.2
	$50,000–$74,999	65.9
	$75,000–$99,000	72.6
	$100,000–$149,999	74.9
	$150,000 and over	78.1
Education (years of school completed):		
	8 years or less	38.1
	High School:	
	1 to 3 years	39.9
	HS graduate	54.9
	College:	
	1 to 3 years	68.0
	Bachelor's degree	77.0
	Advanced degree	82.7

(Continued)

Table 4.2 (Continued)

Social Characteristic		Percentage Voting
Employment status:		
	Employed	65.2
	Unemployed	54.7
Sex:		
	Male	55.7
	Female	60.4
Race:		
	White non-Hispanic	64.8
	African American	60.8
	Asian	32.1
	Latino	31.6
Age:		
	18–24 years old	44.3
	25–34 years old	48.5
	35–44 years old	55.1
	45–54 years old	62.6
	55–64 years old	68.1
	65–74 years old	70.1
	75 years old and over	65.8

Source: Adapted from data found at U.S. Census Bureau, Population Division, Education & Social Stratification Branch. (2009, July 20). Voting and registration in the election of November 2008. *U.S. Census Bureau.* Retrieved from http://www.census.gov/population/www/socdemo/voting/cps2008.html.

economic resources and advantages (with the exception perhaps of women). As such, they are inconsistent with the pluralist argument that when people are dissatisfied because their interests and needs are not being met by existing leadership, they will mobilize their latent interests and participate. If the pluralist argument were correct, one would expect to find that people who are unemployed, poor, and have low education, as well as people of color and younger people to be more likely to vote, not less.

Although those who are more privileged are more likely to vote, there remain significant proportions of people in these categories who still do not. This finding is consistent with the pluralist argument: Such individuals are likely to be satisfied with the existing leadership and policies and are therefore less motivated to feel the need to go out of their way to vote. On the other hand, it would make sense for these individuals to want to participate in order to protect the advantages they already enjoy; were they to leave participation to those who are more dissatisfied they might stand to lose their privileges. Nonparticipation appears to be more widespread than simply relegated among the most disadvantaged in society. Therefore, how do we explain both the electoral participation patterns as well as nonparticipation?

Why Don't People Vote?

Analyses of electoral nonparticipation may be grouped into several categories: those focusing on social psychological explanations, those offering structural explanations, and those pursuing political alienation explanations. Let's examine these in turn.

Social Psychological Explanations

One explanation of the social correlate patterns of participation and nonparticipation is a socialization argument: It might be that those with higher incomes are likely to work in occupations that involve more politically relevant skills and thought processes that easily transfer to interest in politics and electoral participation. For example, higher-income jobs may require a fairly high degree of analysis of information, spoken or written articulation of interests or ideas, networking and interaction, negotiation with colleagues, and the ability to mobilize resources on behalf of an idea or a project. Such jobs may also require independent and critical thinking, personal initiative, and some degree of risk taking. These are important skills for gathering information about candidates and issues prior to an election; critically evaluating these, discussing, and debating issues and ideas with other people; and making an independent assessment before actually casting a ballot at the voting booth.

Furthermore, people in higher-income jobs may have relatively more time to engage in politics; those who are poor may find such time in short supply because they must devote their time to the unrelenting search for the resources of survival. Many, for example, juggle two or more part-time jobs just to make ends meet, putting a roof over their families' heads and food on the table. Political participation would seem to be a luxury indeed. And people without jobs at all are deprived of any cultural environment in which to learn political behavior. This argument explains political participation as the result of a culture of class and of socialization: Jobs in general, and higher-income (and frequently higher-power) occupations, in particular, teach people the skills and values of political activity, while the struggle for living presumably does not. People learn political behavior in their occupational contexts. However, the U.S. Census Bureau offers little support for this analysis. Census surveys report that "too busy, conflicting schedule" was the most commonly offered reason for not voting in the 2008 presidential election, and it was one of the strongest reasons given regardless of annual income levels of the respondents (U.S. Census Bureau, Population Division, 2009). Apparently everyone, from the very wealthy to the very poor, was hard pressed to get away from work to vote. The explanation for this anomaly is far from clear using these data, but it is not consistent with the argument that lower-income people would have stronger priorities for putting food on the table than voting and fewer opportunities to learn valuable political behavior compared with higher-income people.

Research does suggest that organizational involvement is important in providing members with access to opportunities to learn politically significant skills and values and that this may correlate with income levels or class. For example, one study found that higher income levels correlated with higher participation in faith community efforts in charity, public policy, and social justice. Such organizational participation may provide higher-income individuals with more opportunities to learn civic and political skills (Schwadel, 2002). Research also suggests that participation in unions may similarly offer members access to politically relevant skills that translate to voting behavior. That union membership has declined in recent decades may help explain the decrease in working-class voting participation rates (Radcliff, 2001).

On the other hand, studies of organizational involvement and its effect on political participation also suggest that participation in groups in and of itself may not be sufficient to socialize members to vote. McMiller (1999), for example, found that white and African American organizations vary in their ability to translate members' organizational activity into voting. Moreover, some research indicates that organizational involvement and access to information and politically relevant skills may be more likely to extend into individuals' participation in alternative forms of political activity (such as protests and demonstrations) than institutional forms like voting (McVeigh & Smith, 1999).

Although political socialization explanations for voting patterns may be persuasive, they omit the notion that political participation may in fact be the product of a rational calculation of the advantages of participating. Observers using a rational choice perspective argue that people may participate politically because they evaluate the costs and benefits of such an investment of time, money, and energy, and they see a real advantage in getting their interests met by participating (Djupe & Grant, 2001; Opp, 2001). As a corollary, those who do not participate may not do so because after weighing and evaluating the costs and benefits, they see no advantage: Their interests are unlikely to be met or they will have no impact on the outcome by voting and therefore it is not worth their precious time and energy (Verba, Schlozman, & Brady, 2000). According to a rational choice analysis, differences in electoral participation may be a result of a rational calculation of the benefits of participation rather than the result of socialization in one's cultural and occupational environment.

However, while there are fairly strong patterns to participation, there are no such clear patterns describing nonparticipation. In recent decades, low rates of political participation have been widespread throughout the populace. As we saw in Table 4.2, there remain significant segments of even the most advantaged groups who do not participate. Nonparticipation would appear to cut across the social correlates.

Structural Explanations

If participation and nonparticipation are not satisfactorily explained as a product of socialization or of rational choice, then how are we to understand why people in the United States don't vote? Piven and Cloward (2000) argued that structural and mechanical obstacles exist that reduce participation. For example, they cite cumbersome voter registration laws that might discourage eligible voters from registering. Few if any states continue to offer bilingual registration, making it more difficult for citizens for whom English is a second language. This would certainly appear to be an important impediment to participation, since registering is a prerequisite for voting on Election Day. Moreover, each state has the right to determine the deadline for registering to vote, with some states requiring citizens to register at least one month prior to election day and others allowing same-day registration. The U.S. Census Bureau noted that participation rates in 2004 were actually fairly high among those registered and that participation was highest in states that permitted voters to register on Election Day as opposed to states requiring registration by an earlier date (Holder, 2006). Thus, any procedures that hinder registration are likely to pose a structural obstacle to participation.

In addition, there are obstacles to participation created by the structure of election processes. For example, confusion of appropriate voting district for transient populations (such as students) may help explain the low participation rates of younger people. Students who move away from their parents' homes to attend school are often confused about whether their appropriate district is where they go to school or where their parents live. If they determine their district remains with the address where their parents live, they must often use an absentee ballot, because it may be too far away to travel for the one day to vote, and time away from classes, exams, and papers due is not plentiful. But the use of absentee ballots is often confusing: Where does one get an absentee ballot? When are absentee ballots due? How must they be filled out? If they are not filled out exactly as required, they may be discounted and therefore someone who thinks they voted with an absentee ballot may in fact remain uncounted as a participant.

These issues are probably more problematic for students than for military personnel stationed abroad who are often provided the materials for absentee balloting. However, anyone who must use an absentee ballot confronts the problem of decision making with perhaps less information to inform their choices than voters who participate in their home district. Absentee ballots must be submitted a couple of weeks before Election Day in order to have time to be verified and counted. This can discourage participation, because absentee voters must make their decisions at somewhat of a disadvantage: Important news stories and pieces of critical information may occur in the last few weeks of the election campaign, and it is sometimes enough to sway a voter from a previous decision about one's voting preference. The knowledge that one may be forced to choose a candidate with less information than everyone else may dissuade at least some potential voters from participating.

Moreover, electoral participation is actually structured as a two-stage process of registration and voting. For immigrants, that process begins with a prior stage of naturalization. One study found that Asian Americans who have gone through the naturalization and voter registration stages are actually almost as likely to vote as whites (Lien, Collet, Wong, & Ramakrishnan, 2001). This suggests that the dislocation of these stages from each other may affect voting as an outcome by separating voting from the other stages. In that regard, registration drives do matter. Structures promoting registration are likely to result in greater voting rates. Structures that discourage or at least do not promote voter registration interrupt the staging process of electoral participation. Registration drives that target previously underrepresented voters, such as young voters and people of color, are attempts to improve this structural obstacle to participation.

In addition, the structure of maintaining numerous primary elections prior to national elections may give some people the wrong impression that voting in primaries means that they already voted. They are therefore not likely to vote on Election Day if they believe that they have already cast a ballot. Further, the process whereby results are counted and reported out district by district before the entire district's vote has been counted and before the entire election has ended nationwide may depress voter participation rates. Journalists and reporters often attempt to get the "scoop" on the election results by announcing early favorites or projected winners based on returns from states in earlier time zones. This can influence voters to get behind the projected winner, but it can also discourage many voters in the later time zones from bothering to participate at all if it appears that their preferred candidate has already lost or if their preference has already won and more votes cast will not matter any longer.

Finally, many ballots may be confusing in their physical arrangement. Witness, for example, the controversial vote count in Florida in 2000, where voters had to punch a hole in a ballot to register their vote. Many voters were unclear that if they decided they had punched the wrong hole they could get a new ballot and disqualify the one with the mistake. Moreover, the "butterfly" arrangement of candidates' names across a two-page ballot confused even seasoned voters who thought their punch indicated a vote cast for one candidate when in fact it indicated a vote for another. Some voters did not punch the hole fully, resulting in "hanging chads," the little bits of punched paper left attached to the ballot after the vote was cast. In such cases, great controversies ensued over the interpretations of what voters intended when they tried to punch the ballot. Many ballots were declared invalid and not counted, thereby voiding participation by large numbers of voters (Wattenberg, 2002).

These structural impediments might indeed depress voter participation, but at best these can account for only some of the lack of voting. Indeed, structural impediments to participation were among the least-often cited reasons respondents gave to the U.S. Census Bureau for not voting, including inconvenient polling place (2.7% of respondents), registration problems (6%), and transportation problems (2.6%) (U.S. Census Bureau, Population Division, 2009). Structural impediments also cannot explain the significant proportion of nonparticipation among voters in the more advantaged groups for whom these impediments do not matter. For example, highly educated people are less likely to be confused by the structure of primaries or to be swayed by early projections of winners, and they are likely to know where and how to register to vote. Furthermore, an analysis of the structural barriers to electoral participation cannot explain the similarly low levels of participation in other forms of political activity, such as involvement in social movements.

Political Alienation

While social psychological and structural analyses may help explain at least some political nonparticipation, they do not explore the role of estrangement from the dominant political system, or what sociologists call political alienation. Alienation is not the same thing as apathy. People who are apathetic do not care; alienated individuals do care but feel estranged or disaffected from the system or somehow left out of the political process. For those who are politically alienated, voting does not address their interests or their needs and so participation has no meaning for them. They often view political leaders as unresponsive to their needs, pursuing instead the narrow interests of the elite. Although democratic cultural institutions reinforce the notion, "government of the people, for the people, and by the people," for those who are politically alienated the reality of how the political process actually works is a substantial departure from the ideal of how it is supposed to work.

For some, the lack of community structures that encourage participation denies them the opportunity to participate in meaningful civic activities that can contribute to a belief in the efficacy of participation (Docherty, Goodlad, & Paddison, 2001). For others, chronic and widespread unemployment may breed a lack of confidence in the salience and legitimacy of institutions, political leadership, and politics in general, particularly among youth (Bay & Blekesaune, 2002).

Public opinion polls show that while confidence in the meaningfulness of participation in the electoral process remains relatively strong among respondents in the United States, a significant proportion still indicate feelings of alienation from that process. For example, the U.S. Census Bureau found that 13.4% of respondents did not vote in the 2008 presidential election because they were "not interested"; another 12.9% indicated that they "did not like the candidates or issues" (U.S. Census Bureau, Population Division, 2009). A 2009 Fox News/Opinion Dynamics poll found that 91% of the respondents believed that it matters that they vote (Fox News/Opinion Dynamics Poll, 2009). Similarly, 68% of respondents in a 2009 Pew Research Center poll said that "voting gives people like me some say about how government runs things" (Pew Research Center for the People and the Press Values Survey, 2009). Yet surveys show substantial cynicism and political alienation as well: More than one fourth of respondents to a Voters' Experience poll in 2008 indicated that they did not believe that "nearly enough [has been done] to make sure that votes are collected and counted accurately" (Public Agenda Foundation, 2008). These polls suggest that the disaffected may not be the majority, but they are certainly not a small, insignificant group. Moreover, public confidence in public institutions is not strong: Half of the respondents to a 2008 Gallup poll indicated that "most members of Congress" did not deserve to be reelected (Gallup/*USA Today* Poll, 2008). More than half of the respondents in a 2006 health poll indicated that "the government's handling of Hurricane

Katrina [had a] negative impact on their confidence in government overall" (Kaiser Family Foundation, 2006). This lack of confidence in public institutions reflects a sense among significant proportions of the electorate that these elected offices are irrelevant or unresponsive to them. Ironically, one of the fundamental principles of pluralism—emphasizing the power of the masses to control elites and hold them accountable—is a key source of political alienation because such a controlling role by nonelites is not a reality for a considerable proportion of the electorate.

Why Are People Politically Alienated?

That political alienation would occur among oppressed or disadvantaged groups is not surprising, but the fact is that nonparticipation and expressions of lack of confidence in leaders and institutions is evident even among those in the more privileged groups. This raises the following question: Why has this political alienation occurred?

Scandals in Leadership

Cynicism among the electorate toward leaders, both elected and non-elected, is not surprising, given the parade of scandals to emerge over the past several decades. Nearly three-fourths of the respondents to a Council for Excellence in Government (2007) survey cited "low ethical standards among elected officials" as a major reason for reduced public confidence in government. Although political scandals have always periodically punctuated the political landscape, those that have occurred more recently are more likely to affect how current voters feel. The Watergate scandal in which the then president Richard Nixon encouraged illegal activities to undermine his political opponents and his subsequent attempts to cover these up finally forced him to resign in 1974 and became the benchmark defining political scandal. More recent scandals are often named in parodies of Watergate, such as the Irangate and Contragate scandals during the administration of President Ronald Reagan in the 1980s implicating the CIA as well as the White House in illegal interference in other countries' politics. Many politicians have been accused of illegal influence peddling once they leave public service, such as Ed Meese, Lynn Nofziger, and Michael Deaver in the 1980s. More recently, high-level figures in the Bush administration have been indicted or convicted of "outing" a CIA operative in order to punish her diplomat husband for publishing a strong critique of the Iraq War.

Personal scandals have rocked politics and destroyed political careers as well, such as the extramarital affairs of Gary Hart, which caused him to withdraw his presidential candidacy in the 1988 election, and the notorious "Monicagate" affair involving President Bill Clinton's Oval Office dalliances with a young intern. Joseph Biden's bid for presidency in 1988 evaporated in a scandal involving charges that he plagiarized campaign speeches. Several states have suffered scandalous crises of leadership, toppling governors in New Jersey and Connecticut in 2004 and mayors in several major cities as well as members of Congress in at least the past 20 years alone. Revelations of leadership wrongdoings have extended, as well, beyond elected officials. Scandals have surfaced in charges of sexual harassment against Clarence Thomas during his confirmation hearings before the Senate for his seat on the Supreme Court; those charges did not prevent him from being confirmed. Even religious leaders have not been exempt from scandal. The charges of sex abuse of children by clergy have shaken the Catholic Church since at least 2003.

Taken together, such scandals contribute to a heightened disaffection with institutional leadership in general and the political system in particular. Notice that scandal is not restricted to one or the other party; both parties have been sullied. Voters are thus unable to simply say that scandal is a characteristic of one particular party; instead, they are confronted with more widespread unethical or illegal misuses and abuses of power and authority and may thus determine that it does not matter who gets into office.

The Structure of the Political Process

Part of political alienation may also derive from the two-party system in the United States. The two-party system has protected the stability of the dominant sociopolitical and economic institutions and has discouraged changes in the prevailing class system. This is because of several important features of the party system in the United States. First, Democrats and Republicans, as the two parties, may engage in heated debate over such specific issues as spending versus taxing (and whom to tax, the affluent or everyone, including the marginal working class), health care, environment, or affirmative action. But the two parties essentially do not express divergent policy offerings addressing the most basic issues, most pointedly avoiding the question of the sanctity of private profit accumulation. Indeed, to raise such an issue is to invite charges of inciting "class warfare" or of being a "communist," neither of which is likely to raise candidates' political popularity. Apart from the popular notion that the Democratic Party, as the party of the Left, represents the interests of the poor and working class, and that

Republicans, as the party of the Right, represent only wealthy and corporate interests, neither party really reflects clear and divergent class interests. Both parties represent, to varying degrees, the interests of the capitalist class and of capital accumulation. Their disagreements often revolve around differences in how to accomplish a "healthy" economy, largely understood to mean the preservation of the capitalist political economy.

Moreover, elections in the United States are ruled by a "winner-takes-all" principle: Whoever wins the most votes wins the election. This encourages both parties' candidates to try to appeal to as many voters as possible, which generally means charting a broader, more centrist position than staking out an explicit, clearly identified one. The result is that the parties and their candidates do not sharply differ. Potential presidential candidate Joseph Lieberman articulated just this point when he tried to emerge from the pack of Democratic rivals in 2003 by arguing that he was, in fact, the most moderate, centrist candidate and that other contenders who were attempting to appeal to the party's more traditional base of the disaffected were charting the wrong course. Ironically, Lieberman's critics have often charged that his positions are more akin to those of the Republican Party than those of the Democratic base.

Sometimes third parties emerge to try to articulate a clear difference from the fused perception of the two main parties. But when third-party candidates are on the ballot, voters are discouraged from voting for them: to do so is in effect to waste their votes because they have little chance of winning. Worse, voters are warned that third-party candidates "rob" votes from the main party candidate closest to their interests and thus assure that the party candidate least appealing to those wishing to vote for the third-party candidate will get elected. For example, Ross Perot, who ran for president in 1992 and 1996, was an independent billionaire who used his personal fortune to organize his Reform Party in 1996. His affluence and his more libertarian views positioned him closer to the Republican Party platform and were more likely to draw voters from them than from the Democratic Party candidate. Indeed, observers often argued that Perot's candidacy "watered down" the support for George H. W. Bush in 1996 and helped get Bill Clinton elected. Similarly, supporters for Ralph Nader's Green Party candidacy for president in 2000 were often besieged with pleas from the Democratic Party not to vote for him: His ideals of environmental protection and corporate accountability and responsibility made him more likely to take votes away from Democrat Al Gore than Republican George W. Bush. Although Nader did not get widespread support, his candidacy was often accused of ensuring that Bush won the election.

Because they aim for the broadest support from the largest number of voters, the Democratic and Republican Parties tend to emphasize issues of personality and to avoid serious issues concerning the structure and functioning of political and economic institutions. Parties mainly function to nominate, campaign for, and elect candidates; articulating issues and constructing clear and pointed policy programs are secondary and often viewed as strategically unwise during election campaigns. Spelling out specific programs and issues becomes an electoral liability, since it provides opponents with a target and since it may alienate some voters. Candidates commonly work toward developing a "good organization" to win, not toward articulating good ideas for policy. Candidates become packaged for consumption, much like any other consumer product: They are not presented as desirable because of their important positions on a range of critical issues confronting voters; they are presented as desirable because of their personalities or because their opponents' personalities are somehow objectionable. Political debates are consequently highly controlled, limited largely to the two parties, limited by how much time each may spend on any given question, and limited in substance of information offered to voters. It is not surprising, then, to find that voters often find it difficult to identify the important points of divergence between candidates to clearly choose and cynically complain of the lack of choice to be made between "Tweedle Dee and Tweedle Dum."

Further, in the United States, voters do not directly participate in electing the president. Instead, they may elect delegates to send to the Electoral College, where each state has a certain number of votes to cast for president based on their population in the last census count. Highly populous states like California, New York, Illinois, Pennsylvania, Massachusetts, and Florida have far more Electoral College votes than states like Rhode Island, Delaware, Maryland, Iowa, Montana, and New Mexico. All of the Electoral College votes in a given state are awarded to the candidate who wins the most popular votes in that state. Once again, winner takes all: Electoral College votes in a state are not awarded based on the proportion of that state's votes a candidate may win. This gives the more populous states more power in the Electoral College and raises the possibility that a candidate may win the overall popular count of votes in the country at large but lose the election because he or she has won the more populous state's electoral votes. While this rarely occurs, it is possible and has in fact occurred at least twice: Rutherford B. Hayes in 1876 and George W. Bush in 2000. When that happens, it may lead at least some voters to believe that their votes do not count because they either live in less populous states or the majority of voters in their particular state support the candidate with fewer national votes.

In addition, systems of oppression may affect voter participation. Let's explore the impact racism and gendering may have on electoral participation.

Racism in the Electoral Process

Political alienation may also result from problems stemming from racism in the culture as well as in the political process. As one researcher suggested, African Americans have had to struggle to participate in a political system that was "designed to repress them for three centuries" (Covin, 2001). But beyond politically alienating voters, racism may structurally disenfranchise people of color, even if they are not disaffected. Racism frequently taints contentious political competitions, at times more explicitly than others. Barely concealed, for example, was the highly criticized campaign ad in which George H. W. Bush's 1988 campaign suggested that his opponent was soft on crime. The infamous ad showed a picture of Willie Horton, an African American man accused of murder after being freed from a Massachusetts prison by the then governor Michael Dukakis. The ad attempted to capitalize on white voters' fears of a criminal African American population and implied that Bush would be more strict in controlling such dangerous populations.

Dukakis himself was not immune to charges of racism in that election, however. Recall that this was the election in which Jesse Jackson pursued the nomination of the Democratic Party in a run for the presidency. Jackson managed to galvanize a significant proportion of otherwise alienated voters with an aggressive voter registration drive, with the understanding that political participation begins with registration, and an awareness that once registered, voters are highly likely to actually cast a ballot. Jackson's voter registration drive contributed to more minority voters being registered to vote than ever before. But his contribution was not necessarily appreciated by the party: Although he succeeded in registering thousands if not millions of new voters, he lost the party's primaries leading up to its candidate nomination. When Dukakis selected his running mate for the national election, he did not choose Jackson. Nevertheless, Jackson offered to continue his $7 million campaign to register disenfranchised voters, particularly in communities of color. Although Dukakis and the party did not have a voter registration drive of their own planned, the Democratic National Committee chair Paul Kirk demurred, mistakenly assuming that the Democratic Party could simultaneously court the white Southern voters by appearing not to align with people of color and still count on the votes of people of color who traditionally voted with the party. Jackson's ardent supporters expressed insult at the snub. They expressed their dismay by staying away from the polls in droves: African American voter turnout that year was 10% lower than in 1984, despite the progress made by the voter registration drive to bring them into the political process (Jackson, Clemente, & Watkins, 1989). Others expressed their anger by voting for Jackson as a third-party candidate rather than to vote for Dukakis as the Democratic Party's nominee.

The damage from the political miscalculation by Dukakis and the Democrats was costly: Dukakis lost the election to the Republican George H. W. Bush. An analysis of the vote along racial lines clearly indicated just how costly: Dukakis lost by less than 2 million votes in Maryland, Missouri, Pennsylvania, Illinois, Louisiana, South Carolina, California, North Carolina, and Georgia—states that represented 160 Electoral College votes. He lost five of these states by 2 percentage points or less (Jackson et al., 1989). Note that these states have substantial populations of people of color. Had Dukakis at least accepted Jackson's offer to continue his voter registration drive, he might have been able to keep voters of color from abandoning the party, and indeed the election itself, and win the critical Electoral College votes of at least some of these states. The difference was the election itself: Adding the 160 close Electoral College votes to the 112 Dukakis did win would have been enough to produce a very different outcome.

The presidential election in 2000 was no less tainted by charges of racism. The political contest between Democrat Al Gore and Republican George W. Bush was close and highly contentious. The split of Electoral College votes between the two candidates was so close that the election outcome came down to who would win the votes of Florida. The vote was so close as to prompt a recount. The election and recount in that state was troubled by an extremely confusing "butterfly" ballot that listed candidates across two pages, by punch ballots that were ambiguous in the voters' intent, and by irregularities in absentee ballots that were improperly validated by registrars completing incomplete ballot information. Worse, a disproportionate number of votes disqualified by registrars were those cast by people of color. Analyses indicated that the higher the proportion of African Americans in a voting district, the more likely it was to suffer higher rates of invalidated votes. In the most heavily white precincts, about 1 in 14 ballots were thrown out as invalid. In largely African American precincts, more than 1 in 5 ballots were invalidated, and in some African American precincts, almost one-third of the ballots were thrown out (Lichtman, 2003). Worse still were the charges that in the months before the election, the state disqualified thousands of registered voters without telling them, and more than half of these were African American. These voters did not discover their disenfranchisement until Election Day, when they were denied the right to vote (U.S. Commission on Civil Rights, 2000). The disenfranchisement of substantial numbers of voters of color was apparently enough to swing the Florida outcome: In 2000, 90% of African American voters cast their ballot for Gore, while whites accounted for 95% of Bush's support (Wing, 2001).

The 2008 presidential election cycle, however, indicated something of a break in the racialized gap in participation that had previously prevailed, due in part to population dynamics and in part to a newly energized electorate. The number of eligible Latino voters increased by almost one-fourth over the 2004 level, owing to increases in population and citizenship. While the white share of the overall electorate has been declining, that of voters of color has been increasing. By the 2008 presidential election, African Americans, Latinos, and Asians accounted for 22% of those who voted, up from about 12% in 1988. In addition to population dynamics, voters of color were energized and galvanized by the candidacy of Barack Obama, the first major candidate of color to run for the presidency (Roberts, 2009). Clearly, the Obama candidacy was key in challenging the predominant political alienation evident in previous presidential elections among voters of color (Chen, 2009).

On the other hand, although some observers view the election of Obama as evidence that the United States is now a "post-racial" society, there is evidence that a racialized divide remains deep and, for some people, highly charged. For example, the Tea Party began as a seeming grassroots opposition to health care reform under the Obama administration. But much of the rhetoric calls that passion into question: 28% of people in the United States define themselves as supporters of the Tea Party, 55% of these had annual incomes of $50,000 or above, 65% had at least some college, and 79% were "non-Hispanic white" (Saad, 2010). Fifty-three percent of Tea Party supporters responded to a *New York Times*/CBS News poll in 2010 that they were "angry" about the way things were going in Washington (*New York Times*/CBS, 2010). And while ostensibly they were angry about the economy and health care reform, that same poll indicated something deeper: 73% agreed that Obama "does not understand the needs and problems of people like yourself" and 75% agreed that he does not share the values of most Americans. Considering the profile of Tea Party supporters, these frustrated survey responses suggest a sense that Obama's racialized identity appears to them as a barrier to understanding white America. More telling, 52% believed that "in recent years too much has been made of the problems facing black people," and 73% believed that "white people and black people have an equal chance of getting ahead" (*New York Times*/CBS, 2010). Far from a post-racial society, the election of an African American or biracial president has elicited a racialized political alienation, at least among a significant portion of white, educated, and middle-class people.

Beyond the campaign decision making by party leaders, the very structure of the Electoral College commonly alienates voters of color and makes it difficult for them to get their interests heard. The winner-takes-all structure of the Electoral College all but assures that African American, Latino, and Native American voters are being marginalized. This is because in no state do voters of color constitute the majority. Therefore, as white voters go, so go the electoral votes—thus assuring that the preferences of white voters will produce an electoral outcome as if voters of color did not participate at all. Indeed, census data indicate that African Americans, Latinos, and Asians lag seriously behind whites in Congress: By 2007, there were still only totals of 43 (8%) African Americans, 26 (4.9%) Latinos, and 6 (1.1%) Asians in both houses of Congress combined (U.S. Census Bureau, 2009). Clearly, voting districts that are carved out in such a way as to produce white majorities and dilute minority voter strength have resulted in an overwhelmingly white Congress, disproportionate to the overall representation of people of color in the general population.

Large numbers of African American males are also disenfranchised because they are incarcerated or have been convicted of felonies, a punishment one study called "collateral restrictions" that go beyond the jail time (Demleitner, 2002). In many states, convicted felons are denied the right to vote, even after serving their sentence. In the past decade alone, with the adoption of "three-strikes" laws requiring prison time after the third offense (no matter how large or small), the incarceration rate of African American males has increased 10 times faster than that of white males (Common Sense for Drug Policy, 2008). The effect of the denial of voting rights to convicted felons has resulted in widespread disenfranchisement of African American males (Hermon, 2001; Manza & Uggen, 2008; Uggen & Manza, 2002). Then it is not surprising to find that people of color have significantly lower participation rates in electoral politics than whites. And this is not adequately explained by either social psychological or structural explanations. This analysis suggests that it is crucial to analyze participation in the context of cultural and political racism as well in order to fully appreciate the differences in participation. Political alienation would appear to be a more compelling explanation of differential voting rates along racially defined groups than social psychological or structural arguments alone. And the uptick in participation rates of voters of color relative to rates in previous presidential elections suggests that when voters feel less alienated from the candidates and the process of elections, they are more likely to participate.

Is There a Gender Gap?

When we look at comparative participation rates by social background correlates, gender stands out as a departure from the overall pattern in which those who are among the more oppressed categories are the least likely to vote. Data on participation suggest that whatever gap in voting participation rates that may have once existed between women and men in the United States has now disappeared. Census data indicate that the proportion of women who vote is equal to or greater than that of men (see Table 4.2). How do we explain this?

First, the change in the pattern between women and men over time is itself of interest. Prior to 1980, it was more common for women's participation rates to be lower than those for men. One study of voting patterns in the 1952 through 1988 elections points to the significant influence of historical conditioning: Women who were of voting age at the time of the passage of the Nineteenth Amendment giving women the right to vote were less likely than younger women to participate (Firebaugh & Chen, 1995). This suggests that women who came of age prior to the passage of the Nineteenth Amendment were conditioned to accept their political disenfranchisement as a normal state of affairs. Even after the right to vote was extended to women, this older cohort appears to have found it difficult to simply become political participants, while younger women who had come of age assuming the right to vote was a given were more likely to participate as a matter of course.

Another study cites the effects of the gender gap in employment as a factor producing differential participation rates between women and men. Women were less likely than men to participate politically because, the researchers argued, they were less likely to participate in the workforce at all, or, if they did, they were less likely to hold full-time or high-level jobs (Schlozman, Burns, & Verba, 1999). Moreover, still another study suggests women are simply less interested in politics, are less informed, and are less politically effective than men. The researchers found that at least part of this is because of social cues that reinforce politics as a "man's world" (Verba, Burns, & Schlozman, 1997). Taken together, these studies suggest a socialization explanation of women's lower political engagement and participation rates. This might help explain why women were less likely to vote prior to the 1980s. However, this analysis is limited in its ability to explain why women's voting participation rates were, in fact, *higher* than that of men in the presidential elections between 2000 and 2008.

One explanation may be that women's labor force participation rates have, in fact, increased so that women now represent at least half of the labor force in the United States. Indeed, women's unemployment rates in the 1990s were lower than those of men for the first time in history. One study found that women's greater participation in the labor force appeared to translate into an increased likelihood that they will vote (Manza & Brooks, 1998). This analysis suggests a social psychological explanation in that one's job is seen to produce politically relevant skills and viewpoints.

A more compelling explanation may be in terms of political mobilization as opposed to alienation. The 20th-century phase of the women's rights movement spawned several well-developed political organizations, including the National Organization for Women (NOW) and EMILY's List, a political action organization that funnels campaign funds to women running for political office. These organizations have articulated many women's interests and issues, often succeeding in bringing these into the public agenda and helping to win important legislative and court battles and encouraging women to vote in "get out the vote" campaigns. The forward strides in women's rights since the 1950s may have produced a generation of women who have come of age not only assuming the right to vote but also feeling politically entitled and empowered. Indeed, one study found some evidence that feminist consciousness was an important element affecting women's political behavior (Manza & Brooks, 1998). Serious political challenges to women's reproductive rights, for example, may spark renewed interest in political participation to preserve those rights. Notice the popular bumper sticker "I am pro-choice—and I vote!"

While the aggregate gender gap in voting participation rates may have disappeared, there remains a significant gender gap between the main political parties. In the presidential elections between 2000 and 2008, women were more likely to vote with the Democratic Party, while men were more likely to vote with the Republican Party (U.S. Census Bureau, 2009). Why? Since 1980, men in the United States have been found to be increasingly more conservative and thus pro-Republican because of that party's agenda of smaller government in the economic sphere, lower taxes, and less spending. While the Democratic Party is hardly the liberal firebrand it perhaps was in the 1960s and 1970s, some of its leaders have shown a tendency to be somewhat more sympathetic to liberal social policy issues than Republicans. One study suggested that this may explain the party-line gender gap: Women come to politics with a predisposition of empathy for the oppressed, they argued, and are therefore more likely to be drawn to candidates whose agenda supports such things as social welfare programs (McCue & Gopoian, 2000). The researchers were not clear whether they saw women's greater empathy for the oppressed as something innate or a result of their own likelihood of having experienced gendered oppression, but their point was that this predisposition is something that shapes women's political behavior.

Moreover, although women may participate in voting at least as much as men (if not along the same party alignments), there continues to be a gap in women's likelihood of running for and holding elective office. Research shows this pattern to be consistent in most if not all Western democracies, a situation researchers say "relegates women to second class citizenship"

(Praud, 2001, p. 250). One of the reasons for the slow progress in integrating women into the legislative bodies is the continuing effect of institutional history. Women continue to be accorded "outgroup" status by party chairs who are more likely to prefer potential candidates with similar characteristics to themselves. Since party elites have historically been male, this suggests a formidable "barrier to entry" or a political glass ceiling for women (Niven, 1998).

In the United States, incumbents have a strong tendency to return to office, particularly in Congress. Since men have historically dominated elected offices, the power of incumbency creates something of a "political glass ceiling" for women. Indeed, one study found that when women do run for elected office, it is more likely to be for an "open" seat than one in which they would be challenging an incumbent (Palmer & Simon, 2001). The researchers suggested that this implies it would take substantial redistricting or some "unanticipated events and crises" to stimulate greater integration of women into the elected bodies. This analysis also implies that a similar institutional history of racism in which white men dominate elected bodies such as Congress create a political glass ceiling for people of color, as well.

However, it is noteworthy that a swelling antiwar sentiment among voters in 2006 and again in 2008 helped to produce a Congress with the largest number of women in history (at 74 women in the House of Representatives and 16 in the Senate) (U.S. Census Bureau, 2009), and the first female speaker of the house, Representative Nancy Pelosi. It also helped to have a serious presidential candidate who also happened to be a woman, Senator Hillary Rodham Clinton (who thanked the "Sisterhood of the Traveling Pantsuits" in her concession speech to the then-Senator Barack Obama at the Democratic National Convention in 2008). Indeed, the strong Democratic presidential primary contest between Senators Clinton and Obama suggested that perhaps the political glass ceiling confronting women and people of color may be vulnerable to cracks, if not a full shattering.

Radical Objections to Voting

Many political radicals, especially anarchists, oppose voting as a strategy for social transformation on a variety of grounds. First and foremost, voting has been seen as incapable of bringing about the kind of radical changes in society that many dissidents see as necessary. How does one, for example, vote the means of production out of the hands of the ruling class when the state and business interests are so closely tied? How does one vote institutionalized power out of the hands of the few when choosing those leaders through the vote assumes and protects their existence? It was questions such as these that prompted the anarchist revolutionary, Emma Goldman, to say, "If voting changed anything, they'd make it illegal."

Secondly, anarchists see the direct action (more on this later) of the people as the appropriate means to bring about societal changes. Electoral politics, anarchists have noted, are the exact opposite of direct action. Rather than empowering those who vote, it teaches those who do to accept that "politics" means an individual or, perhaps, a party acting on behalf of those who vote—rather than people acting on their own behalf. If we are to create a future participatory world, it requires that people learn to participate rather than rely on politicians for decision making and policy setting. Voting is a part of our political socialization to accept a world in which the state has become a hegemonic institution and efforts to act outside of the logic of the state and capitalism are decried as utopian or extremist.

Thirdly, many radicals raise questions about where political changes actually come from. Rather than political parties bringing about changes in our political and social landscape, many argue that it is actually through pressure from below that politicians grudgingly meet the demands of oppressed groups—albeit often only partially and temporarily. Even socialist political parties, Miliband (1969) noted, can often deter radical social change by attempting to appease capitalist interests by calming the actions of a radical population. However, regardless of what parties control the state apparatus, with enough pressure from below, oppressed groups can force the hand of the elite to act against its own interests (though some have argued that this ultimately serves the interests of the elite by preserving capital accumulation, albeit in some reformed manner).

Finally, anarchists have often raised ethical objections to electoral participation. Who exactly does one vote for if one wishes a world free of political rulers? If one votes for Bill Clinton to be one's ruler, is it not just a quantitative difference between him and some other political ruler ("the lesser of two evils") rather than a qualitative shift in how we organize society? Since anarchists oppose all relations of domination, voting is often seen as a rather dishonest expression of political sentiment. Voting in state political systems, for many anarchists, validates those systems and implicates one in the processes of one's own subordination.

It should be noted, however, that this is not a monolithic position among radicals or even among anarchists. The anarchist, Pierre-Joseph Proudhon, for example, stood for election in the French Constituent Assembly in 1848. Libertarian socialists like Noam Chomsky and Howard Zinn have promoted voting for Democrats in the United States, especially in response to George W. Bush's bid for the White House. Social ecologist Murray Bookchin argued for voting in local elections to help bring about a "libertarian munic-ipalism" that could eventually replace the state. Nevertheless, among many radicals, and especially anarchists, voting is seen as anathema to radical social change and can often serve to stall it.

Power Beyond Voting

It would appear that participation in voting is not necessarily the key to nonelite power: Despite popular media's fascination with "voter rebel-lions" in which the electorate gets fed up with incumbents' nonrespon-siveness or poor leadership and votes them out of office, the fact is that the vast majority of incumbents (with the exception of most modern presi-dents) do return for more than one term. In contrast to pluralists' notion that nonparticipation is an expression of satisfaction with "things as they are," data suggest otherwise. Precisely those whom one would expect to be the most dissatisfied are the ones who are least likely to vote. The disen-franchised are, in fact, most likely to be those who are politically alienated because they do not believe the process speaks to their needs in any mean-ingful way. This suggests that the ability to affect the very identification of the central or most pressing issues for public discourse and policy debate would be a more fundamental expression of power, since setting that agenda precedes the electoral process. Voting becomes a secondary expres-sion of power if nonelites are not able to affect the agenda of public debate and policy-making decisions: Voters are then participating in a process that was decided without them. The question then becomes one of power without necessarily voting: Who shapes the political agenda that defines the issues and public debates, and how do they accomplish this? Also, what other ways can people express themselves politically outside of the purview of the state?

Direct Action

Direct action is any action undertaken by a group or individual to address injustice or oppression that is self-generated rather than controlled from above. It is empowering in that it teaches individuals and groups that they can address and, in some cases, solve their own problems without the need for intervention by elites. Thus, through direct action, oppressed and exploited groups learn self-government—tools that we are not often taught in a world organized on the principles of centralized authority, hierarchy, and control.

Direct action can include a range of possible activities such as work-place occupations and appropriations, squatting (occupying unoccupied houses and/or buildings and using them as living spaces), or sabotage. Direct action has always been a staple of radical politics, and entire move-ments have been built around its practical application to the daily lives of people. Food Not Bombs, for example, is an international network of col-lectives that recovers wasted food and serves vegetarian meals to hungry people. Thus, members of Food Not Bombs see a need (people are hungry) and do something about it themselves rather than rely on the state to do so. Likewise, Indymedia, a loose-knit group of media activists that produce news outside of the corporate and state-run presses, is also a form of the direct action of concerned individuals and groups as they attempt to make sure that stories are covered and disseminated that are ignored by the mainstream press.

The purpose of direct action can be to address problems affecting any given community. For example, Food Not Bombs is a response to the inad-equate methods of food distribution in a capitalist economy and the sheer amount of waste produced by the profit system. Thus, member collectives reclaim wasted food that is still edible and use it to feed anyone who wishes to eat in public spaces. This provides a venue for hungry people to get food and eat and addresses the problem of hunger through collective action rather than relying on the state to fix the problems it is complicit in creating and maintaining. In the process of doing so, people become aware that they are capable of solving their own problems collectively without the need for cen-tralized authority.

Direct action can also be used to bring awareness to social problems and to bring otherwise ignored issues into public discourse. Indymedia, for example, uses independent sources of media distribution to make people aware of otherwise ignored issues. In fact, the Indymedia centers rose ini-tially in response to the lack of coverage, as well as the one-sidedness of what little coverage there was, on the battle of Seattle in 1999 (when a coalition of trade unions, environmental activists, anarchists, church groups, and oth-ers effectively stopped the WTO Ministerial Conference in Seattle). In the labor movement, direct action has a long and proud history. Rather than waiting for the boss to give workers adequate breaks, for example, many workers have organized "slowdowns," when laborers would purposely withdraw their labor away from production. Worker slowdowns have also been used to force concessions from bosses. As well, workers have often just taken their workplaces from their bosses (as happened in the beginning of the Russian Revolution and during the Spanish Civil War) or have appro-priated abandoned workplaces and ran them collectively and democratically without bosses (as in the Zanon ceramics factory in Argentina). However, when attempting to affect the agenda of politicians and the state, other, more conventional, methods are often employed.

Political Action Committees

Another source of power beyond voting is the funding of campaigns that occur well before anyone enters the voting booth. The determination of who runs for office, how they finance their campaigns, and what effect that might have on their decision making once in office are thus critical issues. Since 1974, federal law has set limits on how much individuals or organizations like corporations or unions may contribute to any one candidate in any single election or year. But they may increase their contributions by donating more money through PACs. These committees pool the additional contributions and thus multiply the financial impact donors may have on a political campaign. Most political elites accept campaign contributions from PACs, even though critics often warn of the potential these pose for undue influence on decision making after the election: Those who pay the piper call the tune, they warn. Indeed, it is so rare for politicians to reject PACs' money that those who don't accept these donations stand out as anomalies. But if PACs pose such potential for compromising political leaders' independence to legislate in the common good, why is it such accepted practice to accept their contributions? Why are PACs necessary?

To appreciate the need for the resource PACs offer, one need only look at the cost of running an election campaign. Let's look at the cost of running for a seat in the House of Representatives, as the least costly campaign to run for federal office. Representatives have a relatively small district in which to campaign, compared to senators who must stump across a whole state or presidential candidates who must campaign across the entire country. Since candidates for the House of Representatives only need to cover a single district, their travel expenses are much smaller. Yet the cost of running a campaign even in such a relatively small area is astronomical: According to the Federal Election Commission, the average cost of winning a seat in the House of Representatives in 2006 was nearly $5.9 million; the average cost of winning a seat in the Senate was $17 million (U.S. Census Bureau, 2009). Few individuals are independently wealthy enough to spare that kind of money on the gamble of winning an election.

Anyone wanting to challenge an incumbent has even fewer resources: Incumbents can use the resources of their office, including mailing privileges and existing staff, as well as the office itself to gain free broadcast time by making announcements or public appearances related to their jobs. Yet incumbents running for reelection typically outspend their challengers by substantial margins: In 2007, House of Representatives incumbents spent a total of $527.6 million to campaign for reelection, compared to the total of $246.7 million spent by their challengers (U.S. Census Bureau, 2009). If political candidates, especially challengers to existing officeholders, are to be people other than just the most affluent, campaign financing must come from somewhere. Enter the PACs: They can offer their considerable resources to a campaign.

The potential to expand individuals' and organizations' contributions to political campaigns has clearly gained momentum: The number of PACs has exploded since 1977 (see Figure 4.2), slowing only after 2004. But not all PACs are equal. Notice that there are far more corporate PACs than any other type, including labor. Organized labor certainly has its own PACs, but these are far fewer in number than corporate PACs. Notice, too, that corporate PACs show a much sharper growth curve than all other types of PACs except those that are nonconnected. Most notably, the growth in the number of labor PACs since the early 1980s has been rather flat. It would

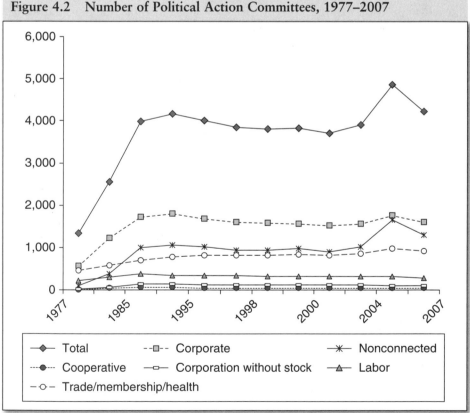

Figure 4.2   Number of Political Action Committees, 1977–2007

Source: Adapted from http://www.census.gov/compendia/statab/2010/tables/10s0410.pdf.

seem that economic actors like corporations have an advantage over workers in their ability to funnel money into political campaigns. However, more important than the number of PACs is the proportion of total PAC contributions each type makes.

Figure 4.3 shows that the biggest PACs are generally corporate PACs, which together make substantially larger donations than labor PACs. Among the corporate PACs, those representing financial, insurance, and real estate corporations are the largest donors, with those representing energy corporations right behind them.

Are there patterns to the distribution of PAC money? The data indicate that PACs overwhelmingly favor incumbents over challengers by a margin of more than 8 to 1, regardless of party or ideology. Researchers suggest that

Figure 4.3   Political Action Committees by Total Contributions to Candidates, 2005–2006

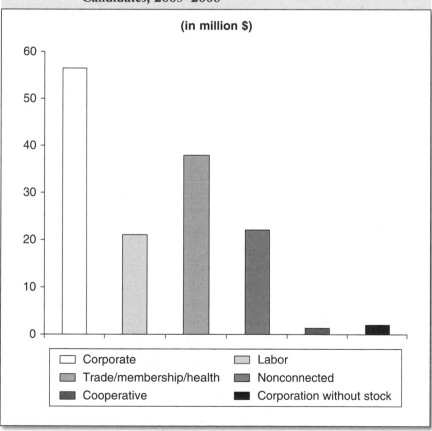

Source: Adapted from http://www.census.gov/compendia/statab/2010/tables/10s0411.pdf.

this is because incumbents are a known entity: Representatives of PACs are likely to have established a working relationship with the incumbents and therefore have a better opportunity to gain their attention when it comes time to make policy. A challenger represents a new, unknown relationship requiring a large investment of time and effort to nurture and may prove to be resistant to lobbyists' efforts at influence. Incumbents are also known actors whose behavior can be more predictable than a newcomer.

And incumbents are more dependent on PACs and therefore more likely to listen to and give in to their demands. Yet while PACs clearly favor incumbents with their donations, they show no such decided pattern in terms of party: PACs donate almost equally to both Democrats and Republicans, although labor PACs tend to give more to Democratic Party candidates, and corporate PACs more to Republican Party candidates (U.S. Census Bureau, 2009).

Does this mean that PACs are buying policy? Researchers do not think so. Clawson, Neustadtl, and Weller (1998) argue that what they are buying is access, not policy. Lobbyists representing PACs are attempting to gain favored attention and time from legislators, so as to shape their perceptions and preferences about which issues matter most and which interests are most akin to the common good. This suggests that PACs function as an important aspect of preemptive power in that their preferential access to legislators makes their voices and their points of view more likely to be heard at all, and that is likely to shape agendas and perceptions for legislators. Indeed, it is not unusual for lobbyists to write bills, in portions or in their entirety, and to provide distilled information to time-starved and overwhelmed legislators, all of which favors the lobbyists' interests. That does not necessarily guarantee a policy outcome desired by PACs and their lobbyists. But a sizable campaign contribution does make the PACs and their constituents more important to legislators than an average citizen. When PACs call or knock on the legislators' doors they are likely to be answered; when an average constituent tries to contact their representatives, they are more likely to get a form letter or be put on hold.

Soft Money

In spite of the decided advantages of PACs, in recent years another form of campaign financing has emerged: "Soft money" derives from a major loophole in federal campaign financing and spending law that exempts from regulation those contributions made for party building in general rather than for specific candidates. Soft money includes contributions made for such things as voter registration drives, get-out-the-vote drives, bumper stickers and posters, and television and radio spots supporting a party platform or idea but not an individual candidate (Liptak, 2010b). Unlike PACs, there are no limits imposed on soft money. And while they are technically supposed to be devoted to party-building efforts, usually on the local and state level, the reality is that they are commonly diverted to such things as office overhead costs, computer equipment, and the like, freeing up the more carefully controlled PAC money to support specific candidates more effectively. And although party-building activities are generally done by local and state-level party officials, raising such funds is most commonly done by federal candidates and officeholders and thus the latter are most likely to control and coordinate the use of soft money funds.

Where federal election law limits individuals' annual contributions to no more than $1,000 per candidate and no more than $20,000 to a specific political party, there have been no such restrictions on soft money. Corporations, labor unions, and highly affluent individuals commonly make soft donations of anywhere from $100,000 to $1 million for party building. The unregulated nature of soft money became such an attractive loophole that it began to replace PAC money as the main source of campaign financing, swelling from just $86 million in 1992 to more than $400 million in 2008 (Open Secrets, 2002; Weissman, 2008). By 2002 it averaged 42% of the total for the Democratic Party and 58% of the Republican Party, a trend that observers believe is likely to continue (Open Secrets, 2002). It is not a surprise, then, to see that the total number of PACs—especially corporate PACs—have shown a slight but notable decline in recent years: Such interest groups have found soft money to be more attractive.

The 2008 presidential election also saw the dramatic rise of 527 and 501 organizations, political organizations so named for the tax codes that allow them to raise and spend unlimited amounts of money. These organizations are not specifically tied to any party, nor are they devoted to any one candidate; therefore, they are not covered by campaign financing limits (which is why candidates, including both presidential candidates in 2008, are increasingly declining public election funds that are subject to federal limits and relying instead on privately raised money) (Mann, 2008). The 527s and 501s are independent organizations that may produce and broadcast their own campaign ads in support of or criticizing one or more candidates or political positions. For example, for the 2004 presidential election, Moveon.org became a significant player in campaigning against the presidency of George W. Bush, and Swift Boat Veterans for Truth strongly campaigned against the challenging candidacy of John Kerry. Neither organization was hired by the Democratic or Republican Parties to participate this way; instead, they were designated as independent organizations of individuals who have a constitutional right to free speech and are thus free to say what they like in the campaign and to spend as much as they like to help others hear it. Although both Moveon.org and Swift Boat Veterans for Truth were clearly advocating a specific candidate, they were not funded by either party, nor did they directly contribute to either party or candidate; they were simply expressing their own point of view—even if that does mean supporting one or the other candidate and thereby avoid governance by campaign financing restrictions. They thus represent a new strategy of soft money in campaign financing.

Soft money contributions, like PAC money, do not explicitly buy donors the candidates or the policies they want, but they do buy access. What they are buying, then, is influence. As former Democratic National Conference fundraiser Johnny Chung has said about such donations, "the White House is like a subway—you have to put in coins to open the gates" (U.S. Congress: Senate, 1998). Big contributions in soft money open doors and set the decision-making agenda by keeping donors' interests front and center for federal policy makers. Some of the most powerful corporate interests are thus among the largest donors of soft money, including major oil and energy companies, the tobacco industry, and pharmaceutical firms. The potential to pose significant influence in shaping legislators' preferences and perceptions is tremendous, and the Supreme Court upheld a ban on the use of soft money in 2010; however, three justices voted to hear the case, leaving the door open to future challenges to the ban.

Citizens United v. Federal Election Commission

Power without participation in electoral politics reached new dimensions in 2010, when the Supreme Court ruled that it was unconstitutional for the state to ban corporate campaign spending in support of candidates running for election. The Court ruled that such a ban violates the First Amendment guaranteeing free speech, particularly political speech. Critics argued unsuccessfully to the Court that corporations do not vote and therefore should not be given free reign to influence political messages or the political process. However, the Court determined that corporations should have the same free speech rights as individuals and allowed full rights to say whatever they like about political candidates or political ideas without restrictions on how much they could spend. Critics, including President Obama, decried this decision as an unprecedented one, reinforcing already-advantaged interests since corporations hold the greatest resources to devote to their own causes and candidates. While the Court's ruling also allows labor unions and social movements the same free speech privileges as corporations, the resources of these groups pale beside the resources of major corporations and capital accumulation interests (Liptak, 2010a). With corporations greatly outspending other interests to skew public perception and influence political conversations, the fear is that other interests will be silenced or outmaneuvered. Only time will tell how much of an alienating effect this court decision will have on future voters and their participation in the political process.

Critics have increasingly raised the specter of influence-peddling by already-advantaged economic interests to the detriment of the ability of the more oppressed interests to be heard by lawmakers. Any campaign finance reforms will undoubtedly have to include some provisions to regulate soft money and corporate campaign spending on ads if it is to truly curb the financial excesses of political campaigning. But while congressional leaders often acknowledge the great need to close the soft money loophole and further regulate campaign finance law, they have yet to follow through with any real legislation. Most if not all of them are at least in some part dependent upon the largess provided by donors and are unlikely to bite the hand that feeds them without any real pressure from other interests. This alone raises the question of the neutrality of the state and its administrators. The issue of congressional reluctance to control soft money points to at least one area where the interests of the political elites themselves have superseded the interests of the common good. And this raises the question of the extent of voters' ability to wield great power over elected leaders simply by voting.

Structural Factors of Power Without Voting

In addition to the effects of PACs and soft money on the political process, there are structural factors that are likely to privilege some interests over others in policy making. For example, the state remains dependent upon tax revenues in order to perform its functions. Limited revenues mean the state will have to curtail its expenditures, including defense, social welfare, education, and so forth. Its ability to raise tax revenues in a capitalist political economy is highly dependent on the activities of major corporations, in part because they provide the jobs that will produce income tax revenue (and the largest proportion of the federal tax burden is borne by individuals' income taxes). In addition, multinational corporations can avoid paying federal taxes by shifting production and jobs abroad. Witness the increasing corporate interest in offshore production, a decision that could mean a severe loss of federal tax revenues. Moreover, offshore banking can also mean the loss of federal tax revenues both from the banks themselves and from affluent individuals who can shield great portions of their wealth from income, capital gains, and estate taxes.

Thus, the great dependence of the state on dominant economic actors is likely to make policy makers more sensitive and responsive to these interests not necessarily only because these interests deliberately manipulate them with PAC and soft money or vote against them but because legislators have little choice. To ignore dominant economic interests or to make policy that specifically contradicts their interests is to increase the likelihood that the state will suffer major losses of tax revenues either because corporations cannot maximize their profits or because restrictive legislation may encourage them to shift production elsewhere. This becomes power that does not require voting or participation in the campaign process; it is an advantage produced by the structure of the political economy.

The significance of this structurally rooted power thus mitigates the effect of nonelite participation in electoral politics and as such is likely to render nonelite participation less meaningful if their needs and interests are inconsistent with those of economic elites. Note, too, that dominant economic elites are not held accountable by nonelites' participation in electoral politics. This is because nonelites do not elect them and thus have no control over the decision-making process of the corporation: No matter how nonelites may vote, they have no input into corporate decisions that will fundamentally affect their lives as well as the welfare of the state itself. Corporate elites may decide where to base production, whom to employ and at what rate, what to produce, whom to sell their products to, and what price to charge. They may, in fact, decide to massively downsize even though they may be highly profitable, because the concerns of major stockholders, including the biggest financial institutions, take precedence over those of other stakeholders in the firm, including workers, the community, consumers, and the state.

Structures of patriarchy, racism, and heterosexism also reproduce power beyond voting for men, whites, and people with normative sexual and/or gender practices. Male privilege and white-skin privilege have over centuries of cultural and political practice become institutionalized, so that these systems of oppression are reproduced without the need for people to vote to keep them in place, as have been privileges accorded to those with normative sexual and/or gender practices. It is not necessary, for example, for whites to deliberately vote to keep people of color in relative poverty, or to prevent them from living in good neighborhoods or to get a good education, or to get (and keep) good jobs and promotions. The use of property tax revenues to support public schools means that schools in neighborhoods predominated by people of color and poor people will suffer meager budgets and therefore struggle to provide adequate education for their students. That means students of color will be less able to compete against more affluent white students for jobs. Seniority rules of "last hired, first fired" institutionalizes white advantage to keep one's job in an era of downsizing, since people of color are likely to be historically among the last hired.

While women are certainly less likely to be segregated from men in their housing than people of color to be segregated from whites, women do confront the institutionalization of oppression, such as patriarchy in seniority rules in employment. Since women are relative newcomers to many job categories, they are likely to be the first fired. Moreover, historically powerful assumptions of gendered family responsibilities and parenting institutionalize the oppression of women because employment structures are still not structured to accommodate a balance between work and family. This makes it difficult for women to rise in their occupations or, often, to keep their jobs. Where racism is a structure of oppression reproducing white privilege beyond voting, patriarchy is a structure of oppression reproducing male power beyond voting. The structures of patriarchy and racism mean that those already in power are likely to remain more sympathetic and responsive to dominant interests. And that does not require voting to accomplish. It is difficult indeed to use voting to hold accountable employers, landlords, banks, judges, police, or educational institutions whose structures of opportunity reproduce inequality and oppression.

Does this mean that dominant economic elites are completely beyond the ability of nonelites to hold them accountable? Hardly. As we will explore in Chapter 6, political participation is not restricted to voting alone. Indeed, for the oppressed, nonelectoral political activism may be a more viable avenue for empowerment. Organized resistance can apply substantial pressure to challenge dominant economic interests and elicit some change. Such was the case of an internationally organized campaign against the racist apartheid policies of South Africa in the 1980s. Although it was not an overnight success, persistent pressures against universities and other major investors to withdraw or disinvest their holdings in corporations doing business in and with South Africa eventually caused corporate interests to press for dismantling of apartheid policies as a prerequisite for their continued economic support of that country. Note that this ability of nonelites to affect significant policy change did not occur as a result of electoral politics. Rather, it occurred because a highly organized effort of nonelites was able to reshape the preferences and perceptions of economic and ultimately political elites by applying economic pressure. We will turn to this question of political participation beyond voting in Chapter 6.

Discussion

1. How might campaign financing be reformed to avoid the problems that currently exist? Should soft money and 527 and 501 organizations be controlled? If so, how? If not, why? What alternatives to the current campaign financing mechanisms might there be?

2. Is the Electoral College still useful? Why or why not? How might voting for president of the United States be done differently?

3. Consider the recall election of the governor of California in 2003. Does a recall challenge the concept of democracy? Why or why not? What does the recall suggest about the role of power in electoral politics? What might it suggest about the role of the media? About the role of money in politics? Does the recall election represent power to the people? Why or why not?

4. Does "one person, one vote" ensure equality of political power for each citizen? Why or why not? Is it possible to produce equality of political power in electoral politics? Why or why not? What are some possible alternative ways of leveling the playing field?

5. Can anyone effectively run for political office? Why or why not? How might someone who is poor run for office?

6. Did you vote in the last election? Why or why not?

References

Bay, A. H., & Blekesaune, M. (2002). Youth, unemployment and political marginalisation. *International Journal of Social Welfare, 11*(2), 132–139.

Chen, M. (2009). *Giving them back their vote*. Retrieved from http://colorlines.com/archives/2009/07/giving_them_back_their_vote.html

Clawson, D., Neustadtl, A., & Weller, M. (1998). *Dollars and votes: How business campaign contributions subvert democracy*. Philadelphia: Temple University Press.

Common Sense for Drug Policy. (2008). Race and prison. Retrieved from http://www.drugwarfacts.org/cms/node/64

Council for Excellence in Government. (2007). Survey done February 20–24, 2007. Retrieved from http://webapps.ropercenter.uconn.edu

Covin, D. (2001). The length of memory: The black population and the presidential election of 2000. *Black Scholar, 31*(2), 33–37.

Demleitner, N. V. (2002). "Collatoral damage": No re-entry for drug offenders. *Villanova Law Review, 47*(4), 1027–1054.

Djupe, P. A., & Grant, J. T. (2001). Religious institutions and political participation in America. *Journal for the Scientific Study of Religion, 40*(2), 303–314.

Docherty, I., Goodlad, R., & Paddison, R. (2001). Civic culture, community and citizen participation in cotrasting neighbourhoods. *Urban Studies, 38*(12), 2225–2250.

Firebaugh, G., & Chen, K. (1995). Vote turnout of Nineteenth Amendment women: The enduring effect of disenfranchisement. *American Journal of Sociology, 100*(4), 972–996.

Fox News/Opinion Dynamics Poll. (2009, June). Retrieved from http://webapps.ropercenter.uconn.edu

Gallup/*USA Today* Poll. (2008). Survey done July 25–27, 2008. Retrieved from http://webapps.ropercenter.uconn.edu

Hermon, G., Jr. (2001). Putting election 2000 in perspective: A declaration of war. *Black Scholar, 31*(2), 11–13.

Holder, K. (2006). Voting and registration in the election of November 2004. *Current population reports* (P20–556). Washington, DC: U.S. Census Bureau.

Jackson, J., Clemente, F., & Watkins, F. E. (1989). *Keep hope alive: Jesse Jackson's 1988 presidential campaign.* Boston: South End Press.

Kaiser Family Foundation. (2006). Survey done June 12–19. Retrieved from http://webapps.ropercenter.uconn.edu

Lichtman, A. J. (2003). What really happened in Florida's 200 presidential election? *Journal of Legal Studies, 32*(1), 221–243.

Lien, P.-T., Collet, C., Wong, J., & Ramakrishnan, S. K. (2001). Asian Pacific-American public opinion and political participation. *Political Science and Politics, 34*(3), 625–630.

Liptak, A. (2010a, January 21). Justices, 5–4, reject corporate spending limit. *New York Times.* Retrieved from http://www.nytimes.com/2010/01/22/us/politics.22scotus.html

Liptak, A. (2010b, June 29). Supreme Court affirms a ban on soft money. *New York Times.* Retrieved from http://www.nytimes.com/2010/06/30/us/politics/30donate.html

Mann, T. E. (2008, July 1). Money in the 2008 elections: Bad news or good? Retrieved from http://www.brookings.edu/opinions/2008/0701_publicfinance_mann.aspx

Manza, J., & Brooks, C. (1998). The gender gap in U.S. presidential elections: When? Why? Implications? *American Journal of Sociology, 103*(5), 1235–1266.

Manza, J., & Uggen, C. (2008). *Locked out: Felon disenfranchisement and American democracy.* New York: Oxford University Press.

McCue, C. P., & Gopoian, J. D. (2000). Dispositional empathy and the political gender gap. *Women and Politics, 21*(2), 1–20.

McMiller, D. L. (1999). Race, associational involvement, and political participation. *Race and Society, 2*(1), 83–95.

McVeigh, R., & Smith, C. (1999). Who protests in America: An analysis of three political alternatives—inaction, institutionalized politics, or protest. *Sociological Forum, 14*(4), 685–702.

Miliband, R. (1969). *The state in capitalist society.* New York: Basic Books.

New York Times/CBS. (2010). *National survey of Tea Party supporters.* Retrieved from http://documents.nytimes.com/new-york-timescbs-news-poll-national-survey-of-tea-party-supporters

Niven, D. (1998). Party elites and women candidates: The shape of bias. *Women and Politics, 19*(2), 57–80.

Open Secrets. (2002). *Soft money backgrounder.* Retrieved from http://www.opensecrets.org/parties/softsource.php

Opp, K. D. (2001). Why do people vote? The cognitive-illusion proposition and its test. *KYKLOS, 54*(2–3), 355–378.

Palmer, B., & Simon, D. (2001). The political glass ceiling: Gender, strategy, and incumbency in U.S. House elections, 1978–1998. *Women and Politics, 23*(1–2), 59–78.

Pew Research Center for the People & the Press Values Survey. (2009). Retrieved from http://webapps.ropercenter.uconn.edu

Piven, F. F., & Cloward, R. A. (2000). *Why Americans still don't vote: And why politicians want it that way.* Boston: Beacon Press.

Praud, J. (2001). French women and the liberal model of political citizenship: From exclusion to inclusion? *Contemporary French Civilization, 25*(2), 250–270.

Public Agenda Foundation. (2008). Survey done November 5–16. Retrieved from http://webapps.ropercenter.uconn.edu

Radcliff, B. (2001). Organized labor and electoral participation in American national elections. *Journal of Labor Research, 22*(2), 405–414.

Roberts, S. (2009, April 30). No racial gap seen in '08 vote turnout. *New York Times.* Retrieved from http://www.nytimes.com/2009/05/01/us/politics/01census.html

Saad, L. (2010). *Tea partiers are fairly mainstream in their demographics.* Retrieved from http://www.gallup.com/poll/127181/tea-partiers-fairly-mainstream-demographics.aspx

Schlozman, K. L., Burns, N., & Verba, S. (1999). "What happened at work today?" A multistage model of gender, employment, and political participation. *Journal of Politics, 61*(1), 29–53.

Schwadel, P. (2002). Testing the promise of the churches: Income inequality in the opportunity to learn civic skills in Christian congregations. *Journal for the Scientific Study of Religion, 41*(3), 565–575.

Uggen, C., & Manza, J. (2002). Democratic contraction? Political consequences of felon disenfranchisement in the United States. *American Sociological Review, 67*(6), 777–803.

U.S. Census Bureau. (2009). *Statistical abstracts of the United States, 2009.* Retrieved from http://www.census.gov/compendia/statab

U.S. Census Bureau, Population Division, Education & Social Stratification Branch. (2009, July 20). *Voting and registration in the election of November 2008.* Retrieved from http://www.census.gov/population/www/socdemo/voting/cps2008.html

U.S. Commission on Civil Rights. (2000). *Voting irregularities in Florida during the 2000 presidential election.* Retrieved from http://www.usccr.gov/pubs/vote2000/report/exesum.htm

U.S. Congress: Senate. (1998). *Investigation of illegal or improper activities in connection with 1996 federal election campaigns.* Final report of the Committee on Governmental Affairs (Senate report 105-167—105th Congress 2d Session—March 10). Retrieved from http://www.fas.org/irp/congress/1998_rpt/sgo-sir/1-10.htm

Verba, S., Burns, N., & Schlozman, K. L. (1997). Knowing and caring about politics: Gender and political engagement. *Journal of Politics, 59*(4), 1051–1072.

Verba, S., Schlozman, K. L., & Brady, H. E. (2000). Rational action and political activity. *Journal of Theoretical Politics, 12*(3), 243–268.

Wattenberg, M. P. (2002). *Where have all the voters gone?* Cambridge, MA: Harvard University Press.

Weissman, S. (2008). *Fast start for soft money groups in 2008 election.* Retrieved from http://www.cfinst.org/Press/PReleases/08-04-03/Fast_Start_for_Soft_Money_Groups_in_2008_Election.aspx

Wing, B. (2001). *White power in election 2000.* Retrieved from http://colorlines.com/archives/2001/03/white_power_in_election_2000.html

5

Who's in Charge Here?

The State and Society

Power structure theories imply some notion of the relationship between the state and society. Consider, for example, how the state may affect you. Perhaps you or someone you know has been deployed to serve in Afghanistan or in the war in Iraq. Whose interests are served when the state determines that it is time to go to war? Sometimes the state reaches out to aid the poor and needy; other times the state reduces or withdraws such support. Similarly, sometimes the state reinforces racialized inequality, as it did in support of slavery and Jim Crow laws; other times the state acts to reduce racialized inequality, as it did with civil rights legislation. Sometimes the state ignores women's needs, as evidenced when women were denied the right to vote; other times the state withdraws support for patriarchy, as seen in equal rights and affirmative action legislation. And there are times that the state reinforces heteronormativity, as is the case in "don't ask, don't tell" policies in the military, and times when the state withdraws that support for heteronormativity and recognizes, for example, the right of gay and lesbian couples to marry. Who decides if antipoverty support will be available, and who will be eligible for it? Who decides whether underrepresented populations are equally entitled as dominant populations to rights and privileges? For that matter, who decides who gets to vote, who is a citizen, and why? Who decides who gets to make such decisions? These questions concern the role of the state in society. But what is "the state"? How is it different from government? How powerful is the state? Is the state all powerful and autonomous, captured or dominated by specific interests, or is it *relatively* autonomous? If the state is not entirely autonomous, whose interests are more persuasive than those of others? Whose interests does the state support?

The *state* is the organization of political positions and the structure of political relations in society. The state is different from *government,* which refers to the people who occupy positions within the state. Individuals may come and go in government, and as such, specific policies may change in part because of individuals' personal styles, perspectives, party affiliations and other allegiances, interests, and so forth. However, the structure of political relations (electoral processes, policy-making processes, and relations between the government and corporations, labor, consumers, and others) remains intact no matter who occupies positions in the state. We will examine the relationship between workers, private corporations, and the state and consider how this relationship affects the functioning of government in policy making.

As you will recall from Chapter 2, pluralist theory asserts that the state is the embodiment of power in a capitalist political economy. It stands above influence from the pressures applied by all interest groups, presumably including economic interests. The state thus acts as the neutral arbiter weighing all competing interests to legislate in the common good, striking some balance between the competing demands of these interests. The pluralist analysis places economic interests on a par with noneconomic interests, as if all were equal in power and strength in their ability to influence the state and to get their respective agendas addressed. While political sociologists frequently disagree with this pluralist characterization of the relationship between the state and society, there is much debate concerning the intersection of the state and economy and the role of the state in capitalist society.

Power elite theorists, on the other hand, place economic interests in the very center of their analysis of the relationship between the state and society. They offer a one-class analysis of power, interpreting power and political dynamics in terms of the interests and positions of economic elites as the dominating class. They tend to assume that policies, decisions, and actions originate at the top of the social and political hierarchy. Some power elite theorists (particularly C. Wright Mills) asserted bluntly that the masses were largely irrelevant and powerless to confront the elites since elites so dominate the power structure as well as the ideological frameworks that justify it. This viewpoint ignores the struggle between antagonistic classes or groups as the impetus for action, discounting the role of agency among the masses to effect change. Here, the source of any change occurs from the top down rather than from the bottom up. Society and the state are thus the product of elite class interests, rather than the product of antagonisms and conflicts resulting from relationships of oppression.

While pluralist and power elite theories offer strong contrasts for analyzing the relationship between the state and society, they share a common adoption of a stratification model of power and the state: Society is stratified hierarchically, and those at the top of state institutions make the decisions that matter. Their disagreement stems in part from their view of the ability of those at the lower end of that stratification system to get their interests met. Where pluralists argue that those on the bottom have just as much opportunity and chance as those at the top to eventually get their needs addressed, power elite theorists argue that they have little or no chance at all—at least in a society where the current state exists. The contrast between pluralism and power elite theory, then, is a stark one wherein the masses either have equal power to the dominants in society or little to no power at all. Marxist theories of the state reject this stratification perspective as insufficient to understand the relationship between the state and society, but they disagree greatly as to what that relationship does look like and why.

Marxist Theories of the State

Marxist theories of the state reject the stratification model of the relationship between the state and society offered by pluralists and power elite theorists and instead begin with the assumption of antagonistic classes whose conflict is built into the structure of society. There are several contrasting models of Marxist theories of the state, but each contains an implicit, and, at times, explicit analysis of the relationship between the state and a capitalist political economy.

Interestingly, although much of the spirited debates that have occurred between the models we will examine in this section are derived from analyses of Karl Marx and Friedrich Engels's work, they themselves never offered a fully developed theory of the state. But they did assert some observations that have stimulated much of the contemporary debate. In particular, Marxist scholars have long debated the meaning of a single sentence in *The Communist Manifesto* (Marx & Engels, 1967): "The executive of the modern state is but a committee for the managing of the common affairs of the whole bourgeoisie" (p. 18).

This quote raises several pertinent questions: Does the state act as the coercive instrument of the capitalist class? If it does, what is the process by which that happens? If it does not, what *is* the role of the state in modern capitalist society?

Instrumentalism/Business Dominance Theory: "Capture" or Domination?

The earliest variant of a theory of the state in which economic interests control or dominate the state is *instrumentalism*. Theorists using this model did not frame their analysis in terms of class struggle. Rather, early instrumentalists offered a "capture" theory of the state in which capitalists virtually captured key positions of the state apparatus to use the state as their tool to legislate in their own interests (Domhoff, 1970, 1987, 1991a, 1992b; Miliband, 1969, 1973, 1983; Weinstein, 1968). Capitalists captured the state by running and getting elected to office, such as Senator (previously Governor) Jay Rockefeller of West Virginia, Vice President (to President Gerald Ford and previously Governor) Nelson Rockefeller of New York, President John Fitzgerald Kennedy, Senator Ted Kennedy of Massachusetts, Representative Joseph P. Kennedy II of Massachusetts, Governor Pierre Du Pont of Delaware, Governor Jeb Bush of Florida, and President George H. W. Bush, and President George W. Bush. Each of these men are/were scions of major industrial capitalist families. Alternatively, individual capitalists may capture the state to make it their instrument by consciously and deliberately applying their considerable economic power to bear on the state itself.

While this scenario would seem plausible, and many examples would seem to be readily available, the fact is that few capitalists ever actually captured the state outright, a criticism that more recent theorists took to heart. Indeed, some argued that capitalists actually would have an easier time getting their interests met if they did *not* sit in the command positions of the state: Such blatant and obvious power grabs would quickly lose legitimacy. These theorists offer instead a view of *business dominance* rather than the more extreme view of individual capitalists consciously and deliberately capturing the state. In this more recent variant, capitalists do not own the state or capture its key positions. Instead, they dominate the state by sitting on important advisory groups like the Council on Foreign Relations (CFR), heading regulatory agencies, using political action committees (PACs) in electoral and legislative processes, carefully lobbying key legislators in support of corporate interests, and more recently by funding private political organizations through the "soft money" of 527 organizations (see Chapter 4) (Akard, 1992, 2005; Benoit, 2007; Burris, 1992; Domhoff, 1990, 2000, 2005; Lugar, 2000; Prechel, 1990, 2000; Useem, 1984).

The CFR is an important advisory committee to the president on foreign policy. Its membership is heavily corporate and thus their worldview and perspectives regarding national interests are shaped by their corporate and capital accumulation interests. Since the president relies heavily on the analyses supplied by the CFR, corporate viewpoints and interests are likely to shape presidential pronouncements of foreign policy, including whether or not to sign international treaties and accords, go to war against another nation, or invest huge proportions of the federal budget into Department of Defense projects.

Regulatory agencies are commonly headed by people drawn from the industries these agencies are supposed to govern. This is because regulators often oversee complex industries such as nuclear power, banking, and communications. Individuals from within these industries are presumed to possess important expertise regarding how they operate, what issues they must confront, and what particular problems might arise. However, their ties within the industry make their independence as regulators questionable, and the fact that most of them cycle back into the industry from which they arose when their time is done as regulators (and commonly at a more lucrative position than before) makes it unlikely that they will enforce regulations the industry views as particularly harmful to its interests.

Finally, PACs and 527 organizations may not buy a political candidate outright, but their contributions to political campaigns do buy them access to legislators and give them a stronger voice in shaping legislators' viewpoints, perspectives, and priorities. These mechanisms of corporate participation in the processes of decision making thus enable capitalists to dominate and influence the state. Importantly, that dominance occurs not by capturing the decision-making positions themselves but by providing key resources to those that do (Clawson, Neustadtl, & Weller, 1998).

Although not necessarily conspiratorial, the business dominance position implies that business leaders operate on the basis of a clear, fairly unified conception of both corporate and capital accumulation interests and the policies necessary to address those concerns. Given sufficient threat to their interests and adequate mechanisms granting them access to the policy formation process, business leaders consciously organize the political and economic resources of the corporate community around successful passage and enactment of pro-corporate policy. This analysis also implies that the state is the locus of power; this is why capital accumulation interests find it so necessary to capture or dominate it. The state exists in a capitalist society.

The instrumentalist and business dominance perspectives suggest that individuals make a difference: If the individuals who occupy the important seats of power or the key organizational mechanisms of influence were to change, the state would presumably legislate to protect other, noncapitalist interests. That is, if labor leaders were to get elected to Congress and the White House, or to take control of the CFR and the regulatory agencies and to become the largest, most important PACs and 527 organizations, legislators would have to accede to labor interests instead of capital accumulation interests.

This analysis discounts the role of political socialization in the production of policy in the interests of corporate concerns. The legitimation process facilitates the general acceptance by the wider population of the belief that societal interests and business interests are one and the same: "What's good for General Motors (or Walmart) is good for the United States," or "The business of the United States is business." As such, legislators and policy makers are likely to frame their perspectives in corporate terms because the dominant ideology with which most people are socialized in the United States filters and frames perspectives in such terms. Blatant seizing of the policy-making process or decision-making positions is not necessary if the dominant ideology legitimates such interests as the common good anyway.

Finally, the business dominance and instrumentalist analyses ignore the working class's role in policy making and the effect resistance may have on those processes. They imply that the working class tacitly accepts without resistance what capital accumulation interests and actors force the state to do, even if it is not in workers' interests. However, history is replete with instances of resistance, which have at times facilitated the production of policy that business interests found abominable, such as the right of workers to collectively bargain or the Community Reinvestment Act (CRA) that forced banks to negotiate with community activists to reinvest in underserved communities. The notion that resistance could have the effect of thwarting or at least defying oppression is a significant challenge to the instrumentalist and business dominance positions.

If the state is not merely an institutional actor within a capitalist society, what then is its relationship to society?

Capitalist State Structuralism

Where the instrumentalist and business dominance analyses see a state in a capitalist society, and therefore the state as simply an actor within that society, other theorists using a structuralist perspective see a *capitalist state*. That is, the very structure of the state itself is capitalist. That is why this particular theoretical perspective is referred to as *capitalist state structuralism*. Instrumentalist and business dominance theorists imply that the backgrounds and interests of individuals in key positions are the sources of power and policy; capitalist state structuralists argue, in contrast, that state policies are forged by the structure of the state itself and its position within the larger capitalist economy. State managers are constrained by the imperatives of the capitalist political economy to create and implement policies that reproduce the conditions of capital accumulation and to thwart the conditions that create accumulation crises. State managers have no choice but to legislate this way: Were the state to somehow operate outside of these structural parameters it would court economic crises, which in turn would create political legitimacy crises that state managers can ill afford (Block, 1987; Glasberg, 1989; Glasberg & Skidmore, 1997; Mandel, 1975; Poulantzas, 1968, 1978; Valocchi, 1989; Wright, 1978).

Moreover, because the state is the structural unification of contradictory class relationships, it remains free from direct control by class-based organizations. Pro-capitalist state economic intervention is not, therefore, produced by the participation of business organizations and corporate actors in the policy formation process. Rather, policy is a product of the contradictory relations of power embedded within state structures themselves. It is an expression of the state's underlying, pro-capitalist structural bias.

Capitalist state structuralists and business dominance theorists agree as to *what* the state does: It legislates to secure the conditions of capital accumulation and in the interests of capitalists. But they disagree as to *why* the state does so. Instrumentalists and business dominance theorists argue that the state legislates this way because state managers are either capitalists themselves or they are dominated by such interests. Capitalist state structuralists argue that the state legislates as it does because state managers simply have no choice: Their range of alternative actions is restricted to only those decisions that will not threaten capital accumulation or risk economic collapse and hence loss of control of the polity and their position of political leadership. This does not require dominance of the state by corporate interests.

In fact, capitalist state structuralists argue that the state is "relatively autonomous" from individual competitive capitalists; the fundamental requirements of capital accumulation at the core of the capitalist political economy delimit the state's range of discretion, not competitive individual capitalists. In contrast to the instrumentalist and business dominance perspectives, capitalist state structuralism implies that the structure of the state is impervious to changes in personnel: Regardless of the types of individuals in the state apparatus, the state is structurally constrained to operate for the benefit of the capitalist class. What's good for General Motors or Walmart is good for the United States not because everyone has been politically socialized to accept that this is true or because the capitalists have seized control or dominance of the state to make this so but because it simply is.

Capitalist state structuralism shares a view of the masses with instrumentalism and business dominance analyses in its discounting of class struggle as a factor in policy-making processes. But where instrumentalist and business dominance analyses focus on corporate elites and their role in the state to the exclusion of an examination of resistance from below, capitalist state structuralist analyses acknowledge that such resistance might occasionally occur, but they minimize its importance. Class struggle is viewed by capitalist state structuralists as highly mechanistic, devoid of class consciousness. The state's role is to preserve the organization and coalescence the capitalist class by arbitrating and cooling out the divisive structural contradictions and antagonisms within that class and to cool out antagonisms between capitalists and the working class. For example, the state uses regulatory policy and antitrust legislation to reduce conflicts between capitalists that might threaten the underlying conditions of system-wide capital accumulation and therefore the general health of the political economy, if not the welfare of specific capitalist individuals. The state similarly chills potentially damaging antagonisms between labor and capital by institutionalizing class conflict with such mechanisms as legislation guaranteeing labor the right to collectively bargain with capitalists. Another example of the state's ability to institutionalize and control class conflict is the Taylor Law in New York that forbids workers of "essential services" such as police, firefighters, sanitation workers, air traffic controllers, teachers, and the like from striking. Workers who go on strike risk losing two or more days' pay for every day they remain on strike or may even lose their jobs. This antistrike clause weakens labor power and reduces the potential of class conflicts to damage the conditions of capital accumulation.

While the capitalist state structuralist model explains *why* the state operates in the interests of capital accumulation, it does not specify *how* the state accomplishes this. It does not provide a description of the mechanisms by which the state produces policies in the interest of the capitalist class without being run by that class. Is there some overt process by which new members of the legislative body are socialized or come to understand that they must legislate this way? What mechanisms remind legislators that they must operate in the interests of capital accumulation? Is it a conscious observation by legislators that they have no choice but to address capital accumulation interests?

Further, capitalist state structuralism does not define the mechanisms on which the "relative autonomy" of the state might hinge. The concept is not operationalized in any empirically useful way. Were one to explore the question of the state's relative autonomy, there is little direction in the theoretical model to guide how to measure or document it or to evaluate its relativity: Relative to what? How much or how little relativity might be construed as autonomous? The capitalist state structuralist model itself does not clearly identify what the mechanisms of "relative autonomy" might be or how to empirically evaluate these.

In addition, if state policy making is centered and shaped by the imperatives governing capital accumulation, how do we explain noneconomic policy making? For example, what guides the development of civil rights legislation, women's rights legislation (particularly reproductive rights), gay and lesbian rights, the Americans with Disabilities Act (ADA), and legislation protecting endangered species, just to name a few. Capitalist state structuralism does not provide a mechanism to explain the production of policy that is not driven by capital accumulation interests. Moreover, if state policy is compelled to comply with the requirements of capital accumulation, how is it possible that such interests do not always gain their objectives? How do we explain the production of state policy that would appear inconsistent with capitalist class interests? For example, how do we explain the passage of workers' rights legislation (including worker safety and health policy, minimum wage policy, the right to collective bargaining, and so forth)? Indeed, this is a problem shared by the instrumentalist/business dominance model: If capitalist class actors and interests so dominate the state, whether because of their greater power or because their interests structurally shape the very existence of the state, how is it possible that they at times fail to thwart policy that contradicts their interests?

Finally, capitalist state structuralism and instrumentalism/business dominance theory share a similar focus on the internal structure of the state as a national structure. This focus tends to treat the state in isolation of its global context and thus omits an analysis of the external or international forces that might affect the state. Yet there is some evidence that such forces may indeed matter. For example, when Mexico nearly went bankrupt in 1982, an organized banking community largely from the United States refused to negotiate the nation's loans until the International Monetary Fund (IMF) imposed some very strict austerity conditions on Mexico's domestic policy. Among these conditions was the devaluation of Mexico's currency, the privatization of key industries that had previously been owned by the Mexican state (such as oil), and sharp curtailing of social welfare expenditures in favor of devoting substantial proportions of the national budget to paying their debt to private banks in the United States (Glasberg, 1989). Thus, the Mexican state managers lost control of their own domestic policy making to international forces outside their own state structure. The capitalist state structuralist model does not provide a theoretical mechanism for exploring this.

Class Dialectic Perspective: "Bringing Class Back In"

Business dominance and capitalist state structuralist analyses ignore or discount the role of class struggle in the production of policy in the state. In contrast, the *class dialectic perspective* complicates the analysis of state policy formation by examining the role of labor as well as the state and capitalists in the decision-making process. In this model, class struggle processes affect the state and its policy making. As such, organized resistance from below can in fact apply substantial pressure to the state to legislate in their interests or otherwise address their needs, even if these are not entirely consistent with those of capital accumulation interests (Eckstein, 1997; Esping-Anderson, Friedland, & Wright, 1986; Jackson, 2008; Levine, 1988; Whitt, 1979, 1982; Zeitlin, Ewen, & Ratcliff, 1974; Zeitlin & Ratcliff, 1975). Resistance from below is most effective, then, when working-class interests are organized, mobilized into social movements, and able to create mass disruptions (e.g., with labor strikes) (Jenkins & Brents, 1989; Quadagno, 1984, 1992; Quadagno & Meyer, 1989). When the state cannot legally and institutionally mediate class conflicts it may resort to its sole legitimate use of force and violence to repress labor unrest and mass disruption (Lenin, 1976). But the state actually resorts to the use of force and violence relatively rarely, because such physical coercion risks a legitimacy crisis. More often than not, the state will seek instead to mediate and cool out the conflict before working-class organizations can create mass turmoil by legislating to co-opt labor interests without seriously eroding capital accumulation interests (Galbraith, 1985; Levine, 1988; Schmitter, 1974; Swenson, 2002; Witte, 1972).

This analysis might help explain what previous models could not: How is it possible for capitalists and capital accumulation interests to fail to gain their objectives every time if they are either so powerful or if their interests are so embedded in the state structure itself? The class dialectic model suggests that this is possible because capitalist and capital accumulation interests are not all powerful; they are subject to organized struggles from below and so is the state. Were they impervious to resistance, workers would never be expected to gain their objectives at all. Yet a casual observation of the development of labor law in the United States and elsewhere suggests that capitalist class interests do not always fully dominate the state and the policy-making process.

Does that mean that when workers' interests gain advantage in policy making by the state that capital accumulation interests necessarily lose? Not at all. The state on occasion may produce policies that benefit labor while simultaneously supporting and legitimating the broader political economy (Quadagno, 1992). State policy in this model is the mediation of labor and corporate conflicts and is linked to dynamic struggles between business and labor that is played out in the state. The policies that emerge out of these struggles organize labor into institutionalized forms such as trade unions (as opposed to the more generalized industrial unions that represent all workers in a single, large union) amenable to capitalist interests.

For example, far from acceding entirely to labor interests, labor laws in the United States allow for the right to collective bargaining and the formation of labor unions but impose restrictions such as no-strike clauses and binding arbitration to the deal. Workers enjoy safety and health protections by law but must often bargain for extensions of these as contractual issues. And although workers have won a federal minimum wage policy, there is no guarantee that their wages will be any higher; since minimum wages are set by political process rather than tied to inflation, it is possible for the standing minimum wage to be far below poverty levels. To gain sufficient wages above the legal minimum, workers must negotiate contractually with employers. And to get federal mandates to define the minimum wage at higher rates, workers must often struggle against the dominating influence of corporations and small businesses alike, who typically apply their considerable resources to influence policy makers.

While the class dialectic model does introduce the role of an organized working class and resistance to a model of the relationship of the state and society, it is less specific as to the mechanisms that might animate dynamic class relations that might produce policy that is inconsistent with capital accumulation interests. What sparks class conflicts enough to erupt in struggles over policy? When do antagonistic interests mobilize into action, and why? What are the conditions that might be necessary and sufficient to make interests become action? Specifically, under what conditions does the working class assert its interests? Under what conditions is it more or less successful in pressing for state redress of their grievances?

The class dialectical model also shares the focus of other models on economic and class-based policy. How do we explain noneconomic struggles over policy? Since not all struggles over policy necessarily play out between capital accumulation interests and worker interests—or between the affluent and the poor—how do we understand the dynamics that animate conflicts over other policy domains? How do we explain gendering and sexuality policies or policies affecting and defining the racial formation process?

Finally, the class dialectic model shares the implication of other models that the state is an object and an arena of struggle between accumulation and nonaccumulation interests. But might the state also be an actor itself, with its own interests?

State-Centered Structuralism: "Bringing the State Back In"

In contrast to both business dominance and capitalist state structuralist theories, *state-centered structuralists* argue that the state is the site of bureaucratic political power. The state is neither necessarily capitalist in nature nor subject to capitalists' demands. As an institution, the state has interests separate from the demands of external groups or economic pressures, making it possible for state managers to create policy to which all interest groups might actually object. State policy is shaped not by the class backgrounds of its personnel or by the nature of the capitalist political economy but by the imperatives of bureaucracies. The state, as a bureaucratic and political structure, is separate from the economy. As such, state policy is shaped by past policy precedents, political and party needs, and state managers' interest in expanding their administrative domain and autonomy. In sum, the state is impervious to mechanisms of intraclass unity identified by business dominance theory and unaffected by the "capitalist nature" of state structures assumed by capitalist state structuralists (Amenta & Halfmann, 2000; Amenta & Parikh, 1991; Amenta & Skocpol, 1988; Chorev, 2007; Hooks, 1990, 1991, 1993; Skocpol, 1985, 1988, 1992; Skocpol & Ikenberry, 1983). It is also, according to this perspective, impervious to pressures from below.

Here, the state is once again depicted as neutral relative to competing interests as it was in the pluralist model. The state is, in this model, a structure that transcends the pressure and influence these interests might exert, regardless of the resources these interests might control and regardless of the structure of the economy. But instead of describing the state as legislating in the interests of the common good, state-centered structuralists argue that the state legislates in the interests of the bureaucracy itself, including the interests of bureaucratic agencies to expand their bureaucratic realm of power and of political parties to enhance their legislative power. However, this characterization of the state as a class-neutral or class-transcendent structure raises questions concerning the past backgrounds, allegiances, and interests of state managers themselves. Who are the state managers, and what are their class backgrounds? How do they shed their past class allegiances and interests when they become state managers? Is it possible for state managers to fully divorce themselves in any meaningful way from their class backgrounds and experiences?

This analytical model does leave more room for analyzing and perhaps understanding the production of state policy that is not governed by capitalist class interests or the need to strengthen the conditions supporting capital accumulation. Here, noneconomic policies such as reproductive and civil rights, LGBTQ (lesbian, gay, bisexual, transgender, and queer) rights, the rights of people with disabilities, endangered species protection acts, environmental laws, and the like may be understood as the product of party politics or the interest of some bureaucratic agencies to expand their administrative sphere.

Further, is it realistic to expect state managers to ignore altogether the requirements of the political economy to remain healthy? If state managers are guided by their political party and bureaucratic interests, is it reasonable to expect them to discount the effects of their decisions on the health of the economy? Might their policy decisions based on bureaucratic and party interests threaten the very administrative domain they presumably seek to expand if these decisions in fact undermine the economy?

Finally, state-centered theory shares a focus on elites with instrumentalist and business dominance theorists. Where instrumentalist and business dominance theorists focus on economic and corporate elites, state-centered structuralists focus on political elites among state managers as separate and distinct from economic elites. This focus omits an analysis of the role of resistance and challenge by the masses or the working class. What is the role of resistance from below?

Anarchist Theory

Anarchist theory, as opposed to Marxist theories, stresses the illegitimacy of the state, regardless of the mode of production that a given society might have (i.e., capitalism, socialism, communism). Thus, while Marxists analyze and critique the capitalist state (as in capitalist state structuralism) or the state in capitalist society (as in instrumentalism/business dominance theory), anarchists lodge their critiques at the state *as such*. The state to anarchists is an institution based on hierarchy, coercion, and control and is illegitimate regardless of the character of the people who occupy it. Thus, anarchists differ on whether the nature of the state (apart from some left-wing Marxists [see, e.g., Flank, 2007; Pannekoek, 2003]) is in its *postrevolutionary* form, with anarchists remaining critically opposed to *any* state and denying the very possibility of a workers' state.

Marx argued for what he called "the dictatorship of the proletariat," envisioning a state apparatus occupied and run by workers after the workers carried out a successful revolution. According to Marxist theory, the state exists to manage divergent class interests. Thus, after the workers occupied the state (or constructed their own "worker's state") and social classes were eventually abolished, the state would "wither away" along with class society, as there would no longer be any use for the state.

Anarchists, however, argue that the state will never simply wither away and that the assumption that any centralized power structure will gradually allow itself to simply disappear is faulty. Rather, anarchists predicted that pursuing socialism through the use of the state would end in tyranny. This idea prompted the anarchist Mikhail Bakunin (1964), to remark that "freedom without Socialism is privilege and injustice, and . . . Socialism without freedom is slavery and brutality" (p. 269). Some anarchists have argued that the experiences of the USSR, China, and Cuba have vindicated this idea. For this reason, as previously discussed in Chapter 4, anarchists typically prefer direct action to electoral strategies for bringing about social changes, arguing that in the process of pressuring elites to meet the needs of the masses, people are empowered and learn collective self-management rather than rule from above (as is the case in statist societies).

While anarchists have no comprehensive theory of the state (for a beginning, see Harrison, 1983; Price, 2007), one can see points of agreement within anarchist theory with some of the theories previously outlined. For example, anarchists have noted that the capitalist state functions to serve the interests of capital accumulation like capitalist state structuralists (Berkman, 2003). Likewise, they see the direct action of nonelites to be an influence on state policy like those employing the class dialectic perspective. Further, like state-centered structuralism, anarchists note that the state has interests of its own—regardless of whether or not it is a *capitalist* or *socialist* state. What anarchists bring to the table in this discussion, then, is a theory of the state in postrevolution, again, in which they argue that, since the state has interests of its own, the working class must abolish it in order to achieve an egalitarian future rather than occupy it or create a "worker's state." In fact, in the anarchist analysis, a "worker's state" is an oxymoron, as those who have control of the state apparatus are placed above society, effectively distinguishing them from mere workers without access to state power.

Interest in anarchism has grown in recent years, and anarchist theory has been adapting to theoretical developments outside of the anarchist milieu. While classical anarchism focused on the state and capitalism as central locations of power, many anarchists today argue against *domination* more generally (see, e.g., Gordon, 2008). As such, in contemporary anarchist theorizing, social class is often described as closely intertwined and intersecting with other modes of domination, such as patriarchy, white supremacy, and heteronormativity. While the working class was seen as *the* agent of revolutionary social change by many past anarchists, most contemporary anarchists argue for a more intersectional approach (see, e.g., Shannon & Rogue, 2009). However, anarchists (and many Marxists, feminists, critical race theorists, and queer theorists, as well) are just beginning to theorize about the multiple layers of oppression that exist in contemporary society and how they interact (and, ultimately, how to destroy them and replace them with something more just and humane).

Theories of the State and Oppression

The models described so far (except anarchist theory) have dominated political sociology for at least 5 decades and, with the exception of state-centered structuralism and anarchist theory, tend to revolve around questions concerning how or why corporate interests seem to dominate the political landscape and policy making in the state (see Table 5.1). While class dialectic analyses introduce the working class into the dynamics affecting the relationship between the state and society, it still suggests that corporate interests manage to thwart outright challenges to its preeminence and advantage in the political economy. And while state-centered structuralism leaves room for corporate interests to be ignored in favor of bureaucratic state managers' interests, it does not suggest how these might be completely divorced from class-based interests or influence from these. None of the models presented so far thus adequately explains the full range of policy arenas.

Table 5.1   Comparison of Theories of the State

Theory	Critical Social–Political Units	Form of Conflict	Basis of Political Power	Nature of the State	State Autonomy	Goal of Conflict
Pluralism	Interest groups, political parties	Competition among interest groups	Elections, public opinion, lobbying	Government	Little, highly responsive to public	Balance competing demands in the common good
Instrumentalism/ Business dominance	Elites and masses	Elite pressures for cohesion; domination or co-optation of the masses	Occupation of key institutional positions; elite coordination, control of agendas, and control of mass media	Institutional organization, particularly in the state, the corporate economy, and the military	Highly limited: Elites face few limits	Capture of domination of the state by corporate interests in service of their needs above all others
Capitalist state structuralism	Class positions and economic structures	Economic, political, and ideological	Functional role in the mode of production	Organizer of class dominance, the steering function of capitalism	Limited, "relative," within basic capitalist principles and imperatives	Secure the conditions of capital accumulation

(Continued)

Table 5.1 (Continued)

Theory	Critical Social–Political Units	Form of Conflict	Basis of Political Power	Nature of the State	State Autonomy	Goal of Conflict
State-centered structuralism	Organizations, institutions, bureaucracies	Competition among state managers for institutional resources and administrative power	Organizational capacity, economic and legal resources	Organization and unit in a system of increasingly complex bureaucracies	Significant but varies by state capacity	Expand the bureaucratic domain of power of state managers
Class dialectic perspective	Politically active and organized movements and classes	State-based repression, mass protests	Capacity to organize, ability to disrupt business as usual	A site and an object of struggles among classes	Relative, varies by issues and historical situation	Address needs of labor as well as capital
Anarchist theory	Politically active individuals and groups	State-based ideological co-optation, repression, mass actions	Ability to organize, disrupt business as usual, and challenge ideological and legal restraints	A site and an object of struggles embedded in the political economy	Relative, within basic imperatives & ideologies of political economy before revolution; decentralized, horizontal (nonhierarchical) after	Obtain freedom from institutionalized hierarchy, constraint, and oppression

In particular, there are whole areas of social and political policy making relative to oppression that are not adequately covered by these models. How do we explain the dominance of patriarchal, racist, or heteronormative policy making with the existing theoretical frameworks these models offer? Is it sufficient to simply replace the existing concepts of class domination with concepts describing gendered, racist, or heteronormative domination? As we will discuss in Chapter 7, the answer is no: While some analyses have in fact tried to do just that, the concepts do not lend themselves easily to such a simple transplant. What is needed is a model of the relationship between the state and society that allows for an analysis of multiple oppressions.

Discussion

1. Select an issue currently being debated in Congress. What state project might this issue join? How is the issue framed? What are the various interests that might have a stake in the outcome of the debate? Are these unified, or are they split by conflicts? If unified, what are the possible mechanisms of that unity? If they are split by conflicts, what are some of these? What resources do each of these have that might affect the balance of political forces involved? Are there potential interests that might have a stake in the outcome of the debate but who are not heard?

2. Are there policies that might straddle several state projects? Select one, and discuss how it might resonate with more than one state project. What are the political forces involved? How might the political forces of one state project affect those of another?

3. Select a feature-length film about power, politics, and oppression and discuss which of the theories of the state might best explain what is going on in the film. What are the limitations of the different theories of the state in explaining the film?

4. The Supreme Court currently is more diverse than it has ever been. How might that diversity affect their role in the development of state projects, if at all? Why? What does your answer suggest about power and the state?

References

Akard, P. J. (1992). Corporate mobilization and political power: The transformation of U.S. economic policy in the 1970s. *American Sociological Review, 57,* 597–615.

Akard, P. J. (2005). No room for compromise: Business interests and the politics of health care reform. *Research in Political Sociology, 14,* 51–105.

Amenta, E., & Halfmann, D. (2000). Wage wars: Institutional politics, WPA wages, and the struggle for U.S. social policy. *American Sociological Review*, 65(4), 506–528.

Amenta, E., & Parikh, S. (1991). Comment: Capitalists did not want the Social Security Act: A critique of the "capitalist dominance" thesis. *American Sociological Review*, 56, 124–129.

Amenta, E., & Skocpol, T. (1988). Redefining the New Deal: World War II and the development of social provision in the U.S. In M. Weir, A. S. Orloff, & T. Skocpol (Eds.), *The politics of social policy in the United States* (pp. 81–122). Princeton, NJ: Princeton University Press.

Bakunin, M. (1964). *The political philosophy of Bakunin* (G. P. Maximoff, Ed.). New York: Free Press.

Benoit, D. (2007). *The best-kept secret: Women corporate lobbyists, policy, and power in the United States*. Piscataway, NJ: Rutgers University Press.

Berkman, A. (2003). *What is anarchism?* Oakland, CA: AK Press.

Block, F. (1987). *Revising state theory: Essays in politics and postindustrialism*. Philadelphia: Temple University Press.

Burris, V. (1992). Elite policy-planning networks in the United States. *Research in Politics and Society*, 4, 111–134.

Chorev, N. (2007). *Remaking U.S. trade policy: From protectionism to globalization*. Ithaca, NY: Cornell University Press.

Clawson, D., Neustadtl, A., & Weller, M. (1998). *Dollars and votes: How business campaign contributions subvert democracy*. Philadelphia: Temple University Press.

Domhoff, G. W. (1970). *The higher circles*. New York: Vintage.

Domhoff, G. W. (1987). Corporate liberal theory and the Social Security Act: A chapter in the sociology of knowledge. *Politics and Society*, 15, 297–330.

Domhoff, G. W. (1990). *The power elite and the state: How policy is made in America*. New York: Aldine De Gruyter.

Domhoff, G. W. (1991a). American state autonomy via the military? Another counterattack on a theoretical delusion. *Critical Sociology*, 18, 9–56.

Domhoff, G. W. (1991b). Class, power, and parties during the New Deal: A critique of Skocpol's theory of state autonomy. *Berkeley Journal of Sociology*, 36, 1–49.

Domhoff, G. W. (2000). *Who rules America? Power and politics* (4th ed.). New York: McGraw-Hill.

Domhoff, G. W. (2005). *Who rules America? Power, politics, and social change*. New York: McGraw-Hill.

Eckstein, R. (1997). *Nuclear power and social power*. Philadelphia: Temple University Press.

Esping-Anderson, G., Friedland, R., & Wright, E. O. (1986). Modes of class struggle and the capitalist state. *Kapitalistate*, 4–5, 184–220.

Flank, L. (2007). *Philosophy of revolution: Towards a non-Leninist Marxism*. St. Petersburg, FL: Red and Black Publishers.

Galbraith, J. K. (1985). *The new industrial state* (4th ed.). Boston: Houghton Mifflin.

Glasberg, D. S. (1989). *The power of collective purse strings: The effect of bank hegemony on corporations and the state*. Berkeley: University of California Press.

Glasberg, D. S., & Skidmore, D. L. (1997). *Corporate welfare policy and the welfare state: Bank deregulation and the savings and loan bailout.* New York: Aldine De Gruyter.

Gordon, U. (2008). *Anarchy alive: Anti-Authoritarian politics from practice to theory.* London: Pluto Press.

Harrison, F. (1983). *The modern state: The anarchist analysis.* Montreal: Black Rose Books.

Hooks, G. (1990). The rise of the Pentagon and U.S. state building: The defense program as industrial policy. *American Journal of Sociology, 96,* 358–404.

Hooks, G. (1991). *Forging the military-industrial complex: World War II's Battle of the Potomac.* Urbana: University of Illinois Press.

Hooks, G. (1993). The weakness of strong theories: The U.S. state's dominance of the World War II investment process. *American Sociological Review, 58,* 37–53.

Jackson, M. I. (2008). *Model city blues: Urban space and organized resistance in New Haven.* Philadelphia: Temple University Press.

Jenkins, J. C., & Brents, B. G. (1989). Social protest, hegemonic competition, and social reforms. *American Sociological Review, 54,* 891–909.

Lenin, V. I. (1976). *The state and revolution.* Peking, China: Foreign Languages Press.

Levine, R. (1988). *Class struggle and the New Deal: Industrial labor, industrial capital and the state.* Lawrence: University of Kansas Press.

Lugar, S. (2000). *Corporate power: American democracy and the automobile industry.* New York: Cambridge University Press.

Mandel, E. (1975). *Late capitalism.* London: New Left Books.

Marx, K., & Engels, F. (1967). *The Communist manifesto.* Baltimore: Penguin.

Miliband, R. (1969). *The state in capitalist society.* New York: Basic Books.

Miliband, R. (1973). Poulantzas and the capitalist state. *New Left Review, 82,* 83–92.

Miliband, R. (1983). *Class power and state power.* London: Verso.

Pannekoek, A. (2003). *Workers' councils.* Oakland, CA: AK Press.

Poulantzas, N. (1968, November/December). The problem of the capitalist state. In R. Blackburn (Ed.), *Ideology in social science* (pp. 238–253). New York: Pantheon Books.

Poulantzas, N. (1978). *State, power, and socialism.* London: Verso.

Prechel, H. (1990). Steel and the state. *American Sociological Review, 55,* 634–647.

Prechel, H. (2000). *Big business and the state.* Albany: State University of New York Press.

Price, W. (2007). *The abolition of the state: Anarchist and Marxist perspectives.* Bloomington, IN: AuthorHouse.

Quadagno, J. (1984). Welfare capitalism and the Social Security Act of 1935. *American Sociological Review, 49,* 632–647.

Quadagno, J. (1992). Social movements and state transformation: Labor unions and racial conflict in the war on poverty. *American Sociological Review, 57,* 616–634.

Quadagno, J., & Meyer, M. H. (1989). Organized labor, state structures, and social policy development: A case study of old age assistance in Ohio, 1916–1940. *Social Problems, 36,* 181–196.

Schmitter, P. C. (1974). Still the century of corporatism? *Review of Politics*, *36*(1), 85–127.

Shannon, D., & Rogue, J. (2009). *Refusing to wait: Anarchism and intersectionality*. Retrieved from http://www.anarkismo.net/article/14923

Skocpol, T. (1985). Bringing the state back in: Strategies of analysis in current research. In P. B. Evans, D. Rueschemeyer, T. Skocpol (Eds.), *Bringing the state back in* (pp. 3–37). Cambridge, UK: Cambridge University Press.

Skocpol, T. (1988). The limits of the New Deal system and the roots of the contemporary welfare dilemmas. In M. Weir, A. S. Orloff, & T. Skocpol, *The politics of social policy in the United States* (pp. 293–311). Princeton, NJ: Princeton University Press.

Skocpol, T. (1992). *Protecting soldiers and mothers: The political origins of social policy in the United States*. Cambridge, MA: Harvard University Press.

Skocpol, T., & Ikenberry, J. (1983). The political formation of the American welfare state in historical and comparative perspective. *Comparative Social Research*, *6*, 87–148.

Swenson, P. A. (2002). *Capitalists against markets: The making of labor markets and welfare states in the United States and Sweden*. New York: Oxford University Press.

Useem, M. (1984). *The inner circle*. New York: Oxford University Press.

Valocchi, S. (1989). The relative autonomy of the state and the origins of British welfare policy. *Sociological Forum*, *4*, 349–365.

Weinstein, J. (1968). *The corporate ideal in the liberal state, 1900–1918*. Boston: Beacon Press.

Whitt, J. A. (1979). Toward a class dialectic model of power: An empirical assessment of three competing models of political power. *American Sociological Review*, *44*, 81–100.

Whitt, J. A. (1982). *The dialectics of power: Urban elites and mass transportation*. Princeton, NJ: Princeton University Press.

Witte, E. E. (1972). Organized labor and Social Security. In M. Derber & E. Young (Eds.), *Labor and the New Deal* (pp. 241–274). New York: DeCapo Press.

Wright, E. O. (1978). *Class, crisis, and the state*. London: Verso.

Zeitlin, M., Ewen, L. A., & Ratcliff, R. E. (1974). New princes for old? The large corporation and the capitalist class in Chile. *American Journal of Sociology*, *80*, 87–123.

Zeitlin, M., & Ratcliff, R. E. (1975). Research methods for the analysis of the internal structure of dominant classes: The case of landlords and capitalists in Chile. *Latin American Research Review*, *10*(3), 5–61.

6

From the Bottom Up?

Social Movements and the State

W hile the power of economic, gendered, and race dominants in society is formidable in advantaging and privileging them and oppressing others, their power is not absolute. Indeed, nonelites may pose a countervailing force. Nonelites may resist, challenge, subvert, and otherwise alter power relationships and the policies that emerge from the state, prompting change from the bottom up through large-scale social movements. When do social movements emerge? How do they come about? What is the relationship between social movements and the state?

Defining Social Movements

Social change does not just happen randomly or by some mysterious accident. People's action can shape the power structures of society, whether these actions are by dominating economic and political elites or by oppressed nonelites. That is not to suggest, however, a pluralist assumption of equality of the ability of elites and oppressed groups to affect power structures. Dominating elites have access to important resources that certainly pose daunting obstacles and disadvantages to the oppressed to seek redress of grievances. But it is clear that social changes do occur—and sometimes over and above the strenuous objections of the advantaged and privileged elites. How do nonelite and oppressed people affect power structures and elicit social change if so much occurs by and for the already privileged?

Individuals have very little ability by themselves to effectively challenge the privilege and power of elites and the power structures that reinforce that advantage. A single, solitary voice alone is unlikely to gain much attention and indeed may not even be heard. However, individuals acting together can. An important key, then, to social change from below is collective, organized action (Cazenave, 2007). Organized, collective efforts by many individuals working together have historically launched potent challenges to the powerful. History is replete with dozens of examples of revolutions of the oppressed overthrowing entire regimes, including the American Revolution and French Revolution in the 18th century and the Chinese and Russian Revolutions in the 20th century, to name just a few. Other examples of organized resistance with more limited but still significant results punctuate history throughout the world. For example, when 19th-century British factory owners redefined the production process in the stocking industry by using machinery, Luddite workers collectively rebelled by destroying the machines that displaced their labor (Rude, 1964, 1985). The rebellion only succeeded in temporarily delaying the introduction of the new machinery, but it represented a call to collective action as resistance to the use of technology that benefitted factory owners but hurt workers. This organized action of rebellion and resistance was so significant that it has earned a place in modern language. People who resist the introduction of new technologies (especially those that threaten to displace human labor) are often pejoratively called Luddites, a reference to these 19th-century rebels.

Persistent, organized, and collective efforts to resist existing power structures, cultural repertoires, and practices and elite dominance and oppression or to introduce changes in them are called *social movements*. They are organizational structures and strategies that may empower oppressed populations to mount effective challenges and resist the more powerful and advantaged elites. Social movements may provide organizational opportunities for producing change from the bottom up within nations. In addition, they may allow the relatively powerless to affect international relations as well. The antiwar movement during the 1960s and early 1970s intensified the pressure on the United States to cease its military involvement in Vietnam. Beyond this specific impact of the antiwar movement, however, was its longer-term effect on U.S. foreign policy. Congress passed the War Powers Act to restrict the ability of U.S. presidents to militarily intrude into other nations' domestic affairs. This is an example of a social movement providing an organizational structure empowering individuals to collectively address and affect issues that would otherwise be too big, too daunting, and too overwhelming for individuals to tackle.

Social movements are commonly "umbrella" structures, or networks of many social movement organizations working on issues of mutual interest.

The civil rights movement, for example, has been a broad network of groups such as the National Association for the Advancement of Colored People (NAACP); Southern Christian Leadership Conference (SCLC); Congress of Racial Equality (CORE); Student Nonviolent Coordinating Committee (SNCC); the Commission for Racial Justice, By Any Means Necessary; and scores of professional organizations such as the Association of Black Sociologists (ABS), among perhaps hundreds of other local and national groups. While each organization pursues its own specific agenda and set of activities, together they work to apply collective pressure to local, state, and federal governments to adopt and enforce policies protecting equal civil rights of all regardless of racial identification and to challenge cultural and ideological perceptions of the significance of "race."

In addition to the loose networking and collective efforts of many social movement organizations, broad social movements may often contain several branches differentiated by their goals and strategies, and these may coexist as part of the larger, more general movement. Consider the feminist movement. While it generally addresses the empowerment of women, it is not a uniform social movement with a single goal and agreed-upon strategies. Rather, it consists of several different movements, each with a defining agenda or strategy for action that sets it in contrast with the others, even if all branches more broadly attempt to address women's oppression (Ferree, Lorber, & Hess, 1999). For example, the liberal feminist movement, expressed through organizations such as the National Organization for Women (NOW), is a reformative movement within the feminist milieu. Its focus is women's rights and equal participation in society and greater integration of women into society's political, social, and economic institutions. Reformative feminist organizations like NOW do not challenge the existing social institutions; instead, they accept these institutions as given and challenge the gendered discrimination that disadvantages women within those institutions. Their strategies for achieving greater integration and rights of women, therefore, involve legislative lobbying, antidiscrimination suits in the courts, and public education and consciousness raising.

The liberal feminist movement contrasts sharply with the radical feminist movement, which identifies men as the cause of women's oppression. Its goal is to fundamentally change existing institutions its adherents see as patriarchal. Since the institutions themselves are patriarchal, it is not sufficient to simply reform them. Instead, they must be radically altered or replaced. Radical feminists define marriage in particular as an especially oppressive institution for women. They therefore seek to restructure the institution of family so as to eliminate the traditional gendered roles that impede women's development as independent individuals. Families of women living together, for example, are structured to support one another and any children they may have. These families of choice do not include men and thus eliminate gendered divisions of labor that privilege men and oppress women. Radical feminists act as a social movement advancing the goal of women's empowerment and rights by reinforcing one another's individual resistance to oppressive institutions. Radical feminists' ultimate goal is institutional change resulting from many women's individual resistance to the existing institutional arrangements. As such, radical feminists' strategy is not to apply pressures for legislative reforms but to persuade individual women to reorganize their personal living arrangements.

Marxist feminists contrast with radical feminists in that they view capitalism rather than men per se as the source of women's oppression. To Marxist feminists, both men and women are oppressed by a political economy that is arranged to exploit masses of people for the benefit of relatively few in the capitalist class. They perceive the antagonism between men and women as a problem of false consciousness created by the capitalist class as a "divide and conquer" strategy. Men and women are pitted against each other to drive a wedge within the working class so as to reduce the chance that workers will transcend gendered differences to organize and challenge capitalism. Unlike the goal of liberal feminists, the goal of Marxist feminists is not greater integration of women into the political, social, and economic institutions of society; integration simply legitimates the existing social arrangements that promote oppression. And in contrast to radical feminists, Marxist feminists do not view men per se as the cause of women's collective oppression; such a view distracts attention away from capitalism as the real source of women's oppression. The goal of Marxist feminists is for both women and men to realize that sexism and patriarchy are strategies of capitalist oppression and to cooperate together to replace it with a socialist society. Their view is that eradicating sexism in general and women's oppression in particular requires eliminating capitalism.

In contrast to both Marxist and radical feminists, socialist feminists see women's oppression coming from the "dual systems" of capitalism and patriarchy (see, for an interesting analysis, Young, 1981). Socialist feminists argue that while women are oppressed under capitalism, their oppression cannot be reduced to economic exploitation. Rather, one must also take into account the system of patriarchy or men's domination of women (which existed well before the development of capitalism). Thus, socialist feminists share the goal of the elimination of capitalism with Marxist feminists but argue that socialism will not guarantee the emancipation of women. Men and women must work together to also rid society of patriarchal values and how those values diminish women and subordinate their interests to those of men.

Likewise, anarcha-feminists argue that we should eliminate capitalism and patriarchy, but extend that argument to all institutions based on coercion, domination, and control (see, e.g., Dark Star Collective, 2002). Thus, to anarcha-feminists, the fight for women's emancipation is connected to all struggles against domination. Their major contrast with Marxist and socialist feminists is their position on the state. While Marxist and socialist feminists have argued for seizing the state, or in some variations destroying the existing state and replacing it with a "worker's" state, anarcha-feminists argue that human emancipation, and by extension women's emancipation, will not be complete without also eliminating hierarchical structures like the state. Thus, anarcha-feminist activism includes mass revolutionary strategy to destroy the state and capitalism but also focuses on changing our everyday lives to create a culture consistent with non-hierarchical, egalitarian values.

Although differences of goals and strategies may splinter social movements into several branches, these divergent branches often share a need to change some specific system of oppression. This question still remains: Why do social movements occur in the first place, and how do individuals' grievances become collective efforts to challenge oppression?

Explaining Social Movements

Absolute and Relative Deprivation Theories

Some observers explain the rise of social movements in general and revolutions in particular as prompted by deprivation: When people are deprived of what they need, or what they believe they need, they will rebel. For example, Karl Marx and Friedrich Engels (1967) argued that the capitalist political economy is arranged in such a way as to polarize the working class and the capitalist class: The rich will get richer because of their control over labor and the means of production, and the poor will get poorer because of their lack of such control. Eventually, the workers would suffer immiseration, or *absolute deprivation*: The most basic requirements of survival would be unaffordable for them. In order to survive, workers who are lucky enough to still be employed would have to work longer hours at lower wages; more and more workers would be entirely unemployed as their labor was displaced by machines or their work was exported to other shores where labor was exploited at even cheaper wages. Marx and Engels argued that intolerably immiserated workers would eventually collectively revolt to overthrow the social structure that caused their oppression because they would have nothing more to lose.

Popular media analyses of the civil rights movement in the United States often apply a variation of an immiseration thesis. They commonly describe the civil rights movement as ignited by a single act of resistance: When Rosa Parks could no longer tolerate chronic racist oppression, she expressed her resistance by refusing to give up her seat on a Birmingham, Alabama, bus to a white man. The application of immiseration, or absolute deprivation, theory here points to one of its limitations: Not all social movements are prompted entirely by economic deprivation. Rosa Parks may certainly have suffered from deprivation of civil rights, but the fact that she was employed in a cultural context of minimum wage laws suggests that she had at least a minimum, if not middle-class, ability to purchase what she needed for basic survival.

Some sociologists have pointed to other, empirical problems of the thesis of absolute deprivation. James Davies (1962, 1969, 1974), for example, examined when revolutions, as extreme forms of social movements, occurred. He found that, historically, revolutions did not occur when people's material conditions reached a level below basic survival. Rather, he noted such organized rebellions occurred in response to people's *perceptions* of deprivation, or *relative deprivation*. That is, Davies argued, people's perception of deprivation is *relative* to conditions around them, conditions they expect, or conditions that previously existed but no longer do (see Figure 6.1). People were more likely to revolt when a gap opened, over time, between the material conditions they expected and the material conditions that actually existed (see also Klandermans, Roefs, & Olivier, 2001). Although Davies's notion of relative deprivation referred primarily to people's material conditions as economic circumstances, his thesis can also be applied to social and political conditions.

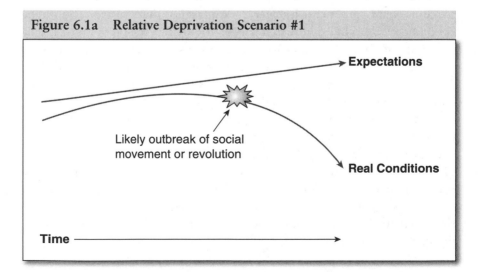

Figure 6.1a   Relative Deprivation Scenario #1

Figure 6.1b   Relative Deprivation Scenario #2

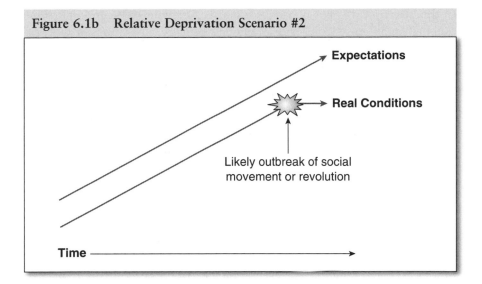

Figure 6.1c   Relative Deprivation Scenario #3

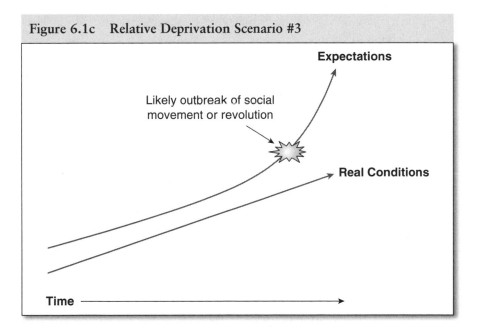

For example, people's expectations of their material, political, or social conditions may gradually rise; at the same time, real conditions may gradually improve, too, even if they don't quite match people's full expectations. According to Davies, people can commonly live with that difference between their expected and their real conditions without resistance; revolutions will not occur until real conditions begin to deteriorate relative to expectations.

In this scenario, it is not necessary for real conditions to deteriorate to the point of immiseration, as Marx and Engels believed; it is sufficient that real conditions simply get worse while expectations continue to rise.

In another scenario, people's expectations for improved conditions may rise sharply, and their real circumstances may also improve sharply but not quite enough to match expectations. It is unlikely for a revolution to occur until real conditions level off, but people's expectations continue to rise. In this scenario, people's real conditions need not worsen at all; it is sufficient that real conditions stagnate while expectations continue to rise.

A third theoretical scenario of relative deprivation describes a situation in which people's expectations for improved conditions may sharply increase, and their real conditions may show an equally sharp degree of improvement. In this scenario, revolutions are likely to occur when people's expectations for better conditions rise more sharply than their real circumstances. It is not necessary for real conditions to deteriorate or even stagnate at all; for revolutions to occur, it is sufficient, even in the face of significantly improved real conditions, that expectations dramatically increase to an even greater degree. Here, even vastly improved conditions would not satisfy the populace: They expect increasingly better conditions than they have.

As persuasive as the theses of absolute and relative deprivation may be, both explanations imply a sort of spontaneous combustion of social dissatisfaction. They assume that at some point conditions will become absolutely intolerable or the difference between expectations and real conditions will suddenly become intolerable, and a large group of people will rise together and revolt. While such dissatisfaction may be necessary for social movements and revolutions to erupt, it may not be sufficient. What is missing here is an analysis of what people would need to see the situation similarly, notice that others share that vision and a vision of what to do about it, and have the resources to realize that vision.

Resource Mobilization

No matter how intolerable conditions may be, people may not form social movements or revolt unless they have access to resources to help them organize a shared definition of their situation and develop a shared vision of strategic responses. They need human resources to articulate their frustration and formulate a strategy for response; leadership to organize and mobilize others; tangible resources, such as financial backing, to disseminate their message, support and legally defend endangered or jailed participants, and communicate widely with other potential supporters; and networks of other groups of people or existing organizations that can contribute their resources in a combined effort (McCarthy & Wolfson, 1996). Thus, revolutions and other social movements are unlikely to occur in the absence of access to critical supportive resources. Sociologists refer to this explanation of social movements as *resource mobilization theory.*

Aldon Morris (1984, 1999) found resource mobilization theory a useful framework to help explain the rise of the civil rights movement in the United States. Using extensive interviews with activists and participants, he found that African Americans everywhere did not suddenly and simultaneously get frustrated enough to rebel against racist oppression. Instead, he found that leaders in several African American organizations mobilized resources and combined their organizational efforts to become a powerful collective force in challenging segregation and other forms of racialized discrimination in the United States.

Morris's analysis reframed popular accounts that personalized the civil rights movement in the defiance of Rosa Parks and in the charismatic leadership of Martin Luther King Jr. Morris demonstrated that the civil rights movement was much greater than one person. Reverend King was certainly the most visible and stirring speaker articulating the issues, able to galvanize and mobilize great numbers of individuals. But Morris found that the civil rights movement was actually the result of the collective efforts of the NAACP, the SCLC, the SNCC, and CORE, as well as African American churches, white faith communities, labor unions, student organizations, and local small businesses. Together these organizations combined their efforts and mobilized vast resources in support of the movement. Instead of having to organize individuals one at a time in support of the civil rights movement, the leadership was able to tap into their existing organizational leadership, memberships, communication networks, and monetary resources to quickly and effectively mount boycotts, marches, voter registration drives in hostile Southern states, and acts of civil disobedience such as sit-ins at lunch counters.

Morris's research illustrates how social movements rely on the strategic mobilization of resources to empower people who are relatively powerless, disadvantaged, oppressed, and largely disenfranchised from the dominant institutions of society. The civil rights movement managed, against overwhelming odds and historical tradition, to push for reform of oppressive and rigidly racist cultural repertoires, practices, and laws that had denied African Americans basic civil rights.

In addition to organizational mobilization by movement leaders around a common issue, social movement organizations frequently grow and new ones emerge through a "demonstration effect": When some initial organizations become large enough to gain public attention, their existence broadcasts a sign of increasing public support for the movement (Isaac & Christiansen, 2002; Meyer & Minkoff, 2004; Olzak & Ryo, 2007). On the other hand, once a social movement has succeeded in generating multiple social movement organizations around its common focus, it is likely for conflict between these organizations to emerge as they compete for the same resources, including membership (Carroll & Hannan, 2000). When that happens, social movement organizations are likely to develop specialized foci related to their common issue, enabling them to continue to coexist and collaborate rather than compete and splinter the movement in competition for increasingly scarce resources (Bernstein, 2003; Minkoff, 1999). Levitsky (2007) refers to this phenomenon as "niche activism."

How do social movements, then, mobilize and apply the resources they access?

Political Process Perspective

Deprivation, perceived or absolute, and supportive resources and their mobilization, and a unifying collective identity may be necessary conditions for social movements, but they are not sufficient. There must also be access to dominant political structures, or opportunities for people to apply these resources to disrupt business as usual, or to create their own opportunities for such disruption (McAdam, McCarthy, & Zald, 1996; McAdam, Tarrow, & Tilly, 2001; Meyer & Staggenborg, 1996; Tilly & Tarrow, 2006). Sociologists refer to this as *political process theory*, which Goodwin and Jasper (1999) argued "is currently the hegemonic paradigm among social movement analysts" (p. 28). According to this model, social movements emerge when shifting political conditions open opportunities for disruption and the activities of social movements in turn can alter political policies and structures. These altered political structures then may become a new opportunity for social movements (Tarrow, 1998).

Researchers using the political process model have variously suggested at least four dimensions of opportunities for social movement emergence: (1) access to political structures and the perception of ability to influence policy affects mobilization; (2) instabilities in political alliances that can open opportunities for the creation of new coalitions, primarily in party politics; (3) influential allies among legislators and jurists that can enhance the likelihood of affecting policy and practice; and (4) conflicts between elites that can create political schisms as opportunities for disruption (Kolb, 2007; McAdam, 1994; McAdam et al., 1996; Tarrow, 1998).

As we previously noted, popular cultural mythology of the civil rights movement often point to Rosa Parks's seemingly spontaneous refusal to give her seat on the Birmingham bus to a white person as the original precipitating event. But Morris's research documents that Parks was, in fact, an active member and the first secretary of the local NAACP. She had been arrested several times before that incident for the same action. Rosa Parks's famous act of defiance was part of an organized, conscious resistance strategy rather than an isolated, spontaneous reaction to racism. She herself insisted, "My resistance to being mistreated on the buses and anywhere else was just a regular thing with me and not just that day" (Morris, 1984, p. 51). Here, Parks's act of defiance, and many other, similar acts at lunch counters, stores, and public restrooms, as well as mass demonstrations across the bridge to Selma, Alabama, and boycotts of public transportation, together created political opportunities to disrupt business as usual, even if temporarily.

Doug McAdam's (1982, 1988) research of the civil rights movement also noted the role of the state as a factor in the rise and fall of social movements as a political process. For example, elimination of racist barriers to blacks' voting enhanced the likelihood of electing well-placed sympathetic elites such as John F. Kennedy or encouraging politicians such as Lyndon B. Johnson to become more sympathetic. However, McAdam also emphasized that federal support for the goals of the civil rights movement came not so much in response to electoral politics but in response to insurgency and violent and nonviolent acts that subverted civil order. That is, the state responded to mass disruptions created by strategic actions of civil rights movement organizations. Similar findings on the role of insurgent disruptions and their effect on the state can be seen in analyses of other movements, such as the labor movements in Brazil and South Africa (Seidman, 1993) and the antinuclear movements in the United States and Germany (Joppke, 1993; Meyer, 1993).

If social movements require the mobilization of organizations and other resources, and the application of these in opportunities to create mass disruption, how do some of the most oppressed and deprived people in society get their needs addressed? In their comparative study, *Poor People's Movements*, Frances Fox Piven and Richard Cloward (1977) argued that only insurgency and mass rebellions like strikes and riots have encouraged elites to make concessions for poor people. They argued that when people formed organizations it tended to sap their energies, divert their attention, and co-opt the poor into nonthreatening actions and that created the false perception that the political system was fair and responsive to their needs. But when the poor rebelled, rioted, and staged strikes in massive eruptions of insurgency (as they did in the welfare rights, the unemployed workers', the industrial workers', and the civil rights movements), it disrupted business as usual and elicited the state's legislative and judicial response to address their needs and quell the insurgence.

Resource mobilization, organization, and political opportunity appear to be critical as well to the increasing activism of the more recent welfare rights movement. For example, the Kensington Welfare Rights Union (KWRU) organized a variation of the civil rights freedom riders in their national bus campaign in 1998 to gather testimonials from those harmfully affected by welfare reform. They marched across the main bridges and streets of New York City to the United Nations to present thousands of these testimonials to the United Nations, demanding a human rights violation investigation, which the UN agreed to do. The KWRU remains highly visible and active: It has launched a Poor People's Economic Human Rights Campaign, participated in demonstrations at the Republican and Democratic National Conventions in 2000, organized a Poor People's World Summit to End Poverty, launched a campaign against predatory lending practices by financial institutions that target the poor and people of color, and maintains a website on the Internet (www.kwru.org) to widely disseminate information (Baptist, Jenkins, & Dillon, 1999; Cress & Snow, 2000). And they continue to find opportunities to use these resources to create disruption. They are among the most economically oppressed and yet they clearly have learned how to mobilize important resources and to apply these in a political process to address their needs.

Research thus suggests that social movements can use the political process to affect policy and cultural practices. But observers do caution that the state is not just an arena for conflicts or a target for social movements; it is also an actor. When social movement actors mobilize resources to create disruption, the state commonly responds. Indeed, the state, as the sole legitimate user of force and violence, may resort to immense means of repression against insurrection (Davenport, Johnston, & Mueller, 2005; McAdam, 1996). Consider, for example, the common reports of police riots and abuse at the 2009 Copenhagen Climate Summit, the G20 Protests in Pittsburgh, Pennsylvania, and the protests in Minneapolis, Minnesota, at the Republican National Convention.

However, although overt and violent repression is a common state response to insurgency and challenge, researchers note that repression may take other forms. Ferree (2005) distinguished between hard repression (including military action and corporal punishment) and soft repression (such as the use of public ridicule and stigmatization and silencing insurgents). Indeed, a heavy-handed use of hard repression can backfire against the state, galvanizing more people to join in the resistance. Such appeared to be the case in the aftermath of the killing by the National Guard of four college students protesting the Vietnam War at Kent State University in Ohio in 1970. This likewise seemed to be the case after police killed a young anarchist teenager, Alexandros Grigoropoulos, in December 2008 in Greece. Students and workers, in solidarity with anarchists in Greece, occupied high schools, universities, and workplaces and in many cases even fought with police in the streets, expelling them from their neighborhoods. This generalized rebellion reoccurred, albeit on a smaller scale, in early December 2009—the year's anniversary of Alexandros's killing.

In contrast, the use of the USA PATRIOT Act in the wake of the September 11, 2001, attacks to brand antiwar activists as unpatriotic and worthy of intense surveillance has had a chilling effect on many people's willingness to overtly challenge the state, with relatively little protest against the state. The state in the United States has also instituted a well-documented "Green Scare," mimicking in many ways the anti-Communist "Red Scare" of the Cold War (see Potter, 2010 for documentation and analysis). These current attacks on the civil liberties of dissenting citizens, however, has been used to target environmental activists rather than communists, oftentimes frightening would-be activists from participating in social movements making environmental demands. This is an example of the power of preemptive soft repression.

The question of the response of the state to social movement challenges raises the question of opposition movements that arise as part of the equation affecting movement success. That is, social movements do not emerge and operate in a vacuum; nor do they encounter resistance to their efforts solely from the state itself. Oppositional interests are likely to emerge to counter the activities and goals of a social movement and organize their opposition using similar tactics and resources and sometimes gaining insider access to the resources and power of the state (McAdam et al., 2001). Indeed, the more successful a social movement is in securing attention and progress toward achieving its goals, the more likely it is to elicit a counter-movement (Meyer & Staggenborg, 1996). Political process theory, then, takes into account not only the processes by which social movements may emerge and mobilize resources in opportunities for mass disruption but it acknowledges the ebb and flow of social movements, their rise and abeyance, and their successes and failures as part of a larger political process (Koopmans, 2007; Taylor, 1989).

Moreover, many political opportunity structure theorists acknowledge the dialectical relationship between political opportunities, resource mobilization, and movement success (McAdam, 1982; Soule & Olzak, 2004). That is, political opportunities affect social movement success by creating windows for mobilizing resources in meaningful ways, and these are likely to attract more members and enhance opportunities for success; successful opportunities, particularly those that result in some positive response or change, are likely to open more opportunities and spark more interest. At the same time, success is also likely to elicit oppositional activity. Strong oppositional activity, however, does not necessarily mean the movement's efforts have failed or have been obstructed; indeed, sometimes a social movement may be temporarily halted in its efforts but gain in support and membership as a result of perceptions of increased oppression (Tilly, 1999) and frequently create mutual opportunities to sustain movement momentum (Dugan, 2004, 2008; Meyer & Staggenborg, 1996). As such, political opportunity theory suggests the value of exploring social movement *consequences* as part of an ongoing political process rather than focusing on the elusive measurement of social movement "success" as a final outcome (Amenta & Caren, 2007; Giugni, 1998).

Globalization and Social Movements

Interestingly, most explanations for social movements look at the internal dynamics of individual societies. But globalization processes that have increasingly concentrated economic power in fewer and fewer dominating corporate hands have also inspired increasingly globalized social movement efforts to resist them. Social movements can, in fact, become external forces that spark pressures for change from below within individual nations (Tilly, 1998; Wright & Middendorf, 2007). Frequently these involve networks of transnational organizations (Smith, 2007). For example, the student movement against sweatshops in the United States has begun to have an effect on conditions of production around the world. An organized international boycott and disinvestment campaign against corporations doing business in and with the white minority apartheid government in South Africa was a crucial factor in toppling a brutally racist institutional policy and practice.

Similarly, debt crises in developing countries that have prompted the imposition of International Monetary Fund (IMF)–sponsored austerity programs have elicited resistance movements. Walton and Ragin's (1990) study of debt-ridden nations found that the likelihood of political protest and mass disruption, as well as the intensity of such responses, was enhanced by increased external pressures by the IMF for countries to adopt the austerity programs. Walton and Ragin found that although deprivation and hardship of living conditions certainly contributed to people's grievances, these were not strongly related to the protests. Deprivation was not sufficient to instigate insurgency and neither were the internal dynamics of each individual nation. Rather, a global context of resource mobilization and political process were the key ingredients. Echoes of this can be seen in the global support of the Zapatista uprising in Chiapas, Mexico. Due to international mutual aid and meetings at the "encuentros" organized by the Zapatistas, movements across the globe found support and inspiration in each other in their efforts to organize against neoliberalism and global capitalism.

Feminist movements with the goal of promoting the well-being of women within nations are expanding their efforts beyond individual national borders as well. The Internet is helping national women's rights organizations throughout the world to form international networks. These networks operate to raise consciousness among women locally about their rights. In addition, they increasingly work together to apply pressure on governments and international agencies in their efforts to secure women's political and human rights and access to education, health care, and jobs (Ferree & Subramaniam, 2000).

Here is one note of caution, however: The term *globalization* can be a bit misleading here. What is, in fact, taking place is a globalization from above. Indeed, if wealthy capitalists or corporations wish to move around from country to country in "free" trade regions like those found in the North American Free Trade Agreement (NAFTA), they may move around and do business as they wish. But if workers try to move around as they like in search of better working conditions, better standards of living, or any jobs at all, they are labeled "illegals" and subject to arrest and fines. This insight highlights the need for the kind of intersectional analysis that we are suggesting in this book.

For example, while workers in general suffer the brunt of the ill effects of globalization from above, workers of color are much more heavily policed. Note, for example, the kinds of measures taken to keep Latino migrant workers from entering the United States and working. Even as of the writing of this chapter, Arizona has enacted new, draconian laws allowing law enforcement officers to stop anyone "suspected" of being "illegal," and therefore designed to profile and drive out Latino workers. This is in conjunction with a new bill designed to outlaw ethnic studies classes in Arizona school systems.

Moreover, migrating women workers of color have also reported added, gendered hardships due to globalization processes. Frequent reports of sexual assaults, rapes, and harassment have followed women migrant workers as they attempt to enter the United States to find paying work to help support their families. Likewise, in zones where companies have hired predominantly women of color because they are considered a compliant workforce that can be paid low wages, similar reports have been made about the treatment of women. And it does not require migration for these attacks on women of color to take place. Consider, for example, the commonly reported murders, rapes, and assaults of women of color who work in Juarez, Mexico.

As we noted before, despite the deck being seemingly stacked in favor of the wealthy, there is a large alter-globalization movement. This movement stresses the need for globalization from below. As wealthy corporations globalize, so must resistance movements. Thus, the *encuentros* we mentioned served as meeting spaces for activists spanning the globe. The World Social Forum (WSF) was set up in opposition to the World Economic Forum (WEF), highlighting the needs and desires of ordinary working people rather than the wealthy and powerful. Despite structural difficulties due to lack of resources, workers all over the world are increasingly able to use technologies to organize with one another and collectively develop theory and political practice. These observations about globalization from below pose some interesting implications and challenges for state theory.

Social Movements and State Theory

Taken together, the material on social movements suggests that even those who would appear to be among the most oppressed are not victimized bystanders in the political process of oppression. While these theories of social movements may disagree about how and why social movements develop and operate, they share the observation that the oppressed often respond collectively to the institutions and cultural repertoires and practices that produce and reinforce their oppression. Some observers note that social movement organizations may not have singular goals but rather can alternate between policy change and cultural transformation (Bernstein, 2003, 2008; Snow, 2004; Whittier, 2002). Moreover, while observers may dispute the meaning of "success" of social movements in attaining their goals, they largely share an understanding that social movements can have an effect on state policies and cultural and political practices (Goldstone, 2003; Stetson, 2005). How do we reconcile these observations with state theory?

With the exception of the class dialectic perspective and anarchist theory, state theories largely focus on the behavior of elites or the structures that empower elites over and above the oppressed. That focus would appear to be a limited piece of the larger picture of the relationship between the state, society, and oppression. Social movement literature suggests that the oppressed and their political responses to their circumstances must be incorporated into a larger vista of the political institutions, relationships, processes, policies, and practices that define and shape oppression. Moreover, although the obvious target of social movements would seem to be the state, often social movements target other institutions instead—for example, major corporations, to accomplish goals that would take far longer to achieve with the state itself (Armstrong & Bernstein, 2008; Van Dyke, Soule, & Taylor, 2004). How do we blend the insights of the various state theories with those of social movement theory for a broader understanding of the relationship of the state, society, and oppression? To explore that challenge, we turn in the next chapter to working toward a framework that conceptually blends these literatures and that allows us the flexibility for understanding multiple oppressions rather than being limited to economic and class oppression.

Discussion

1. Consider activism on your campus. Which of the social movement theories best explains what you see happening there, and why? Are students powerless to effect change? Why or why not?

2. Is terrorism a social movement? Why or why not? How might we explain the rise of terrorism in the past several decades?

3. What sorts of evidence do you see of globalization from above around you? What sorts of evidence do you see of globalization from below? Are we powerless in the face of globalization from above? Why or why not?

4. What is the meaning of social movement "success"? What sort of evidence do you see that might suggest the importance of social movements to effect change? What sort of evidence do you see that might suggest they are not useful in effecting change? How might it be possible to understand a social movement as both a "success" and a "failure"?

5. Social movements were extremely active during the 1960s and 1970s. Are they still as relevant today? Why or why not? What might explain the tumultuous period of the 1960s and 1970s compared to today?

References

Amenta, E., & Caren, N. (2007). The legislative, organizational, and beneficiary consequences of state-oriented challengers. In D. A. Snow, S. A. Soule, & H. Kriesi (Eds.), *The Blackwell companion to social movements* (pp. 461–488). Malden, MA: Blackwell Publishing.

Armstrong, E. A., & Bernstein, M. (2008). Culture, power, and institutions: A multi-institutional politics approach to social movements. *Sociological Theory, 26,* 74–99.

Baptist, W., Jenkins, M. B., & Dillon, M. (1999). Taking the struggle on the road: The new Freedom Bus—Freedom from unemployment, hunger, and homelessness. *Journal of Progressive Human Services, 10*(2), 7–29.

Bernstein, M. (2003). Nothing ventured, nothing gained? Conceptualizing social movement "success" in the lesbian and gay movement. *Social Science History, 26,* 531–581.

Bernstein, M. (2008). The analytic dimensions of identity: A political identity framework. In J. Reger, D. J. Meyers, & R. L. Einwohner (Eds.), *Identity work in social movements* (pp. 277–301). Minneapolis: University of Minnesota Press.

Carroll, G., & Hannan, M. T. (2000). *Demography of corporations and industries.* Princeton, NJ: Princeton University Press.

Cazenave, N. (2007). *Impossible democracy: The unlikely success of the war on poverty community action programs.* Albany: State University of New York Press.

Cress, D. M., & Snow, D. A. (2000). The outcomes of homeless mobilization: The influence of organization, disruption, political mediation, and framing. *American Journal of Sociology, 105*(4), 1063–1104.

Dark Star Collective. (Eds.). (2002). *Quiet rumours: An anarcha-feminist reader.* Oakland, CA: AK Press.

Davenport, C., Johnston, H., & Mueller, C. (Eds.). (2005). *Repression and mobilization.* Minneapolis: University of Minnesota Press.

Davies, J. (1962). Toward a theory of revolution. *American Sociological Review, 27*(1), 5–19.

Davies, J. (1969). The J-curve of rising and declining satisfactions as a cause of some great revolutions and a contained revolution. In H. D. Graham & T. R. Gurr (Eds.), *Violence in America* (pp. 671–709). New York: Signet.

Davies, J. (1974). The J-curve and power struggle theories of collective violence. *American Sociological Review, 39,* 607–610.

Dugan, K. B. (2004). Strategy and spin: Opposing movement frames in an antigay voter initiative. *Sociological Focus, 37,* 213–233.

Dugan, K. B. (2008). Just like you: The dimensions of identity protest in an antigay contested context. In J. Reger, D. J. Meyers, & R. L. Einwohner (Eds.), *Identity work in social movements* (pp. 21–46). Minneapolis: University of Minnesota Press.

Ferree, M. M. (2005). Soft repression: Ridicule, stigma, and silencing in gender based movements. In C. Davenport, H. Johnston, & C. Mueller (Eds.), *Repression and mobilization* (pp. 138–155). Minneapolis: University of Minnesota Press.

Ferree, M. M., Lorber, J., & Hess, B. B. (Eds.). (1999). *Revisioning gender.* Thousand Oaks, CA: Sage.

Ferree, M. M., & Subramaniam, M. (2000). The international women's movement at century's end. In D. Vannoy (Ed.), *Gender mosaics: Social perspectives* (pp. 496–506). Los Angeles: Roxbury.

Giugni, M. G. (1998). Was it worth the effort? The outcomes and consequences of social movements. *Annual Review of Sociology, 24,* 371–393.

Goldstone, J. A. (Ed.). (2003). *States, parties and social movements.* New York: Cambridge University Press.

Goodwin, J., & Jasper, J. M. (1999). Caught in a winding, snarling vine: The structural bias of political process theory. *Sociological Forum, 14,* 107–125.

Isaac, L., & Christiansen, L. (2002). How the civil rights movement revitalized labor militancy. *American Sociological Review, 67,* 722–746.

Joppke, C. (1993). *Mobilizing against nuclear energy: A comparison of Germany and the United States.* Berkeley: University of California Press.

Klandermans, B., Roefs, M., & Olivier, J. (2001). Grievance formation in a country in transition: South Africa, 1994–1998. *Social Psychology Quarterly, 64*(1), 41–54.

Kolb, F. (2007). *Protest and opportunities: The political outcomes of social movements.* Frankfurt, NY: Campus Verlag.

Koopmans, R. (2007). Protest in time and space: The evolution of waves of contention. In D. A. Snow, S. A. Soule, & H. Kriesi (Eds.), *The Blackwell companion to social movements* (pp. 19–46). Malden, MA: Blackwell Publishing.

Levitsky, S. R. (2007). Niche activism: Constructing a unified identity in a heterogeneous organizational field. *Mobilization: An International Journal, 12*(3), 271–286.

Marx, K., & Engels, F. (1967). *The Communist manifesto.* Baltimore: Penguin.

McAdam, D. (1982). *Political process and the development of black insurgency, 1930–1970.* Chicago: University of Chicago Press.

McAdam, D. (1988). *Freedom summer.* New York: Oxford University Press.

McAdam, D. (1994). Social movements and culture. In J. R. Gusfield, H. Johnston, & E. Larana (Eds.), *Ideology and identity in contemporary social movements* (pp. 36–57). Phildelphia: Temple University Press.

McAdam, D. (1996). Conceptual origins, future problems, current directions. In D. McAdam, J. D. McCarthy, & M. N. Zald (Eds.), *Comparative perspectives on social movements: Political opportunities, mobilizing structures, and cultural framings* (pp. 23–40). Cambridge, UK: Cambridge University Press.

McAdam, D., McCarthy, J. D., & Zald, M. N. (Eds.). (1996). *Comparative perspectives on social movements: Political opportunities, mobilizing structures, and cultural framings.* Cambridge, UK: Cambridge University Press.

McAdam, D., Tarrow, S., & Tilly, C. (2001). *Dynamics of contention.* Cambridge, UK: Cambridge University Press.

McCarthy, J. D., & Wolfson, M. (1996). Resource mobilization by local social movement organizations: Agency, strategy, and organization in the movement against drinking and driving. *American Sociological Review, 61*(6), 1070–1088.

Meyer, D. S. (1993). Institutionalizing dissent: The United States structure of political opportunity and the end of the nuclear freeze movement. *Sociological Forum, 8*(2), 157–180.

Meyer, D. S., & Minkoff, D. (2004). Conceptualizing political opportunity. *Social Forces, 82*, 1457–1492.

Meyer, D. S., & Staggenborg, S. (1996). Movements, countermovements, and the structure of political opportunity. *American Journal of Sociology, 101*(6), 1628–1660.

Minkoff, D. (1999). Bending with the wind: Strategic change and adaptation by women's and radical minority organizations. *American Journal of Sociology, 104*, 1666–1703.

Morris, A. D. (1984). *The origins of the civil rights movement: Black communities organizing for change.* New York: Free Press.

Morris, A. D. (1999). A retrospective on the civil rights movement: Political and intellectual lankmarks. *Annual Review of Sociology, 25*, 517–539.

Olzak, S., & Ryo, E. (2007). Organizational diversity, vitality, and outcomes in the civil rights movement. *Social Forces, 85*(4), 1561–1592.

Piven, F. F., & Cloward, R. (1977). *Poor people's movements: Why they succeed, how they fail.* New York: Vintage.

Potter, W. (2010). *Attorney Matthew Strugar explains the AETA 4 case.* Retrieved from http://www.greenisthenewred.com/blog

Rude, G. F. E. (1964). *The crowd in history: A study of popular disturbances in France and England, 1730–1848.* New York: Wiley.

Rude, G. F. E. (1985). History from below: *Studies in popular protest and popular ideology in honour of George Rude* (F. Krantz, Ed.). Montreal: Concordia University.

Seidman, G. (1993). *Manufacturing militance: Workers' movements in Brazil and South Africa, 1970–1985.* Berkeley: University of California Press.

Smith, J. (2007). *Social movements for global democracy.* Baltimore: Johns Hopkins University Press.

Snow, D. A. (2004). Social movements as challenges to authority: Resistance to an emerging conceptual hegemony. *Research in Social Movements, Conflicts and Change, 25*, 3–25.

Soule, S. A., & Olzak, S. (2004). When do social movements matter? The politics of contingency and the Equal Rights Amendment. *American Sociological Review, 69*, 473–497.

Stetson, D. M. (Ed.). (2005). *Abortion politics, women's movements, and the democratic state: A comparative study of state feminism.* Oxford, UK: Oxford University Press.

Tarrow, S. (1998). *Power in movement: Social movements and contentious politics.* Cambridge, UK: Cambridge University Press.

Taylor, V. (1989). Social movement continuity: The women's movement in abeyance. *American Sociological Review, 54*, 761–775.

Tilly, C. (1998). Social movements and (all sorts of) other political interactions: Local, national, and international, including identities. *Theory and Society*, 27(4), 453–480.

Tilly, C. (1999). From interactions to outcomes in social movements. In C. Tilly (Ed.), *How social movements matter* (pp. 253–270). Minneapolis: University of Minnesota Press.

Tilly, C., & Tarrow, S. (2006). *Contentious politics*. Boulder, CO: Paradigm Publishers.

Van Dyke, N., Soule, S. A., & Taylor, V. (2004). The targets of social movements: Beyond a focus on the state. *Mobilization*, 25, 27–51.

Walton, J., & Ragin, C. (1990). The debt crisis and political protest in the Third World. *American Sociological Review*, 55(6), 876–890.

Whittier, N. (2002). Meaning and structure in social movements. In D. S. Meyer, N. Whittier, & B. Robnett (Eds.), *Social movements: Identity, culture, and the state* (pp. 289–307). Oxford, UK: Oxford University Press.

Wright, W., & Middendorf, G. (Eds.). (2007). *The fight over food: Producers, consumers, and activists challenge the global food system*. University Park: Penn State University Press.

Young, I. (1981). Beyond the unhappy marriage: A critique of the dual systems theory. In L. Sargent (Ed.), *Women and revolution* (pp. 43–70). Boston: South End Press.

7

State Policies and Practices

Racialized, Class-Based, and Gendered Oppression

with Sandra Bender Fromson

Much of the lively debate in political sociology concerning state theory has tended to be centered on stark claims and counterclaims of which of these models is "correct" and which ones so flawed as to be useless (see, e.g., the exchanges between Miliband, 1973, and Poulantzas, 1978; and between Skocpol, 1988, and Domhoff, 1991a, 1991b). Notably, all of these models have found some support in empirical research, if not completely vindicated. Further, analyses examining the same policy arenas, particularly the New Deal legislation, have drawn very different conclusions concerning each of these models. How is it possible for so many researchers to look at the same policy arena and draw different theoretical conclusions?

For example, what is the role of the state in the byplay between labor and capital? How does the state relate to the political economy and the processes and relationships of work and production? How do state projects of economic intervention affect class relations and the system of class oppression? Similarly, what is the role of the state in gendering, racial formation, and sexuality relations and processes? How does the state's relationship to society affect the processes of gender, racial formation, and sexuality? How do gendering, racial formation, and sexuality state projects affect systems of gendered, racialized, and heteronormative oppression? How do social movements affect the relationship between the state, society, and oppression?

In addition, class, gendered, racialized, and heteronormative systems of oppression do not operate in isolation of one another but rather intersect and resonate in significant ways to produce a "matrix of domination" (Collins, 1990). What is the relationship between the state and social relations that affect and are affected by this intersectionality? How does the matrix of domination affect resistance, and how might that resistance affect the state?

Many sociologists have increasingly called for an analytical framework for reconciling the strengths that each perspective of the state–society relationship might have to offer (Gilbert & Howe, 1991; Hooks, 1991; Jenkins & Brents, 1989; McCammon, 1994; Prechel, 1990, 2000). We argue that we also need an analytical framework that provides the ability to understand multiple oppressions and the role of the state in that relationship. And we need to incorporate how resistance might affect that relationship. This calls for a reconceptualization of state theory.

The models described so far (with the exception of anarchist theory) have dominated political sociology for at least 5 decades, and, with the exception of state-centered structuralism, tend to revolve around questions concerning how or why business interests seem to dominate the political landscape and policy making in the state. While class dialectic analyses introduce the working class into the dynamics affecting the relationship between the state and society, it still suggests that corporate interests manage to thwart outright challenges to its preeminence and advantage in the political economy or at least succeed in co-opting any changes so as to remain consistent with capital accumulation interests. And while state-centered structuralism leaves room for corporate interests to be ignored in favor of bureaucratic state managers' interests, it does not suggest how these might be completely divorced from class-based interests or influence from these. None of the models presented so far thus adequately explains the full range of policy arenas.

In particular, there are whole areas of social and political policy making relative to oppression that are not adequately covered by these models. How do we explain the dominance of patriarchal, racialized, or heteronormative policy making with the existing theoretical frameworks these models offer? Is it sufficient to simply replace the existing concepts of class domination with concepts describing gendered, racialized, or heterosexist domination? As we will discuss in this chapter, the answer is no: While some analyses have in fact tried to do just that, the concepts do not lend themselves easily to such a simple transplant. What is needed is a model of the relationship between the state and society that allows for an analysis of multiple oppressions.

The problem may not be that any one of the models is more powerful than the others but rather that each model may simply be focusing on a different corner of the big picture; if taken together, they may actually contribute to a fuller understanding of that bigger picture. Consider an analogy to a box of 1,000 jigsaw puzzle pieces. If we select just one piece out of the box, or even work to fit together all the pieces of a small area of the puzzle, we will not be able to see the fuller picture. But if we look at the picture of the completed puzzle on the box cover, we might get a fuller understanding of the role of that single piece or that small area to the larger picture. State theory may actually be quite similar: Each model is like a smaller area of the bigger picture, and each model's central concepts are like a single piece of the puzzle. The task before political sociologists, then, is to design a theoretical framework for fitting together all of these pieces of the bigger picture in a synthesis of theoretical models. While no one has yet devised such a model, we can suggest some concepts that might facilitate its development. Let us now turn to an exploration of a model that incorporates the significant concepts of the competing models we have already examined and that might allow enough flexibility to examine the relationship of the state and society in all its realms of oppression: What are the conditions under which some interests dominate and others might challenge that domination in state policy making?

Toward a Multidimensional View of the State, Society, and Oppression

A contingency framework of the relationship between the state, society, and oppression offers one way to forge a synthesis of the strengths of existing theories as it seeks to outline the conditions under which varying interests are likely to prevail at a given interval. Bob Jessop (1990) offered some concepts that can be useful for organizing important elements of existing state theories. His concepts of *state projects, selectivity filters*, and *balance of class forces* are particularly helpful here (see Glasberg & Skidmore, 1997). Jessop suggested that the relationship between the state and society is not one-dimensional, nor is it necessarily the same at all points in time for all actors and participants. Instead, the relationship may change as a result of previous struggles and their resolution. In that sense, the relationship between the state and society is a dialectical one in which earlier conflict resolutions set the stage for later ones so that the relative positions and resources of participants are likely to vary from one struggle to another.

The state itself is limited in its ability to exercise power on its own. State managers can be extraordinarily significant in shaping society, but they must gain support from some sectors of civil society (including economic actors) for their initiatives. Otherwise, state managers would have to impose their will by force upon civil and economic society, a risky proposition as most dictators and fascists sooner or later discover. Jessop (1990) argued instead that the need of the state to elicit support for its interests produces more of an interactive relationship between the state and society as state managers seek to gain such support and legitimacy and other actors and interests seek to elicit state support and legitimacy for their interests. What can be accomplished simply through coercion or highly developed bureaucratic capacities is extremely limited. Does this mean that all participants have equal power? Hardly. One must look for the resources and the processes affecting the efficacy of those resources in the process of the struggle.

While Jessop (1990) offered his concepts as tools for analyzing the relationship between state and society relative to class antagonisms, we can reconceptualize them to capture the relationship built around multiple oppressions. A contingency framework highlights the importance of understanding the historical and situational conditions that exist at the time of policy formation and implementation. These shape the conditions under which various interests are more or less likely to have their needs met with policy and under which oppressions may be altered.

We do not assume that "the state" is a monolithic and unchanging structure with a coherent and compelling agenda. Rather, we view the state as both a structure and a participant in power processes. The interactive relationship between the state and society may affect not only various interest groups in society but also the state itself (Pringle & Watson, 1992). The state becomes a dynamic product of these interactions rather than a static structure that can be anticipated to always act to maintain and reproduce capitalist, patriarchal, white superiority, or heteronormative relations, even if it can be found to do so in a given society. What matters is not *whether* the state necessarily reproduces these relations of oppression by conscious purpose or by structural constraint but rather *how* that may happen *if* that is, in fact, the observed pattern. Thus, gendered, racialized, class, and heterosexist oppressions may be embedded in the state and the state embedded in the oppressions. The point is to examine the conditions under which that occurs. It is important to note, however, as we learned from anarchist theory and state-centered structuralism, the state has interests of its own and can act to reinforce its own power. Thus, as the state is a hierarchical institution, even if under certain conditions it did not reproduce structured inequalities on the basis of race, class, gender, or sexuality, it would still reproduce state power over those citizens that it rules. And were the state organized horizontally, rather than hierarchically, it would no longer be recognizable as a "state."

When we use the term *structure* we do not mean that the state is ossified into a rigid, unchanging, and unchallengeable entity. "Structure" indicates the organization of social relations and institutional arrangements that constitute the state. Over time these may together reproduce patterns of racialized, class, gendered, and sexualized privilege and disadvantage, but it is not presumed to necessarily be constrained to do so. The structure of the state can affect and be affected by organized resistance from below as well as from elites. This does not necessarily mean an assumption that all interests are equal. Some interests may certainly be better positioned to increase their likelihood of affecting the state. The key is to examine the conditions under which that likelihood becomes real and the conditions under which less advantaged interests may gain support from the state in policy.

Let's look now at how Jessop's concepts can be useful in braiding together the significant elements identified by various state theories.

State Projects

We begin with the assumption that policies are not isolated, singular initiatives but rather are part of larger *state projects*. A state project is a *set* of state policies and/or agencies unified around a particular issue or oppression. Policy is not random; more recent policies build on, are shaped by, or challenge prior policies (see Quadagno, 1992). State projects thus involve dynamic and ongoing claims processes in which social constructions (such as gender, race, class, and sexuality) may be reinforced or challenged and altered.

For example, one can analyze the social construction of race by examining the historical establishment of state policy and practice through legislation such as the Civil Rights Act, through a set of agencies built around agencies such as the Bureau Citizenship and Immigration Services, the Commission on Equal Opportunities, the Bureau of Indian Affairs, and so on, and through practices such as school desegregation. Similarly, one can understand patriarchy by examining the historical patterns of state policy and practices around the notion of "gender" through legislation such as the equal rights amendment (which even if not enacted demonstrates a process of the struggles over the social construction of gender) and affirmative action, through a set of agencies built around these policies and practices (such as the Commission on the Status of Women), and through practices implementing policy (such as budget decisions made to comply with or defy Title IX provisions of civil rights legislation mandating equal opportunity for females in schools). And one can understand heteronormativity by examining the history of patterns of state policy and practices around the notion of sexuality through legislation such as the right to civil unions and same-sex marriage as well as policies in defense of traditional marriage (as defined as that between one man and one woman) and the military practice of "don't ask, don't tell" through a set of agencies built around these policies and practices (such as the State Department or the Department of Defense), and through practices implementing policy (such as state recognition of same-sex marriages that have occurred in other states).

Using the notion of state projects, we can see that the formation of current policy is contingent upon unified, historical state policy precedents and the state agencies and actors that implement these policies. The concept of "state projects" does not suggest a cogent, centralized state with a clearly defined goal motivating decision making. Rather, the state itself is both an arena of struggle and an actor that above all other actors has the unique authority to codify social constructions into legalized norms and to enforce these in ways that shape cultural repertoires and social behaviors. And, as the concept of state projects suggests, the state is also subject to resistance and modification from below (see Connell, 1990). State projects are not necessarily only produced and reproduced by the state but are the ongoing production of struggles between the state and political forces over the contested terrain that is state policy. Indeed, the state may at times even enact policies that contradict the interests of capital accumulation, patriarchy, white-skin privilege, and heteronormativity as a result of those struggles. What shapes the struggles themselves?

Selectivity Filters

The notion of state projects must include a mechanism through which policy and the struggles over the policy process are shaped and framed. Jessop (1990) called that mechanism *structural selectivity*: State structures "offer unequal chances to different forces within and outside the state to act for different political purposes" (p. 367). State structures and state projects are filters or lenses that frame the issues, debates, and definitions of programs by "selecting against" some policy alternatives and political organizations. For example, cultural and ideological frames such as free market, Protestant work ethic, and culture of poverty contour policy makers' collective perceptions so as to preclude consideration of policy alternatives that are inconsistent with private capital accumulation, personal responsibility for one's own economic fate, and competitive individualism. Cultural and ideological frames such as "anatomy is destiny," "men are from Mars and women are from Venus," "God intended marriage to be between one man and one woman," and the like contour policy makers' collective perceptions so as to drastically reduce the probability that they will consider policy alternatives that seriously challenge male privilege and dominance and heteronormativity. And cultural and ideological frames such as "white supremacy," "natural law," and the like are likely to substantially shape policy makers' collective perceptions so as to mitigate the probability that policy makers will consider policy alternatives that significantly undermine white skin privilege and dominance.

This does not suggest that the state is neutral in the mediation process. Rather, as the notion of structural selectivity implies, the state's definitions of crisis and appropriate responses may be narrowed by a biasing or filtering process in which only some interests or points of view become part of the process while others are ignored, silenced, or never considered. The state becomes more responsive to some strategies and resources than to others; few of the possible policies and organizations surrounding a given issue receive serious political consideration. Over time, selectivity perpetuates biases in the state-society relationship.

Since the policy process selects some interests in and others out, what affects that selectivity? We turn now to the notion of the balance of forces.

Balance of Political and Institutional Forces

Jessop (1990) argued that the balance of *class* forces is a crucial factor influencing whether and when class groups are more or less likely to be selected into the policy process and gain advantageous state policies. That balance will be affected by a variety of conditions, including (1) the extent of unity or disunity with each class relative to other participants in the process, as well as the extent of unity or disunity between the various branches and agencies within the state, (2) the resources available to the classes and the state to bring to bear on struggles over policy creation and implementation, and (3) the opportunities to apply these resources to create mass disruption. Note that the concept of balance of class forces does not suggest that all classes are equally likely to gain advantageous policies; rather, it speaks to factors that may enhance or inhibit a given class's chances of doing so relative to other classes in the political economy.

While the concept "balance of *class* forces" may help us appreciate economic and class-centered policy processes, it is less helpful for understanding other forms of oppression. That is, we would be hard-pressed to explain gendered, racialized, and heterosexist oppression in terms of class alone. However, the notion of the balance of class forces can be reconceptualized to a notion of the *balance of political and institutional forces* in order to capture an analysis of multiple oppressions. The balance of political and institutional forces includes not only class forces but gendering, heteronormative, and racial formation forces as well. By gendering and heteronormative forces we are referring not to male interests versus female interests but rather to socially constructed sets of interests that may privilege one sex over another (in a patriarchal society, this is likely to mean male privilege relative to female oppression, and heteronormativity as a basis for privilege relative to the oppression of sexual minorities of all kinds) as opposed to those that seek to produce greater equality regardless of sex, gender, and sexual practices. It may very well be that one will find people of all genders and a whole range of sexual practices in each set of gendering forces.

Likewise, when we refer to racial formation forces, we do not mean groups or interests defined by the physical or cultural characteristics culturally constructed to have biological significance. Rather, we are referring to socially constructed sets of interests that may privilege one racially formed group over another (in a society based on white superiority, this is likely to mean white-skin privilege relative to oppression of people of color) as opposed to those who seek to produce greater equality regardless of social categorizations defined as "race." Thus it may very well be that one will find people of color as well as whites in each set of racial formation forces.

The notion of "balance" of gendering or racial formation forces refers to the processes and dynamics of struggle between such sets of interests to redefine the social construction of gender, sexuality, and race. The conditions and dynamics affecting these forces, we argue, are similar to those affecting the balance of class forces.

How do we use the concepts of state projects, structural selectivity, and balance of political and institutional forces to frame an understanding of the state and oppression? Let's look at what such a framework might be.

Modeling a Multidimensional View of the State, Society, and Oppression

We can organize the factors suggested as important by the prevailing theories of the state to identify the significant dimensions of the balance of political and institutional forces and of selectivity filters (see Table 7.1). In particular, such factors include (1) organization, including the extent to which classes, gendering forces, heteronormative forces, and racial formation forces are unified and the extent to which they may develop networks and coalitions, as well as these same factors within competing groups; (2) access to and ability to mobilize resources; (3) structural conditions, including the health of the economy, constitutional constraints on policy creation

Table 7.1   Dimensions of Balance of Forces and Selectivity Filters

Balance of Political and Institutional Forces	Selectivity Filters
Opportunity for disruption	Political economy structure
Organization	Party politics
Resource mobilization	Relative autonomy of state actors
Unity within groups	Past policy precedence
Unity within other groups	Ideology & culture
Unity within & between state agencies	

and implementation, existing regulations, and precedence in implementation; (4) opportunity (or perception of potential) for groups to create mass disruption or turmoil; (5) relative autonomy of state actors and agencies; and (6) and unity and organization within and between state agencies.

The interaction between the balance of political and institutional forces and selectivity filters does not end with the passage of a single policy; rather, the process reverberates through the implementation of that policy and sets the stage for later policy creation, modification, and implementation within the larger state project. Individual policy initiatives are framed by the larger state project and prior precedents set by existing policies within that project. The introduction of such initiatives triggers an interaction between the balance of political forces and selectivity filters. The process of resolving the tension between the filters and forces moves policy initiatives toward policy creation. Once policies are created, the dialectic between the balance of political forces and selectivity filters continues as policy initiatives become translated into practice. The resolution of this process shapes the policy as it becomes incorporated into the larger state project and hence part of the selectivity filters that frame subsequent policy initiatives (see Figure 7.1).

State projects are animated, then, by the balance of political and institutional forces in the claims process, producing a dialectic process of policy making and implementation, as well as social practices and repertoires over time. Dominant class, racialized, and gendered interests may be challenged, resisted, and redirected from below in this process.

Taken together the concepts of state projects, balance of political forces, and selectivity filters provide us with useful tools for developing an analytical framework for understanding the relationship between the state, society, and oppression. The notion of "balance" of gendered, sexuality, or racial formation forces refers to the processes of struggle between such sets of interests to redefine the social construction of gender, sexuality, and race. The conditions and dynamics affecting these forces are similar to those affecting the balance of class forces as conceptualized by Jessop (1990). Furthermore, the concept of a balance of political forces expands on the class-centric focus of Jessop's (and much of that of sociological state theory's) conceptual framework to make room for analyses of class formation as well as gendering, sexuality, and racial formation, and the intersections of these. It also becomes possible to incorporate standpoint theory (Smith, 1990, 1999) so that analyses of state projects may begin with the points of view of those from below rather than necessarily beginning only with the state and its policies from above.

In this way, an analysis, for example, of U.S. welfare reform of the 1990s may begin from the standpoint of the poor, particularly women and children, and most particularly women and children of color. In such an approach, the central analytical question is not necessarily why welfare reform occurred in the 1990s. The driving questions instead become the following: What has happened in the lives of the poor, of poor women and children, and of poor women and children of color, since the 1990s, and what factors shaped state policy that affected their lived experiences? It then becomes important to explore the balance of political forces (of both oppression and resistance) before, during, and after the implementation of welfare reform and the selectivity filters that operated to frame public and political discourse. But here the state becomes an actor and the state project an arena of contested terrain, both of which are subject to resistance from below as well as dominance from above. The state thus can become an agent of oppression as well as an agent and object of change, albeit in often limited ways.

Such a reconceptualization of the balance of political forces allows an exploration of class formation, racial formation, sexuality, and gendering state projects (and the intersections of these) through other policy areas as well. For example, one can now examine abortion policy, marriage and family policy (including the struggle over civil unions, legitimacy of parental status for some, and domestic violence), and military policy (including "don't ask, don't tell"), labor laws (including battles over sweatshops, justice for janitors, living wages, and comparable worth), and racial policy (including census definitions of racial categories, immigration laws, racial profiling in police policy, racism in criminal justice and capital punishment, and educational segregation) by beginning from the standpoint of the lived existence of the disadvantaged and oppressed. The analysis can then build out toward the policies themselves and the relationships and processes that ebb and flow to shape them. The state and state projects are then the shapers of notions of race, class, sexuality, and gender, and shaped by the resistance of the oppressed.

A contingency framework of the state, society, and oppression as an interactive process may be diagramed as in Figure 7.1. Here, individual policy initiatives are framed by the larger state project and prior precedents set by existing policies within that project. The introduction of such initiatives triggers a dialectical process between the balance of political and institutional forces and selectivity filters. That dialectical process moves policy initiatives toward policy creation. Once policies are created, the continuing dialectic between the balance of political and institutional forces and selectivity filters reverberates through the process of translating de jure policy into de facto implementation. The resolution of that dialectical process shapes the policy that becomes incorporated into the larger state project and contributes to the selectivity filters that frame subsequent policy initiatives.

Let's now examine oppression and state projects.

Figure 7.1   Modeling a Contingency Perspective of the State

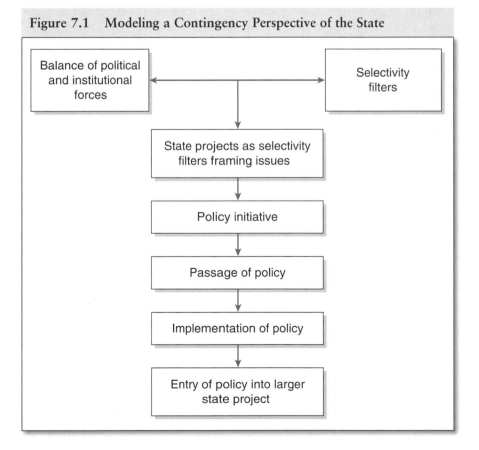

The State and Class-Based Oppression

The main state theories discussed in Chapter 5 largely emphasize the class character of the relationship between the state and society. Their main focus derives from questions concerning how economic and class inequality affects state policy: How or why do economic elites or capital accumulation interests gain their agendas in state policy, largely at the expense of the poor and working class members of society? And while at least some of these analyses (especially those using a class dialectic model) acknowledge that economic elites do *not* always prevail because of class struggle processes, the analysis remains focused on class relations and the state. Regardless of why the state legislates as it does, or how it does, the major state theories suggest that the predominant state project is one of economic intervention, usually defined as the state's attempts to preserve and protect the conditions that facilitate capital accumulation. They thus imply that economic-intervention state projects are essentially class-oppression state projects masquerading as neutral attempts to maintain a healthy economy in everyone's best interest.

State Projects of Economic Intervention and Class Oppression

There is ample evidence in policy processes to suggest that economic-intervention state projects may indeed be thinly disguised class oppression. Even when working-class interests appear to prevail, argue class dialectic theorists, the resulting policies are framed so as not to contradict or hinder conditions favoring capital accumulation. Look, for example, at labor laws governing the relationship between capitalists and workers. During the Industrial Revolution, the state essentially worked to maintain a laissez-faire approach to the economy, allowing capital the freedom to develop as capitalists saw fit. The state's neutrality meant, however, that capitalists were free to enrich themselves, if not the overall national economy, at the expense of workers. Those who toiled in the earth's deep recesses to mine the coal and oil that fueled industrial production, as well as those who labored in the factories and fields of that production, worked in highly unsafe conditions and under extremely exploitive conditions. Workers, who were often new immigrants desperate for work and unfamiliar with the language and customs of their newly adopted home, were paid starvation wages for long hours, with no control over their livelihood or their lives. Company towns emerged in the geographically isolated hills of coal towns, where a single employer provided all the jobs. That same company also owned the houses the workers and their families lived in, the shops where they bought everything they needed to survive, the schools that educated their children, and the churches where they worshipped. Workers were often paid in company scrip rather than dollars, which meant they could not shop anywhere but the company store at any inflated prices the company chose to charge. Consider the power imbalance such a situation created: Workers were not free to dissent or to challenge the employer—to do so was to risk one's livelihood and that of one's entire family. So long as workers existed under a system of competitive individualism, the power remained firmly in the hands of employers who could pay workers as little as they wanted, under any conditions they wanted, and charge as much as they wanted for their goods and services.

By the turn of the 20th century, however, workers increasingly resented and resisted this arrangement and struggled to demand that the state guarantee them the right to collectively bargain with employers for better wages and safer working conditions. The unionization movement that blossomed throughout Europe began to spread in the United States with the help of the (largely anarcho-syndicalist) Industrial Workers of the World (IWW, or the Wobblies). They advocated an international industrial union of all workers, regardless of industry or type of work. The struggle for unionization became quite violent, as capitalists clearly recognized their monopolistic power edge was being threatened, and they fought back with everything they could. But storm clouds were gathering as the Wobblies increasingly appealed to highly exploited and impoverished workers, and capitalists soon appealed to the state for help. Capitalists were quite divided on how and why the state should respond, with big business and the National Association of Manufacturers (NAM) reluctantly favoring trade unions within industries as the lesser evil to national or international industrial unions, and small business and local chambers of Congress favoring no unions at all. But they all wanted the state to step in and legislate labor and production relations to quell labor unrest. Ultimately, big business interests prevailed: In the interest of maintaining a stable, crisis-free economy, Congress intervened in 1935 and passed the National Labor Relations Act (more commonly referred to as the Wagner Act) that provided workers with the right to collective bargaining (Domhoff, 1990; Levine, 1988; Weinstein, 1968).

While this would appear to be a major victory for labor, state governance of labor relations and its endorsement of the right to collective bargaining came at a hefty price: In New York, the Taylor Law prohibits workers in essential services from striking. Among those the state defines as essential services are police, firefighters, sanitation workers, transportation workers, and teachers. So are steel, coal, and oil workers, shipyard workers, and munitions-plant workers, especially during war and other crises. Since labor strikes were the main source of collective power workers had, this antistrike clause essentially took the teeth out of their resistance against capital. Further, the right to collectively bargain also carried provisions for binding arbitration, in which the state may force workers and employers to accept and be bound by agreements brokered by the state in order to avoid labor strife, production snags, and economic downturns. The Wagner Act thus became part of the state's economic intervention state project that was more a state project of labor control: While it provided workers with the right to collectively bargain in trade unions, it institutionalized labor relations around the boardroom table instead of the streets and legislated the terms and strategies workers could assume in the process. The power imbalance between the working class and the capitalist class remained to advantage capital accumulation interests.

After the Great Depression of the 1930s, Congress again moved to expand the state project of economic intervention to ensure that monopoly capitalists did not greedily threaten the economic well-being of the nation. One of the policies put into effect was antitrust legislation that forbade corporations from developing and maintaining a monopoly that essentially posed a threat to competition and therefore a healthy economy. The sheer size and power of monopolies posed a "barrier to entry" to the industry because smaller, newer firms cannot compete with the much larger firms. Furthermore, monopolies posed a similar noncompetitive edge to workers and consumers who would be denied alternative options for employment and for goods and services and thus monopoly corporations could charge whatever the market could bear and pay as little as they could get away with. Corporations seeking to merge with or buy out their competitors were denied that right by federal legislation. That legislation ultimately led to the breakup of AT&T, the only telephone company prior to 1984, into several smaller competitive firms. Ironically, antitrust legislation has rarely been invoked against corporations since the 1980s but instead has often been called up against unions seeking to merge. So while banks, auto manufacturers, and food processing corporations have been able to merge with little or no interference by the state with its antitrust legislation, workers seeking to gain a stronger power base by merging into larger unions often face legal restrictions against noncompetition as defined by antitrust laws.

Most recently, the North American Free Trade Agreement (NAFTA) and efforts to expand it to Central and South America are often framed as part of the state project of economic intervention by reducing barriers to trade that hurt the United States and U.S. made products and therefore, presumably, jobs for U.S. workers. Yet analyses of the effects of NAFTA after more than a decade indicate that it has erased the political borders that inhibited trade at the expense of workers' jobs in the United States and workers' wages everywhere (Wallach & Sforza, 1999). However, the dialectics of class relations are such that the very same state project that is depressing workers' wages, threatening the notion of a minimum wage, eroding workers' health and safety on the job, and motivating the reduction if not outright elimination of health and retirement benefits may ultimately help unions organize workers across national borders as well. Thus, the state project of economic intervention, while largely favoring capital accumulation interests at the expense of workers' interests, may actually help workers edge closer to the international industrial unions envisioned by the Wobblies after all.

Taken together, then, the dominant state theories frame analyses of the relationship between the state and society as one rooted primarily in economic and class relations. How and why the state legislates in favor of capital accumulation interests are at issue among the various theorists, but they generally agree that the state's role is the continued oppression of the working class. However, sociologists are increasingly aware that class is but one system of oppression. State projects may also be arranged around gendered, heterosexist, and racialized oppression as well.

The State and Gendered Oppression

Feminist theories of the state shift the focus of the analysis from one of class relations to one exploring the role of the state in gendered oppression processes. In particular, much of the focus here is on how the state created and reinforced women's subordinated status as an inferior gender and how differentiated states participate in a dynamic process to produce gender regimes (Brush, 2003; Haney, 2000). Let's examine feminist models of the state to see how this shift in focus helps us to see the hand of the state beyond economic and class relations.

Patriarchal state theorists investigate how the state reproduces patriarchal relations that privilege men and subordinate women, particularly (but not only) through welfare and family policy (MacKinnon, 1989). According to these analysts, welfare policy and the concept of the family wage (with the presumption of males as family breadwinners) buttressed the nuclear family and its gendered hierarchy of male dominance and female dependence on individual men to protect them from poverty (Abramovitz, 1996; Connell, 1990; Hartmann, 1976). Patriarchy and class reproduction thus become linked in support of the capitalist economy where, depending on capitalist need, women's roles alternate between keeper of the home and as a low-cost reserve army of labor (McIntosh, 1978). These sometimes conflicting roles for women highlight the tensions and conflicts of a capitalist society. But some argue that class and capitalist reproduction needs and the accompanying subjugation of women are not constant at all times in all societies and they need to be viewed in their ideological and historical context (Barrett, 1990).

There are slight variations on this theme among researchers using a patriarchal state perspective. Some argue that the welfare state extended women's dependence on individual men to a broader dependence on a male-dominated state (Boris & Bardaglio, 1983; Brown, 1981). Others disagree, noting that the dialectics of patriarchal state processes may in fact produce ample welfare state programs that can serve to actually decrease women's risk of poverty or to provide material resources to help women and children survive when there is no male source of support (Edin & Lein, 1996; Kamerman, 1984; Piven, 1990; Ruggie, 1984). But some see the economic protection these programs may offer as evidence of a patriarchal state seeking to protect women from the brutality and devastation of the male preserve of the economy. Social welfare programs operate under the assumption that women are the "natural" caretakers of children and commonly absolve individual men from any such responsibility. These differing viewpoints on the meaning of the state's patriarchal position do not obliterate what they have in common: the view of the state as a centralized, patriarchal institution that subordinates women.

Gendered state subsystem analysts reject the view of patriarchal state analysts of the state as monolithic and centralized. Instead, they argue that the state is a more complex and dynamic institution and thus so is the relationship between the state and gendering processes (Orloff, 1996). For example, some researchers found that welfare states were actually comprised of layers of institutional subsystems (Gordon, 1990). "Masculine" social insurance programs, such as workmen's compensation, unemployment insurance, and Social Security, responded to the limitations of the private labor market to provide stable, secure, and gainful employment for breadwinners. These programs were based on the assumption that men were entitled to such support to help them fulfill their natural male roles as providers and breadwinners (Nelson, 1990; Sapiro, 1990). In contrast, need-based, means-tested "feminine" social assistance programs like Aid to Families with Dependent Children (now Temporary Assistance for Needy Families, or TANF), Mothers' Pensions, and Aid to Dependent Children (ADC) were based on the assumption that women needed a male breadwinner to avoid poverty and the state would step in only when such a breadwinner was absent (Mink, 1994). When the state does take over the role of the male provider, it also assumes the role of male dominator in women's lives. This often happens in the administration of the highly regulated social welfare programs, which typically subject women to a great deal of observation, evaluation, and control as the state tries to establish women's eligibility for benefits (Nelson, 1990).

While this multilayered structure of the welfare state does indeed offer a more nuanced view than the previous conceptions of a centralized state, it remained focused on income-maintenance programs of the welfare state, particularly in the United States (Gordon, 1994; Orloff, 1996). In contrast, *gendered welfare regime* analysts broadened their focus to examine a wider array of the kinds of policies pursued by welfare states. They found that policies dealing with issues such as citizenship, care for family members, women's employment, and reproduction also affected women's material well-being and contributed to gendering processes and gendered oppression. Furthermore, their expanded view, as well as a more cross-national comparison of welfare state types, revealed wide variations of gendered regimes in welfare states (Borchorst, 1994; Esping-Andersen, 1990; Gustafsson, 1994; Hobson, 1994; Huber & Stephens, 2000; Korpi, 2000; Leira, 1992; Lewis, 1992; O'Connor, 1993; O'Connor, Orloff, & Shaver, 1999; Orloff, 1993; Sainsbury, 1994, 1996; Shaver, 1993). This research suggests that welfare states are not only not monolithic in structure or single-minded in their patriarchal allegiances but there are wide variations on this theme of gendered welfare states.

Gendered state process analysts focus less on redistributive policy and more on processes and relations of discourse and gendered meaning in welfare states. In these analyses, the welfare state is not only a policy-making institution but also an arena of struggles over the contested terrain of the social construction of gender, including the reproductive role of women (Curran & Abrams, 2000; Fraser & Gordon, 1994; Yuval-Davis, 1997; Zylan, 2000). Here, claims processes involve shifting the line between the natural and the artificial or political definitions of gender, which then frames the discourse concerning the identification of needs and appropriate policies to address these (Peattie & Rein, 1983; Pringle & Watson, 1992). The struggle therefore becomes one of defining what is biological or natural and therefore immutable and unchangeable with policy and what is really more a social construction of gender and therefore amenable to policies that redistribute resources, redefine roles and responsibilities, and establish rights. These analyses introduced the notion that the welfare state is not just a masculine structural creation imposing patriarchal gendered meanings and oppressions; it is also an arena in which those social constructions are challenged and resisted, where the very meanings of motherhood and dependency could be fought over and where these contested terrains could affect not just notions of gendering but also the formation of the welfare state itself

(Abramovitz, 2000; Bock & Thane, 1991; Goodwin, 1997; Koven & Michel, 1993; Muncy, 1991; Sklar, 1993; Skocpol, 1992).

Some analysts criticize the overemphasis of this literature on issues of maternalism and welfare and family policies. The state can also be seen to play a powerful role in gendering processes in policy domains such as militarism (Enloe, 1989, 2000), abortion (Luker, 1984; Petchesky, 1984), sexuality (Luker, 1998), and violence against women (Brown, 1995; Elman, 2001). For example, Luker's (1998) analysis of the state's regulation of women's sexuality illustrates how social reform policy concerning social hygiene served to allow the state to regulate women's sexuality. Where women in the reform movement supported greater equality in gender relations, male physicians in the movement militated for the criminalization of prostitution requiring greater scrutiny and regulation of women's private sexual lives that reinforced sexual inequality.

Enloe's (1989, 2000) work pointed out that militaries work to confine women to limited and clearly defined roles such as military wives, prostitutes, nurses, and rape targets and to socialize women in these groups to view each other with suspicion and animosity. But she also noted that the military is not always successful in its gendering mission: The resistance, for example, of military wives cast into the role of bitter and disregarded widows and abused wives, or of men as military "wives" whose partners are the soldiers, often means that the military must confront serious challenges and conflicts. Thus, the work of Enloe, Luker, and others identify what is missing from much of the literature on gendering and the state: the question of the state's use of violence and control in reproducing systems of gendered oppression in a patriarchal state, as well as resistance to that use of violence and control.

Taken together, the abundance of feminist state theory scholarship suggests that the state plays a role in far more than just the management of class relations and the reproduction of conditions that reinforce capital accumulation and systems of class oppression. It is also an active participant in power processes and struggles (including resistance and the state's response to that resistance) of gendered oppression. It is, in short, a patriarchal state, but one subject to alterations prompted by challenges from below (see Connell, 1990).

Gendering State Projects

State projects of gender formation include policy initiatives and issue areas articulated by the executive, policies and budgetary decisions passed by the legislature, constitutional provisions, determinations and rulings by the judiciary (including the Supreme Court), and implementation of policies directly and indirectly affecting the social construction of gender by administrative agencies. Such policies include marriage and family law (including divorce, child custody, adoption, and domestic violence laws), social services (such as Aid to Families with Dependent Children), affirmative action and equal rights laws (such as Title IX and the enfranchisement of women in the political process), reproduction (including abortion laws), and sexual assault laws. These policies, as entries into the state project of gendering, affect the social construction of gender insofar as they participate in shaping and defining the meaning and social significance of sex and sexualities, thereby affecting the life chances of both men and women.

Much of the gendering state project has served to create and reinforce a social construction of gender in a patriarchal society, such that women remain subordinate to men politically, socially, and economically. However, there clearly are policies enacted and implemented by the state that alter the social constructions of gender such that women's social, political, and economic positions in a patriarchal society and thus their life chances are improved. What, then, are the dynamics of oppression and resistance, and how do these affect state policies that perpetuate gendering state projects enhancing patriarchy as well as expand women's empowerment and thus challenging and mitigating patriarchal dominance? What are the lived experiences of women, and how are these enforced from above and resisted from below?

Cultural and ideological frames, as well as prior legislative precedence, act as selectivity filters biasing policy creation and implementation, although these may be challenged by the processes and dynamics of the balance of gendering forces. Unlike cultural and ideological frames that dominate class-based or economic state projects, those that frame the claims processes of gendering state projects commonly include an underlying assumption of biological determinism. For example, the structure of language and its usage contain hidden assumptions about gender, such that males are reinforced as the norm of human existence and are appropriately superior and dominant; women are represented as the other, the invisible, or the inferior and subordinate gender (Sorrels, 1983) and thus symbolically annihilated (Tuchman, Daniels, & Benet, 1978). Language acts as a cultural selectivity filter reinforcing patriarchal assumptions that undergird policy initiatives and the state gendering project. Other cultural selectivity filters that may contribute to the reinforcing of patriarchy include gendered definitions of appropriate and inappropriate behavior and aspirations, such as motherhood norms (Schur, 1984; Zylan, 2000), father-as-breadwinner norms (Curran & Abrams, 2000), appearance norms (Barthel, 1988; Ehrenreich, 1992;

Sutton, 1992; Wolf, 1991), and sexual orientation norms (Blumenfeld, 1992; Duberman, 1993). Such norms and language assumptions often find their way into policy, as we will see shortly.

Cultural frames also include institutional traditions that become routinized as "normal." These include practices that privilege the nuclear, heterosexual, middle-class family form wherein the male adult is rewarded as the dominant force and the breadwinner and the female adult is subordinated as the primary caretaker and unpaid domestic laborer; in cases where the female adult participates in the paid labor market, the cultural expectation is that she remain the primary caretaker with the responsibility of domestic labor (see Hochschild & Machung, 1997). Notably, this gendered frame shifts when it intersects with class, so that welfare reform and workfare policies frame poor women with children as responsible only if they work outside the home in the paid labor market, while cultural norms simultaneously frame middle-class and affluent women with children as responsible only if they remain full-time homemakers and mothers and eschew the paid labor market. The state penalizes women (and their children) who do not conform to the norm of poor mothers as breadwinners by denying them welfare benefits beyond a maximum of 2 years.

Economic institutions reiterate this cultural framing of family structures and roles by maintaining gendered definitions of "men's jobs" and "women's jobs" in segmented labor markets, defined by vague extensions of perceptions of each gender's natural abilities: women as helpers and caretakers and men as leaders and physical and mental laborers (Kessler-Harris, 1980; Padavic & Reskin, 2002; Reskin & Hartmann, 1986; Reskin & Roos, 1990). Economic institutions also reinforce the notion of male superiority and privilege by maintaining differential wages for men and women, even when they do the same work (see U.S. Census Bureau, 2009).

Taken together, institutional patterns frame a biased policy creation and implementation process. Witness the difficulty of introducing or passing and ratifying an equal rights amendment (Mansbridge, 1986) and pay equity or comparable worth policies (Greenberger, 1980; McCann, 1994; Padavic & Reskin, 2002). These patterns of gendering in cultural institutions, which act as frames biasing policy creation and implementation, are further supported by the ideological underpinnings of patriarchy, particularly through notions like "anatomy is destiny." This ideological prism identifying sexism as natural itself becomes a contested terrain in the dynamics and processes in the balance of gendering forces.

Past legislative policies and implementations tend to have the overall effect of acting as selectivity filters biasing the framing of newer policies so as to reproduce previous gendering patterns. Examples include legislative policies and court determinations reinforcing heterosexual marriage as the only legitimate relationships, no-fault divorce laws that impoverish women by routinely denying the need for alimony because of the courts' failure to acknowledge the reality of discrimination in the labor market, and family wage policies based on the assumption of the male as the breadwinner.

The ability of women in a patriarchal society to struggle against the social construction of gender as it appears in gendering state projects and in institutions, and the ability of men to reassert their dominance, is conditioned by the balance of gendering forces. That is, women are more likely to gain passage and implementation of advantageous state policy when there is greater unity of perspective among a large number of women (and often aided and abetted with the support and participation of men in coalitions with women) who are organized in formal organizations and networks. They are more likely to become organized when faced with (or they perceive) an imminent threat to their life chances. For example, increasing participation of women in the paid labor market (either by choice or by economic necessity) is more likely to prompt greater demands for pay equity; family leave policy; legal protection from sexual harassment; equal opportunity and access to education, training, and jobs; enforcement of child support awards; etc. This is especially so when women are their own sole source of income and benefits or when they are the sole or primary source of such support for their families.

Such efforts to gain advantageous legislation and implementation of policies and programs are more likely to succeed when men are less unified in their opposition to challenges to patriarchy or when crises in other institutions increase the legitimacy of women's demands. For example, periods of severe economic downsizing and deindustrialization force increasing numbers of men out of work, thereby necessitating more women to participate in the paid labor market in order to provide income for their families. Other examples of the enhancement of women's power in the balance of gendering forces have occurred when men's dominant cultural or institutional position became diminished. Such was the case during the 1983 copper mine labor strikes in Arizona, when court injunctions forbade men from picketing, thus necessitating the activism of women to continue the strike efforts (see Kingsolver, 1989). Similar processes became apparent during World War II, when men were increasingly pulled from assembly lines to fight overseas, at precisely the point in time when dramatic increases in industrial production were necessary to support the war effort. Women's participation in munitions factories, tank and submarine factories, and other industrial settings became increasingly vital. That new productive role for women shifted the line between the natural and the artificial and altered the claims process and thereby altered the ideological selectivity filters biasing policy.

Supreme Court decisions have also played a role in the dialectics of gendering state projects. For example, the 1973 *Roe v. Wade* decision gave women greater control over their bodies by granting women the right to an abortion anywhere in the United States. That decision has been the object of fierce struggles in Congress and in individual states' legislatures ever since. These struggles have been animated by the dialectical push and pull of the balance of gendering forces between those framing the issue in an ideology of "anatomy is destiny" defining women's proper, biologically determined role as mothers and those framing the issue as a matter of women's individual civil rights (Klatch, 1988; Luker, 1984; Petchesky, 1984). Both sides of the struggle are well organized and networked, with anti-abortionists represented by Right to Life, Operation Rescue, and the Christian Coalition, among others and pro-choice proponents represented by the National Abortion and Reproductive Rights Action League (NARAL), the National Organization for Women (NOW), and others. These organizations have been variably effective in accessing and mobilizing resources, raising considerable funds, lobbying legislators, organizing PACs and petition drives, buying advertising space in print and broadcasting media, and organizing widely viewed rallies and demonstrations. Such mobilized resources within the gendered group opens up access to new ideological frames and state actors, forcing legislators to frame and influence the creation of abortion and other gendering policies in ways that might benefit women.

Furthermore, each of the gendered interest groups has created opportunities or invoked the threat of the potential to create mass turmoil. Pro-choice proponents have frequently organized massive demonstrations in major cities, and in Washington, D.C., in particular, drawing hundreds of thousands of participants and suggesting to legislators that there is widespread support for the right to abortion access and the failure to uphold that access could result in political disaster for members of Congress (witness, for example, the popular bumper sticker, "I support *Roe v. Wade* . . . and I vote!"). On the other hand, the Christian right emerged in the 1980s and 1990s as such an organized and influential force in the Republican Party that the party adopted an anti-abortion plank in its electoral platform. In addition, members of Operation Rescue and other similar organizations have engaged in demonstrations blocking the entrance to abortion clinics, harassing patients and doctors entering clinics. Moreover, there have been increasing attacks against abortion clinics, such as bombings, shootings, murders, and harassment of clinic employees at their homes and other public places. These actions produce or threaten to produce mass turmoil at sites where abortions are performed, making access to the right to abortion increasingly difficult (Mason, 2002).

Anti-abortion proponents have also become relatively adept at accessing the judicial system to chip away at the implementation of the right to abortion access. The result thus far is that although *Roe v. Wade* remains a powerful force in defining women's rights, it has undergone increasing restrictions. In its 1989 *Webster v. Reproductive Health Services* decision, the Supreme Court allowed individual states the right to determine their own abortion policy restrictions, a move that has focused much of the struggle at the individual state level. Each state essentially produces its own set of restrictions, including requirements to secure the permission of the parents or guardians of a minor seeking abortion, refusals to allow Medicaid to pay for the abortions of poor women, and the banning of certain abortion procedures. Such restrictions contribute to the state gendering project in that women who cannot afford to pay to end unwanted pregnancies or women who live in states that restrict access to abortions may find themselves unlikely to be able to access educational or employment opportunities because of the high cost of child care, health care insurance costs, and the expense of child rearing. The result at both the state and federal levels is a gendering that reiterates the subordination of women, particularly women of color and poor women, as more become increasingly dependent either on the state itself or on their husbands or partners for economic security.

Although there has clearly been a shifting of the policy line between the natural and the social construction of gender in the United States, the dialectical process of that shifting has been characterized by both progress and setback. One condition affecting the balance of gendering forces in that process has been the relative unity within gendered interest groups. While "the feminist movement" is often depicted as a unified, monolithic movement, the fact is that it is actually splintered along several dimensions (see Andersen, 1993; Ferree & Hess, 1994). The liberal feminist faction, most visibly organized into NOW, is largely a white, middle-class interest group focused on increasing the opportunities for participation of women in the political, economic, and social institutions of society. They thus accept the existing social structures as a given and seek to reform these, so as to end gendered discrimination. This is in contrast to the smaller "radical feminist" interest group, which defines patriarchy as *the* enemy and seeks to end all institutional structures and roles reinforcing male dominance. Thus, marriage, for example, is seen as a highly oppressive, patriarchal institution that needs to be transcended by a redefined notion of family in which adult women and children create new roles apart from men. Marxist or socialist feminists define capitalism as the root of gendered inequality in which women are the reproducers of the reserve army of workers (Mies, 1998; Millett, 1969; Rich, 1995; Rothman, 1982). They therefore seek the abolition of capitalism as the means to eliminating patriarchy (although those who identify as social-ist feminists sometimes frame patriarchy and capitalism as "dual systems" that are often not easily distinguishable from one another). Finally, anarcha-feminists argue against all forms of domination, seeing the state as a fun-damentally dominating institution that is illegitimate in itself. Thus, anarcha-feminists tend to argue for direct action tactics, increasing the autonomy of women (and all genders) rather than relying on the state for social improvement.

In addition, there are other rifts within gendered interest groups, includ-ing class, racially defined, sexual identity, and religious interests, among oth-ers. These different factions and interests within the "feminist movement" mean that gendered interest groups seeking greater empowerment of women as the subordinated group are not necessarily unified in their goals, their strategies, or their framing of the issues. Those schisms become a condition affecting the balance of gendering forces in the gendering state project.

On the other hand, there have been times when these schisms have been transcended to produce greater unity and therefore a greater opportunity to affect the gendering state project. Such a moment in time could be seen in the struggle for the right of women to vote, resulting in 1920 with the pas-sage and implementation of the Nineteenth Amendment to the U.S. Constitution. While those who fought for over 70 years for this right dif-fered over other important issues defining the role of women in other insti-tutions (such as marriage and the labor market), most agreed on the goal of women's suffrage. That coalescence evaporated after passage of the amend-ment, producing a 4-decade period of abeyance (Cott, 1987; Flexner, 1973; Taylor, 1989). There followed a reiteration of male dominance and patriar-chal privilege that largely remained unchallenged until the demand for female labor during World War II created the economic conditions that mit-igated the ideological frame defining women as biologically unsuited for industrial labor. This ebb and flow of challenge and changes in gendering illustrates how the weakening of selectivity filters greatly affected the bal-ance of gendered forces and thus set the stage for the challenges and alter-ations in the state project from the 1940s onward.

Similar dynamics can be seen at work in heteronormative and racial for-mation state projects.

The State and Heteronormative Oppression

Queer theory, in contrast to race and feminist theory, puts poststructuralism rigorously to use in its attempts to outline the ways that people come to be placed into identity categories and the historical ways identities have been constructed, as well as what gets left out when we rely on these simple identity models for discussing nonnormative sexual and gender practices. Since we have organized this idea of "sexual orientation" around gender practices (hetero, homo, and bi categories assume that sexual orientation can be reduced to the gender of the identified person and the object[s] of their affection), queer theorists stress that we cannot isolate oppression around sexuality from gender. Further, people are disciplined and identities are constructed in often similar ways due to nonnormative sexual *and* gender practices. This opens up queer investigations beyond lesbian, bisexual, and gay identity models to include the experiences of nonnormative gender practices and performances like transgender people, drag queens/kings, gender queers, and so on, as well as sexual practices that are not necessarily organized around gender at all (e.g., polyamory; bondage and discipline, dominance and submission, and sadism and masochism or BDSM; sex work).

One of the ways that investigations into state projects and heteronormative oppression have been articulated by researchers is through the concept of *sexual citizenship* (see, e.g., Evans, 1993). Sexual citizenship troubles the assumed divide between the public and private spheres, which typically relegates the sexual to the private sphere—thus outside of the purview of public policy and state initiatives. This functions as a selectivity filter that can serve as a barrier to sexual minorities having their grievances heard in the formation of public policy. But public policy, as researchers have demonstrated, can curtail access to full citizenship rights for sexual minorities.

Perhaps one of the most obvious examples of this is in state projects around kinship—especially marriage. Indeed, access to marriage and the state benefits that come with it seem, at the outset, to be a very basic requirement for full citizenship—particularly where kinship intersects with state policy. Married partners have access to over one thousand legal rights that are denied to nonmarried persons/partnerships (e.g., immigration and residency for partners from other countries; joint parenting and adopting; benefits such as Social Security and Medicare; joint insurance policies for home, auto, and health; wrongful death benefits for a surviving partner and children). Yet, marriage laws in most countries restrict the institution to opposite sex partnerships.

Further, in the United States, one can see how state projects around kinship and marriage have historically been shaped by oppressions that become embedded in governing structures. For example, anti-miscegenation laws prohibited marriage between whites and blacks. Likewise, before the Civil War, slaves were not allowed to marry at all. And before the year 2000, no gay or lesbian couples were legally recognized in any state in the United States. Slowly, however, this has been changing as a result of changes in the balance of political and institutional forces around gay and lesbian struggles for access to marriage.

Many states began seeing large mobilizations in support of same-sex marriage, challenging the state's right to limit these legal partnerships. For example, in Connecticut, Love Makes a Family mobilized community resources around this support, staging protests, organizing letter-writing campaigns, and holding educational and community events to teach the public about the concerns of lesbians and gays who wanted access to marriage rights (Love Makes a Family, 2009). The state, in turn, under Bill Clinton, signed the Defense of Marriage Act (DOMA) into law to roll back some of these efforts. DOMA defined marriage as a legal union between one man and one woman for the purpose of all federal law. Thus, while individual states could allow legal marriages within their state's borders, other states did not need to recognize these unions, and federal laws and benefits were denied to same-sex marriages (see DOMA Watch, 2008).

As we see with racialized and gendered discrimination, cultural and ideological frames of "normalcy" come into play in these public policy debates. That is, opponents of same-sex marriage mobilize arguments that same-sex relationships are "abnormal" or "unnatural" in order to frame the debate in ways that fundamentally alter the lens of the debate from discrimination and exclusion to "natural" and "normal" cultural and ideological frames of reference that exclude same-sex partnerships. This becomes further complexified by queer theoretical models that argue for the legitimacy of all nonnormative sexual practices.

Indeed, even the legalization of same-sex marriages would continue to exclude multipartnered (non-monogamous) relationships or families of choice that may not be based on romantic involvement and/or relationships. This is because of the assumption that dyadic, monogamous relationships are natural and normal despite the existence of many different kinds of multiple partnerships that fall outside of this normative, patterned expectation. Thus, queer theorists often point to the concept of "normal" itself to critique how we have come to police the sexual and gender practices of others, as well as ourselves (see, especially, Warner, 1999).

This has led to research into the ways in which the state creates legal barriers to free sexual expression of all kinds. Again, since queer theoretical perspectives include investigations into all sexual minorities, then sexual and/or gender practices that fall outside of our heteronormative assumptions but may not necessarily be organized around gender (as in lesbian, gay, bisexual, transgender, and queer, or LGBTQ, models) are included in queer research. This allows us to look into the ways that the state legislates against practices such as BDSM, sex work, non-monogamy, and so on.

For example, in the United Kingdom, it is not legally possible to consent to bodily harm. Thus, any consensual sexual act involving bodily harm is an actionable offense according to the state. This policy led, in one case, to a man being convicted of aiding and abetting in his own assault (see Sadist, 2006, p. 180). Similarly, in Italy, anyone willingly causing "injury" to another is subject to legal penalty. Likewise, in Austria, the law allows for consent in bodily injury except where it offends "moral sensibilities." In the United States, laws surrounding sexual practices differ widely depending on the state and sometimes even the county and/or city in which they occur.

As we saw in the debate over same-sex marriage, cultural and ideological frames of "normalcy" are often employed in the disciplining of consensual sexual practices such as BDSM. As well, ideas of moral rightness and correctness are mobilized to defend normative assumptions about sexual and/or gender practices from cultural as well as legal change. And these frames are used to keep attempts to limit state involvement in nonnormative sexual practices out of public debate.

While there has been a rise in BDSM community organization (sometimes referred to as the "leather community") and attempts have been made to mobilize political and economic resources around changing the legal status of various BDSM practices, this particular struggle has not made much inroad into public debate. Part of this might be due to the ways that sexual identity has been constructed in our society. Indeed, BDSM is typically not even considered a "sexual orientation" due to the fact that it is not organized around gender. This can lead to the mistaken assumption that people who engage in BDSM practices are not actually sexual minorities because there is not a culturally available identity category for them. Thus, the discursive frames that have been historically created in the history of sexuality can also serve as selectivity filters for what gets discussed and what gets ignored in state policy.

As well, notions surrounding equality and domination can preclude some communities from involving themselves in a given struggle, such as the fight for the legal right to free sexual expression as it relates to BDSM practices. Because of this, BDSM has caused a split in feminist theorizing and organizing about the nature of the claims surrounding these practices. Some feminists, for example, have claimed that BDSM represents the internalization and eroticization of a culture based on coercion and control. Therefore, to these feminists, BDSM itself is a practice that reinforces the structured domination so common in patriarchal societies. However, other feminists, often referring to themselves as "pro-sex" feminists, argue that power is not so simple and that consensual sexual practices that "play" with power can actually lead to a deeper appreciation for, and understanding of, the complex ways that power operates in our world. These internal disagreements also have effects on the ability of communities to seek support from other social movements in their attempts to effect changes in state policies as they change the balance of institutional political forces.

Similar processes can be seen at work in struggles over social viability for people who transgress our binary understanding of gender. Indeed, notions of "normalcy" and "naturalness" are mobilized to delegitimize the demands of transgender people, intersex people (people born with male and female sexual organs), and genderqueers (those who completely fall outside of our binary construction of gender). Similarly, some feminists have rejected claims made by transgender people based on essentialist notions of what it means to be a "real" woman (see, e.g., Raymond, 1979), while many feminists accept that if gender is a social construction, then "womanhood" is a social category available to people who might be born biologically "male" or intersex.

While many of the legal claims made by gender-variant people have been centered around simple social viability (e.g., access to public bathrooms, personal gender assignment on legal identifications), the gender-variant community has also struggled to get protections under nondiscrimination laws. Such laws have successfully been passed in 13 states in the United States, and there are proposals for such bills in 20 states. These have come as a result of successful challenges to state policy by the gender-variant community and their allies.

An interesting feature of these debates has been the ways that medicalizing discourses have served as selectivity filters within policy discussions. The *Diagnostic and Statistical Manual of Mental Disorders* (or *DSM*, which is utilized by psychologists and psychiatrists) lists "gender identity disorder" as a mental illness. This effectively frames the problem around those notions of "mental illness" rather than questioning the utility of our binary construction of gender in most modern societies (despite evidence of societies with much more flexible notions around gender and many different available categories for gender than just "woman" and "man").

At play here, then, are the selectivity filters used to frame gender-variant people as "mentally ill" as well as the balance of institutional and political forces being affected by ruptures in progressive movements, such as feminism, which might be seen as natural allies in the fight for transgender rights. Thus, the medicalizing discourses used to treat gender variance as an "illness" that might be "cured" limit the ability of social movements to pressure the state to protect gender-variant people from discrimination. Likewise, ruptures in movement alliances can weaken the ability of gender-variant people to mobilize resources in order to struggle for social viability and protection from discriminatory practices.

Like feminism, part of the struggle of queer movements is toward weakening the selectivity filters that create barriers to inclusion in state policy. Similar objectives are at work in movements that attempt to affect state policy around racialized oppression.

The State and Racialized Oppression

Research in race theory parallels many of the issues raised in feminist state theory and suggests a similar challenge to state theory that focuses exclusively on economic and class relations and oppression. For example, analysts using *racial formation theory* (Haney Lopez, 1996; Ignatiev, 1995; Omi & Winant, 1990; Winant, 1994, 2000) emphasize that conceptualizations of race as a matter of biology have no meaning. Instead, they argue, "race" is *socially* constructed, the product of ongoing political struggles over its very meaning and its implications for people's political, social, and economic rights (Stevens, 1999; Yanow, 2003). This analysis implies a role of the state in the process of socially constructing race, since the state is involved in much policy making and political maneuvering relative to racialized issues. As such, the state is a *racial state* (Calavita, 2005; Goldberg, 2002). Other observers are more explicit: Rather than a racial state in society, the state is a *racist state*, in which racialized inequalities are embedded in the very structure of the state (Feagin, 2001).

At the very least, the state has clearly been an arena for battles over rights, sparked by a claims process challenge posed by civil rights movements. Much like the gendering claims process described by Peattie and Rein (1983), the racial formation claims process involves a struggle over shifting the line between the natural or biological and the artificial or political. How much of racialized inequality and oppression is simply a matter of biology, wherein one race (whites) is inherently genetically superior and all others genetically inferior (see, e.g., Herrnstein & Murray, 1994) and therefore immutable and nonresponsive to reform policy? How much of racialized inequality and oppression is more a matter of social constructions that therefore can be challenged and altered with political struggle and legislation? Historically, civil rights movements around the world have set such claims processes in motion and challenged the racial regimes that are "steeped in discriminatory or exclusionist traditions" (Winant, 2000, pp. 177–178), much like feminist claims processes have challenged gender regimes.

Contemporary racial theory has had difficulty explaining persistent racial inequality and oppression that legislative reform by the state should have been expected to eliminate. For example, *ethnicity-based theories* (see Smith, 2001) of race, which view race as a culturally rooted notion of identity, expect integration, equal opportunity, and assimilation to be the antidotes to prejudice and discrimination: The more contact we all have with one another, the more we will understand, appreciate, and accept one another as equals. However, ethnicity-based theories of race are limited by the fact that despite civil rights legislation, serious structural obstacles persist to limit the success of legislation, which may have mandated the social and political rights of individuals to be included but did not mandate the substantive economic resources necessary for accessing those rights (Lipsitz, 1998; Massey & Denton, 1993). Furthermore, the notion of assimilation was predicated on people of color willingly assimilating to white dominant cultural norms, a prospect that was less than appealing to many. The result of this limitation of ethnicity-based theory is the production of analyses that blame people of color themselves for adhering to a race consciousness that harms their ability to assimilate (Thernstrom & Thernstrom, 1997) or that reasserts the importance of defending a "national culture" threatened by immigration and integration (Balibar & Wallerstein, 1991; Taguieff, 2001).

Class-based analyses of race saw racial conflict as an arena in which class-based struggles were played out: Limited resources and opportunities drove a wedge between members of the same class who were differentiated by their membership in different racial groups and pitted them one against the other (Bonacich, 1972, 1976; Frymer, 2008; Gordon, Reich, & Edwards, 1982; Reich, 1981; C. A. Wilson, 1996). These analysts expected class consciousness to override the racial divide and legislation like affirmative action to correct the effects of prior discrimination. However, that class consciousness has not evolved to transplant race consciousness; indeed, as gainful employment opportunities become scarcer, growing competition causes whites to increasingly seek to protect the invisible privileges of whiteness (McIntosh, 1992) and to resist affirmative action programs, making it more difficult to recognize their common class position with people of color.

Where ethnicity-based and class-based analyses of race and racial inequality focus on individuals in racial groups or the groups themselves, *racial formation theory* focuses on the state and political processes that socially construct the meaning of race. Rather than being an immutable, stable construct of clearly defined categories and dimensions, race becomes an ongoing, shifting process in which meanings, identities, dimensions, rights, and oppression are constantly contested and reformulated politically. Racial formation processes are subject to the discursive and interpretational perspectives and actions of a wide range of actors, from individuals to groups and social movements as well as to structures and institutions, history and politics—both national and international. Here, the state is both an arena and an actor, engaged in these struggles over legislation and meaning.

Like much of the gender and state literature, the literature of race and the state tends to de-emphasize the state's use and sanction of violence in the reproduction of systems of racial inequality and oppression in the racial state (see, e.g., James, 1996, 2000). The state frequently uses racial profiling against people of color in policing, for example, and has historically tolerated lynching of African Americans at the hands of white vigilantes, allowing acquittals of lynchers by all-white juries. Jury selection processes that routinely reject the seating of jurists of color have been challenged in many states as racist and therefore unconstitutional in denying people of color the right to due process and a trial by a jury of peers. This practice of jury selection continues today, contributing in no small way to the overrepresentation of African Americans and Latinos in jail and on death row. In essence, when the state sanctions racism in court proceedings and in policing, it is in fact participating in an institutionalized lynching. And when state policy denies convicted felons the right to vote for life, it is compounding the violence by disenfranchising a substantial segment of the population of color, ensuring a hardening of systems of racial inequality that reinforces white privilege (Uggen & Manza, 2002).

Yet, as powerful as the racial state is, it is nonetheless like the patriarchal state, not inexorable. It is subject to pressures from below to alter and change the form and content of racial formation processes. This becomes evident in the ebb and flow of racial formation state projects.

Racial Formation State Projects

State projects of racial formation contribute to the social construction of race through legislation, policy implementation, and judicial determinations governing such issues as slavery, segregation and integration, civil rights (including enfranchisement of African Americans in the political process), affirmative action, multilingualism, immigration, and census definitions and redefinitions of racialized categories. These policies, as entries into the state project of racial formation, affect the social construction of race insofar as they participate in redefining the meaning and social significance of race, thereby affecting the life chances of both whites and people of color.

Much of the racial formation state project has served to create and reinforce a social construction of race in a society based on white superiority, such that people of color remain oppressed and subordinate to whites politically, socially, and economically (Brown, 1995; Marable, 1983; Neubeck & Cazenave, 2001; Quadagno, 2000; Reese, 2005). However, there clearly are policies enacted and implemented by the state that alter the social constructions of race such that the social, political, and economic positions of people of color in a racialized society, and thus their life chances, may be improved (see Fording, 2001). What are the dynamics of oppression and resistance? How do these affect the state policies that both perpetuate racial formation state projects enhancing racism and white supremacy and expand the empowerment of people of color, thus challenging and mitigating white dominance?

Several researchers have pointed to the role of the state in reinforcing racist stereotypes that reproduce racial inequality. For example, Marable (1983) has forcefully argued that the racist state has served to underdevelop African Americans in the United States through a combination of constitutional amendments, Supreme Court decisions, and institutionalized cultural practices. These include Article I, Section 2 of the Constitution defining slaves as three-fifths of a human being, voting restrictions based on race, chattel slavery, sharecropping, segregated educational institutions, and so on (see also Omi & Winant, 1990; C. A. Wilson, 1996). More recently, welfare reform, with its provisions concerning workfare, has reproduced racist social constructions in that its implementation has primarily harmed women and children of color. This is because women of color face far more limited opportunities than white women in the labor market as a result of institutionalized racist assumptions about work ethic, intelligence, and ability. The state refused to acknowledge racism in the economic institutions as it aggressively enacted and implemented a Draconian welfare system of benefit denial and short eligibility definitions. The state thus contributed to and reinforced racially constructed (and gendered) inequality and oppression (Lieberman, 1998; Neubeck & Cazenave, 2001; Quadagno, 2000). And most recently, predatory lending practices among banks as standard operating procedures have been found to routinely target populations of color such that home ownership, a central element of the American Dream, is denied people of color through foreclosure and thus racialized wealth inequality is reinforced (Beeman, Glasberg, & Casey, 2010).

Taken together, these policy implementations and interpretations serve to reiterate a social construction of race in a society based on white superiority, such that people of color generally remain subordinate to Euro-Americans politically, economically, and socially. Yet, as we saw in the gendering state project, there are obviously policies enacted and Supreme Court determinations handed down that alter the content of the social construction of race so that the life chances of people of color are improved. The question, then, is as follows: What are the dynamics and the conditions under which the racial state participates in the perpetuation of racial formation state projects that enhance white privilege and racism but that may also produce policies expanding the empowerment of people of color to successfully challenge that privilege?

Cultural and ideological frames form institutional selectivity filters biasing and shaping the racial formation state project. For example, language functions to reinforce white superiority by privileging whiteness as the standard of normal. The very word *race* is defined as a biological category defining human differences, such that physical attributes such as color of skin, texture of hair, or shape of lips or eyes, or socially constructed attributes such as language (i.e., Spanish) or geographical location (particularly Asia, Africa, and Latin America) are presumed to indicate different subspecies of humans. These "subspecies" are then hierarchically arranged with whites at the top of the hierarchy and all others arranged below (see, e.g., Herrnstein & Murray, 1994). Pejorative racial epithets and stereotypes used to describe people of color thus underscore assumptions of biological inferiority. While such pejoratives and stereotypes describing white ethnics clearly exist, these are not based on immutable biological characteristics but rather on perceptions of ethnicity as changeable cultural choices (Moore, 1995; C. A. Wilson, 1996).

Racist stereotypes describing people of color as less intelligent, less educated, more violence prone, and less hardworking than whites become institutionalized in the labor market, where people of color are far more likely than whites to be unemployed and poverty stricken (W. J. Wilson, 1987, 1996). Most pointedly, a recent study compared white with African American and Latino job applicants and found that applicants of color were half as likely as white applicants to be called back for another interview or a job offer, even when white applicants had recent criminal records and jail time (Pager, Western, & Bonikowski, 2009). In addition, people of color are also more likely to be underemployed in menial, lower-autonomy, lower-paying, dead-end jobs in the service sector or in nonmanagerial blue-collar jobs. Even when people of color do find employment in managerial jobs, they face a glass ceiling beyond which it is extremely difficult to rise (Benjamin, 1991; Cose, 1992; Feagin, 1991; Feagin & Sikes, 1994; Tomaskovic-Devey, 1993; Turner, Fix, & Struyk, 1991; U.S. Department of Labor, 1991).

Racist cultural stereotypes are reiterated in educational institutions, where children of color are highly likely to be segregated into school systems with inadequate budgets and facilities (Kozol, 1991). African American children are disproportionately tracked into classes for the "educable mentally retarded," and white children are far more likely to be tracked into programs for the gifted and talented or college bound (Edelman, 1988). Textbooks and other materials tend to be written for a predominantly white Anglo student body, with the historical and cultural contributions of people of color largely ignored or accorded such brief coverage as to imply that these are unimportant and that only whites have done anything significant and positive (Apple & Christian-Smith, 1991; McCarthy & Crichlow, 1993), thus symbolically annihilating people of color.

White superiority ideologies and culture together act as selectivity filters reinforcing a framing of racial formation biasing policy formation and implementation. This prism interacts with the balance of raced forces in a dialectical process producing policy creation and implementation. The ability of people of color to gain advantageous policy is shaped by a claims process similar to that in gendering processes in which the line between the biological or natural and the socially constructed notions of race are shifted. This process is conditioned by the balance of raced forces. People of color are more likely to gain passage and implementation of advantageous state policy when there is greater unity of perspective among a large number of people of color (and often with the support of whites, an indication of a lack of unity among whites) who are organized in formal organizations and networks to address racism and racial inequality. They are more likely to become organized when faced with (or when they perceive) an imminent threat to their life chances. For example, increased incidents of police brutality and violent hate crimes targeting people of color have elicited organized protests and demands for legal and legislative action, as has mounting evidence of continued segregation and discrimination in schools (Kozol, 1991), labor markets (Kirschenman & Neckerman, 1991; Wilson, 1987), credit access (Glasberg, 1992; Squires, 1994), housing (Beeman, Glasberg, & Casey, 2010), and the location of toxic waste sites (Bryant & Mohai, 1992; Bullard, 1983, 1993).

Such efforts to gain advantageous legislation and implementation of policies and programs are more likely to succeed when whites are less unified in their opposition to challenges to white superiority, when there is disunity between state branches or agencies, or when crises in other institutions increase the legitimacy of the demands of people of color. For example, the Constitution's usage of *freedom from* (as opposed to *freedom to*) supports a notion of negative freedom rather than positive freedom: "Positive freedom involves the creation of conditions conducive to human growth and the development and realization of human potentials. . . . Negative freedom is freedom from restraints and from government intrusion" (C. A. Wilson, 1996, p. 29; see also Dollard, 1949; Myrdal, 1948/1975).

The emphasis on freedom creates a cultural filter protecting slavery, discrimination, and racism rather than equality of life chances. This cultural filter remained intact until the Supreme Court altered its patterns of decision making from an emphasis on equal treatment to one of fair and equitable outcomes, signaling disunity between state branches and agencies.

That disunity created an opportunity for an alteration in the balance of racially formed forces, such that an organized civil rights movement could become more empowered to press an agenda of resistance and challenge to racism in the state and society. Civil rights organizations also became highly sophisticated at networking, such that black churches, student organizations such as the Student Nonviolent Coordinating Committee (SNCC), labor unions, and other organizations such as the Congress of Racial Equality (CORE) and the National Association for the Advancement of Colored People (NAACP) commonly operated together in developing strategies to challenge institutional racialized practices and traditions (Morris, 1984). Moreover, the balance of political and institutional forces was further affected by the ability of civil rights groups to create mass disruption through boycotts, sit-ins, marches, and other demonstrations and organized protests (McAdam, 1982; Morris, 1984) as well as riots.

In the 1980s and 1990s, with the civil rights movement in a more quiescent, less militant period of abeyance than in the 1950s to 1970s, backlashes and challenges to the shift in the balance of racially formed forces have intensified and redeployed into seemingly nonracial (i.e., class or economic) policy arenas such as welfare reform and attempts to repeal or undermine affirmative action (see Lieberman, 1998; Quadagno, 1994). The effect of the return to unbiased or neutral concepts like "freedom from Big Government" in a context of a less active and vigilant civil rights movement and a more organized, resource-rich, and motivated backlash movement has been a perpetuation of racism.

Cultural assumptions that people of color (particularly African Americans and Latinos/Latinas) are violent and less intelligent than whites are additionally perpetuated by the disproportionate representation of people of color under the control of the criminal justice system, including those on death row (Culver, 1992; Radelet, 1981); police brutality of people of color on the streets, which is frequently condoned by the failure of courts and police review boards to punish such unequal and brutal misapplication of the law (Cashmore & McLaughlin, 1991); differential treatment of people of color relative to whites in bail settings (Houston & Ewing, 1992); political disenfranchisement of significant proportions of populations of color through criminal justice policies permanently denying voting rights to convicted felons (Manza & Uggen, 2008; Uggen & Manza, 2002); underrepresentation of people of color on juries; and the differential treatment of immigrants and the granting of visas based on racist stereotypes (Cose, 1992), including the notion of Asians as "model minorities" (Chou & Feagin, 2008) in contrast to immigrants from Latin America and Africa who are largely considered undesirables (Haney Lopez, 1996; Rose, 1997; Takaki, 1982; van Dijk, 1993; Zolberg, 1990).

This discussion of the ebb and flow of the social construction of race as the result of the dynamics of racial formation processes informed by cultural frames as selectivity filters and the balance of raced forces suggests the usefulness of an expanded use of Peattie and Rein's (1983) notion of the claims process (see also Koopmans & Statham, 1999). Insofar as race is culturally conceptualized around assumptions regarding the biological bases of human differences, there is a claims process marked by struggles over shifting the line between the natural (biological) and the artificial (socially constructed) meaning of race.

Intersectionality of Racialized, Class-Based, and Gendered Oppression and State Projects

Some observers have begun working on questions concerning the intersectionality of race, class, sexuality, and gender and the state. For example, McCall (2001) found that configurations of inequality are indeed not simply dimensionalized inexorably along gender, racial, and class lines but that the intersection of these along with variations in geographic place has a significant effect on inequalities. She argued that this insight must have an effect on the formulation of anti-inequality policies enacted by the state. While her approach is indeed a refreshing departure from literature that focuses on one or the other of the crucial organizing principles in isolation of the others, her analysis treats these as independent variables whose patterns should enter into the formulation of state policy to address them. What remains to be examined is the interaction between these organizing principles, their intersections, and the interaction between these and state policy. That is, the state may affect as well as be affected by the intersecions of race, class, sexuality, and gender.

Nakano Glenn (2002) explored the intersections of racialized, class, and gendered oppressions in the state's development of immigration and labor policy between the end of Reconstruction and the beginning of World War II. The state wrestled with the meaning of free labor and citizenship at a time when the abolition of slavery deeply altered the nation's social construction of labor and huge waves of immigrants fueled the Industrial Revolution and challenged the notion of who was a rightful citizen. The struggles over the redefinition of these twin state projects pitted blacks against whites in the southern United States, Mexicans against Anglos in the Southwest, and Asians against white planters in Hawaii and produced what she termed "unequal freedom" among workers based on their gender and their varying racialized categories and framed the shape and scope of worker resistance to that oppression.

In contrast, other analyses recognize the need to place race, class, sexuality, and gender at the center of the analysis within the context of the society in which they occur as well as in the larger, global context. For example, studies of colonialism highlight the powerful role of military action and economic practices and sanctions in control of nations (Ferdnance, 1998; Sharma & Kumar, 2003). This required the subjugation of women, people of color, and labor on a grand, global scale. Connell (1997) noted that racial and sexual issues were intertwined in the North Atlantic expansion and immigration policies that gave rise to "a growing fear of miscegenation, a hardening color line, contempt of the colonizers for the sexuality or masculinity of the colonized, and fears of racial swamping . . ." (p. 1523). The contemporary imperialism is more subtle but just as powerful as the internal and external colonialism of Europe and the United States. It takes the guise of humanitarian and economic aid—what some have come to call "neo-liberalism." But the end result continues to be power and control over indigenous populations and reproduction of systems of inequality and oppression.

The intersections of state projects and multiple systems of oppression can also be seen in the United States' "war on terror." This state project affects and is affected by the everyday lived experiences of the working class and the poor and people of color, who are most likely to populate the "all-volunteer" military used to wage war and to pay most dearly for it. Increasingly, reports of the daily oppression of women as soldiers in that same military (through sexual assault, harassment, and discrimination in training and in service) and women left behind who are expected to juggle work and family with little institutional or financial support continue to mount. Gays and lesbians in the military are subjected to unequal treatment and consequences through the application of the "don't ask, don't tell" policy that has allowed various military branches to discharge thousands of otherwise highly valued and critical personnel (including many with the crucial ability to speak Arabic and Farsi when the United States is involved in armed conflicts in both Iraq and Afghanistan). And people of color are most likely to be subject to enhanced scrutiny and profiling, compromised civil liberties and rights, and possible loss of rights indefinitely. Moreover, revised and new policies resulting in restricted immigration, reallocation of budget funds in support of war and away from programs that benefit women, children, and the poor (while promoting tax cuts benefitting the wealthy) are ostensibly aimed at containing terrorism but become entries into racialized, patriarchal, and classist state projects of oppression (see War Times, 2010).

Finally, a contingency analysis of the state and state projects framed in the intersections of systems of oppression must include an analysis of the role of communities of the oppressed in resistance and relationship between them and state projects and policies (Cazenave, 2007; Goodwin & Jasper, 1999; McBride, 2001). When resistance and social movements are included in the analysis of the process, the state no longer remains a monolithic, overriding force; it takes its place, instead, as an actor as well as a structure and an arena of struggle. Social movements of the oppressed commonly incorporate challenges to dominant ideologies and cultural prisms in state projects and thus may affect the framing of policies and practices. The ebb and flow of these intersecting systems of oppression and of the actors within the state as well as among the oppressed contours the process of state projects and the relationship of the state and society.

Summing Up

Literatures in state theory, feminist state theory, queer theory, and race theory share some parallel notions of the relationship between the state and society and the state's role in the production and maintenance of systems of oppression. State projects are dynamic processes of both oppression from above and resistance from below.

The state is a multidimensional structure that includes not only the legislature but also the judiciary, the executive, and administrative state agencies vested with the power to implement and interpret policy on a day-to-day basis. Moreover, the state is also an actor, subject to the same forces and conditions affecting other groups engaged in policy formation and implementation processes, including unity and disunity between and within agencies and institutional organizations, resource mobilization processes, and access to opportunities to create disruption. In addition, cultural lenses and practices operate as selectivity filters that shape and define perceptions leading to policy and implementation. When we consider that systems of oppression and the selectivity filters they help create do not operate one at a time or in isolation of the others, it alerts us that a multidimensional approach will help us to explain class-based as well as gender-based, sexuality-based, and racially based policy by using Jessop's concepts as organizing conceptual tools. These concepts allow us to identify the relationship between the state and class relations as well as that between the state and gendering, sexuality, and racial formation. We can then begin to articulate the conditions under which some policies are more or less likely to develop at particular points in time and some interests are more or less likely to gain power and have their interests addressed.

State projects are not discrete, individual projects that are isolated from each other. Indeed, there are many places where economic state projects intersect with racial formation state projects (such as immigration policy) or gendering state projects intersect with racial formation projects (as in affirmative action policy) or heteronormative projects intersect with gendering state projects (as in marriage laws). Additionally, there are policy arenas where multiple state projects may intersect, as is the case in the welfare "reform" of the 1990s and warfare and homeland security policy in 2003. In the case of welfare reform, what appeared to be an economic issue (work as the antidote to poverty) operates as an entry into gendering state projects where gender is socially constructed relative to class: Poor women are socially constructed as good mothers only if they work in the paid labor force and leave the care of their young children to others; middle-class and affluent mothers, in contrast, are socially constructed as good mothers only if they remain dependent on their male partners and stay at home to care for their own young children. Moreover, such welfare reforms are also part of the racial formation state project since they largely affect women and children of color more harshly than whites and imply that the problems besetting welfare are somehow a function of a racially related culture of poverty. Thus, state projects themselves are not isolated one from the other. Rather, they articulate common and intersecting agendas that contribute to intersecting systems of multiple oppressions. A holistic state theory must account for these multiple systems, where they intersect, and how—as well as recognize that the state is an institution that often has interests of its own.

References

Abramovitz, M. (1996). *Regulating the lives of women: Social welfare policy from colonial times to the present* (Rev. ed.). Boston: South End Press.

Abramovitz, M. (2000). *Under attack: Fighting back: Women and welfare in the United States* (Rev. ed.). New York: Monthly Review Press.

Andersen, M. L. (1993). *Thinking about women: Sociological perspectives on sex and gender*. New York: Macmillan.

Apple, M. W., & Christian-Smith, L. K. (Eds.). (1991). *The politics of the textbook*. New York: Routledge.

Balibar, E., & Wallerstein, I. (1991). *Race, nation, class: Ambiguous identities* (C. Turner, Trans.). London: Verso.

Barrett, M. (1990). *Women's oppression today*. London: Verso.

Barthel, D. (1988). *Putting on appearances: Gender and advertising*. Philadelphia: Temple University Press.

Beeman, A., Glasberg, D. S., & Casey, C. (2010). Whiteness as property: Predatory lending and the reproduction of racialized inequality. *Critical Sociology, 37*(3), 1–23.

Benjamin, L. (1991). *The black elite: Facing the color line in the twilight of the twentieth century*. Chicago: Nelson-Hall.

Blumenfeld, W. J. (Ed.). (1992). *Homophobia: How we all pay the price*. Boston: Beacon Press.

Bock, G., & Thane, P. (Eds.). (1991). *Maternity and gender politics: Women and the rise of the European welfare states, 1880s-1950s*. New York: Routledge.

Bonacich, E. (1972). A theory of ethnic antagonism: The split labor market. *American Sociological Review, 37*, 547–559.

Bonacich, E. (1976). Advanced capitalism and black/white relations in the United States: A split labor market interpretation. *American Sociological Review, 41*, 34–51.

Borchorst, A. (1994). The Scandinavian welfare states: Patriarchal, gender neutral, or woman-friendly? *International Journal of Contemporary Sociology, 31*, 1–23.

Boris, E., & Bardaglio, B. (1983). The transformation of patriarchy: The historic role of the state. In I. Diamond (Ed.), *Families, politics, and public policy* (pp. 70–93). New York: Longman.

Brown, C. (1981). Mothers, fathers, and children: From private to public patriarchy. In L. Sargent (Ed.), *Women and revolution* (pp. 239–268). Boston: South End Press.

Brown, W. (1995). *States of injury: Power and freedom in late modernity*. Princeton, NJ: Princeton University Press.

Brush, L. D. (2003). *Gender and governance*. Walnut Creek, CA: AltaMira Press.

Bryant, B., & Mohai, P. (Eds.). (1992). *Race and the incidence of environmental hazards*. Boulder, CO: Westview Press.

Bullard, R. D. (1983). Solid waste sites and the Houston black community. *Sociological Inquiry, 53*(Spring), 273–288.

Bullard, R. D. (1993). *Confronting environmental racism: Voices from the grassroots*. Boston: South End Press.

Calavita, K. (2005). *Immigrants on the margins: Laws, race and exclusion in southern Europe*. Cambridge, UK: Cambridge University Press.

Cashmore, E., & McLaughlin, E. (Eds.). (1991). *Out of order? Policing black people*. New York: Routledge.

Cazenave, N. (2007). *Impossible democracy: The unlikely success of the war on poverty community action programs*. Albany: State University of New York Press.

Chou, R. S., & Feagin, J. R. (2008). *The myth of the model minority: Asian Americans facing racism*. Boulder, CO: Paradigm Publishers.

Collins, P. H. (1990). *Black feminist thought: Knowledge, consciousness, and the politics of empowerment*. Boston: Unwin Hyman.

Connell, R. W. (1990). The state, gender, and sexual politics. *Theory and Society*. 507–544.

Connell, R. W. (1997). Why is classical theory classical? *American Journal of Sociology, 102*(6), 1511–1557.

Cose, E. (1992). *A nation of strangers: Prejudice, politics, and the populating of America*. New York: William Morrow and Co.

Cott, N. F. (1987). *The grounding of modern feminism.* New Haven, CT: Yale University Press.

Culver, J. (1992). Capital punishment, 1977–1990: Characteristics of the 143 executed. *Sociology and Social Research, 76*(20), 59–61.

Curran, L., & Abrams, L. S. (2000). Making men into dads: Fatherhood, the state, and welfare reform. *Gender & Society, 14*(5), 662–678.

Dollard, J. (1949). *Caste and class in a southern town.* New York: Doubleday.

DOMA Watch. (2008). Retrieved from http://www.domawatch.org/index.php

Domhoff, G. W. (1990). *The power elite and the state: How policy is made in America.* New York: Aldine De Gruyter.

Domhoff, G. W. (1991a). American state autonomy via the military? Another counterattack on a theoretical delusion. *Critical Sociology, 18,* 9–56.

Domhoff, G. W. (1991b). Class, power, and parties during the New Deal: A critique of Skocpol's theory of state autonomy. *Berkeley Journal of Sociology, 36,* 1–49.

Duberman, M. (1993). *Stonewall.* New York: Dutton.

Edelman, M. W. (1988). Growing up black in America. In J. H. Skolnick & E. Currie (Eds.), *Crisis in American institutions* (7th ed., pp. 143–162). Glenview, IL: Scott, Foresman.

Edin, K., & Lein, L. (1996). *Making ends meet: How single mothers survive welfare and low-wage work.* New York: Russell Sage Foundation.

Ehrenreich, B. (1992, February 17). Stamping out a dread scourge. *Time,* p. 88.

Elman, A. R. (2001). Unprotected by the Swedish welfare state revisited: Assessing a decade of reforms for battered women. *Women's Studies International Forum, 24*(1), 39–52.

Enloe, C. (1989). *Bananas, beaches, and bases: Making feminist sense of international politics.* Berkeley: University of California Press.

Enloe, C. (2000). *Maneuvers: The international politics of militarizing women's lives.* Berkeley: University of California Press.

Esping-Andersen, G. (1990). *The three worlds of welfare capitalism.* Princeton, NJ: Princeton University Press.

Evans, D. T. (1993). *Sexual citizenship: The material construction of sexualities.* New York: Routledge.

Feagin, J. R. (1991). The continuing significance of race: Antiblack discrimination in public places. *American Sociological Review, 56,* 101–116.

Feagin, J. R. (2001). *Racist America: Roots, current realities, and future reparations.* New York: Routledge.

Feagin, J. R., & Sikes, M. P. (1994). *Living with racism: The black middle-class experience.* Boston: Beacon Press.

Ferdnance, T. (1998). Colonialism and the economic demise and transformation or northern Nigeria's slave fundamental extractors from 1903 to the 1920s. *Journal of Asian and African Studies, 33*(3), 223–241.

Ferree, M. M, & Hess, B. (1994). *Controversy, coalition, and consolidation: The new feminist movement across three decades of change.* Boston: Twayne.

Flexner, E. (1973). *Century of struggle*. New York: Atheneum Publishers.

Fording, R. C. (2001). The political response to black insurgency: A critical test of competing theories of the state. *American Political Science Review, 95*(1), 115–130.

Fraser, N., & Gordon, L. (1994). Dependency demystified: Inscriptions of power in a keyword of the welfare state. *Social Politics, 1*, 14–31.

Frymer, P. (2008). *Black and blue: African Americans, the labor movement, and the decline of the Democratic Party*. Princeton, NJ: Princeton University Press.

Gilbert, J., & Howe, C. (1991). Beyond "state vs. society": Theories of the state and New Deal agricultural policies. *American Sociological Review, 56*, 204–220.

Glasberg, D. S. (1992). Race, class, and differential application of bank bailouts: An emerging sociology of the politics of finance. *Critical Sociology, 18*(2), 51–76.

Glasberg, D. S., & Skidmore, D. L. (1997). *Corporate welfare policy and the welfare state: Bank deregulation and the savings and loan bailout*. New York: Aldine De Gruyter.

Goldberg, D. T. (2002). *The racial state*. Malden, MA: Blackwell Publishing.

Goodwin, J. L. (1997). *Gender and the politics of welfare reform*. Chicago: Chicago University Press.

Goodwin, J. L., & Jasper, J. M. (1999). Caught in a winding, snarling vine: The structural bias of political process theory. *Sociological Forum, 14*, 27–54.

Gordon, D. M., Reich, M., & Edwards, R. (1982). *Segmented work, divided workers: The historical transformations of labor in the United States*. New York: Cambridge University Press.

Gordon, L. (Ed.). (1990). *Women, the state, and welfare*. Madison: University of Wisconsin Press.

Gordon, L. (1994). *Pitied but not entitled: Single mothers and the history of welfare*. New York: The Free Press.

Greenberger, M. (1980). The effectiveness of federal law prohibiting sex discrimination in the United States. In R. S. Ratner (Ed.), *Equal employment policy for women* (pp. 108–128). Philadelphia: Temple University Press.

Gustafsson, S. (1994). Childcare and types of welfare states. In D. Sainsbury (Ed.), *Gendering welfare states* (pp. 45–61). Thousand Oaks, CA: Sage.

Haney, L. A. (2000). Feminist state theory: Applications to jurisprudence, criminology, and the welfare state. *Annual Review of Sociology, 26*, 641–666.

Haney Lopez, I. F. (1996). *White by law: The legal construction of race*. New York: New York University Press.

Hartmann, H. (1976). Capitalism, patriarchy, and job segregation by sex. *Signs, 3*, 137–169.

Hernstein, R. J., & Murray, C. (1994). *The bell curve: Intelligence and class structure in American life*. New York: Basic Books.

Hobson, B. (1994). Solo mothers, social policy regimes, and the logics of gender. In D. Sainsbury (Ed.), *Gendering welfare states* (pp. 170–187). Thousand Oaks, CA: Sage.

Hochschild, A., & Machung, A. (1997). *The second shift: Working parents and the revolution at home*. New York: Viking Penguin.

Hooks, G. (1991). *Forging the military-industrial complex: World War II's Battle of the Potomac*. Urbana: University of Illinois Press.

Houston, B., & Ewing, J. (1992, May 17). Racial inequality still evident in setting of bail. *Hartford Courant*, pp. A1, A6.

Huber, E., & Stephens, J. D. (2000). Partisan governance, women's employment, and the Social Democratic service state. *American Sociological Review, 65*(3), 323–342.

Ignatiev, N. (1995). *How the Irish became white*. New York: Routledge.

James, J. (1996). *Resisting state violence: Radicalism, gender, and race in U.S. culture*. Minneapolis: University of Minnesota Press.

James, J. (2000). The dysfunctional and the disappearing: Democracy, race and imprisonment. *Social Identities, 6*(4), 483–492.

Jenkins, J. C., & Brents, B. G. (1989). Social protest, hegemonic competition, and social reforms. *American Sociological Review, 54*, 891–909.

Jessop, B. (1990). *State theory: Putting the capitalist state in its place*. University Park: Penn State University Press.

Kamerman, S. B. (1984). Women, children, at poverty: Public policies and female-headed households in industrialized countries. In B. C. Gelpi, N. C. M. Hartsock, C. C. Novak, & M. H. Strober (Eds.), *Women and poverty* (pp. 41–63). Chicago: Chicago University Press.

Kessler-Harris, A. (1980). *Women have always worked: A historical overview*. New York: Feminist Press.

Kingsolver, B. (1989). *Holding the line: Women in the great Arizona mine strike of 1983*. Ithaca, NY: ILR Press.

Kirschenman, J., & Neckerman, K. (1991). "We'd love to hire them, but . . .": The meaning of race for employers. In C. Jencks & P. Peterson (Eds.), *The urban underclass* (pp. 203–232). Washington, DC: Brookings Institution Press.

Klatch, R. E. (1988). The New Right and its women. *Society, 25*(3), 30–38.

Koopmans, R., & Statham, P. (1999). Challenging the liberal nation-state? Postnationalism, multiculturalism, and the collective claims making of migrants and ethnic minorities in Britain and Germany. *American Journal of Sociology, 105*(3), 652–696.

Korpi, W. (2000). Faces of inequality: Gender, class, and patterns of inequalities in different types of welfare states. *Social Politics, 7*(2), 127–191.

Koven, S., & Michel, S. (Eds.). (1993). *Mothers of the new world: Maternalistic policies and the origins of the welfare state*. New York: Routledge.

Kozol, J. (1991). *Savage inequalities*. New York: Crown.

Leira, A. (1992). *Welfare states and working mothers: The Scandinavian experience*. New York: Cambridge University Press.

Levine, R. F. (1988). *Class struggle and the New Deal: Industrial labor, industrial capital, and the state*. Lawrence: University of Kansas Press.

Lewis, J. (1992). Gender and the development of welfare regimes. *Journal of European Social Policy*, *3*, 159–173.

Lieberman, R. (1998). *Shifting the color line: Race and the American welfare state*. Cambridge, MA: Harvard University Press.

Lipsitz, G. (1998). *The possessive investment in whiteness: How white people profit from identity politics*. Philadelphia: Temple University Press.

Love Makes a Family. (2009). Retrieved from http://www.lmfct.org

Luker, K. (1984). *Abortion and the politics of motherhood*. Berkeley: University of California Press.

Luker, K. (1998). Sex, social hygiene, and the state: The double-edged sword of social reform. *Theory and Society*, *27*(5), 601–634.

MacKinnon, C. A. (1989). *Toward a feminist theory of the state*. Cambridge, MA: Harvard University Press.

Mansbridge, J. J. (1986). *Why we lost the ERA*. Chicago: University of Chicago Press.

Manza, J., & Uggen, C. (2008). *Locked out: Felon disenfranchisement and American democracy*. Oxford, UK: Oxford University Press.

Marable, M. (1983). *How capitalism underdeveloped black America: Problems in race, political economy and society*. Boston: South End Press.

Mason, C. (2002). *Killing for life: The apocalyptic narrative of pro-life politics*. Ithaca, NY: Cornell University Press.

Massey, D. S., & Denton, N. A. (1993). *American apartheid*. Cambridge, MA: Harvard University Press.

McAdam, D. (1982). *Political process and the development of black insurgency, 1930–1970*. Chicago: University of Chicago Press.

McBride, D. S. (Ed.). (2001). *Abortion, politics, women's movements, and the democratic state: A comparative study of state feminism*. Oxford, UK: Oxford University Press.

McCall, L. (2001). *Complex inequality: Gender, class, and race in the new economy*. New York: Routledge.

McCammon, H. (1994). Disorganizing and reorganizing conflict: Outcomes of the state's legal regulation of the strike since the Wagner Act. *Social Forces*, *72*(4), 1011–1049.

McCann, M. W. (1994). *Rights at work: Pay equity reform and the politics of legal mobilization*. Chicago: University of Chicago Press.

McCarthy, C., & Crichlow, W. (Eds.). (1993). *Race, identity, and representation in education*. New York: Routledge.

McIntosh, M. (1978). The state and the oppression of women. In A. Kuhn & A. Wolpe (Eds.), *Feminism and materialism* (pp. 254–289). London: Routledge and Kegan Paul.

McIntosh, P. (1992). White privilege and male privilege. In M. L. Andersen & P. H. Collins (Eds.), *Race, class, and gender* (pp. 70–81). Belmont, CA: Wadsworth.

Mies, M. (1998). *Patriarchy and accumulation on a worldwide scale*. London: Zed Books.

Miliband, R. (1973). Poulantzas and the capitalist state. *New Left Review*, 82, 83–92.

Millett, K. (1969). *Sexual politics.* New York: Doubleday.

Mink, G. (1994). *Wages of motherhood: Inequality in the welfare state, 1917–1942.* Ithaca, NY: Cornell University Press.

Moore, R. B. (1995). Racism in the English language. In P. S. Rothenberg (Ed.), *Race, class, and gender in the United States* (3rd ed., pp. 376–386). New York: St. Martin's Press.

Morris, A. D. (1984). *The origins of the civil rights movement: Black communities organizing for social change.* New York: Free Press.

Muncy, R. (1991). *Creating a female dominion in American reform, 1890–1935.* New York: Oxford University Press.

Myrdal, G. (1948/1975). *An American dilemma: The Negro problem and modern democracy* (Vol. I). New York: Pantheon.

Nakano Glenn, E. (2002). *Unequal freedom: How race and gender shaped American citizenship and labor.* Cambridge, MA: Harvard University Press.

Nelson, B. J. (1990). The origins of the two-channel welfare state: Workmen's compensation and mothers' aid. In L. Gordon (Ed.), *Women, the state, and welfare* (pp. 123–151). Madison: University of Wisconsin Press.

Neubeck, K. J. , & Cazenave, N. (2001). *Welfare racism: Playing the race card against America's poor.* New York: Routledge.

O'Connor, J. S. (1993). Gender, class, and citizenship in the comparative analysis of welfare state regimes: Theoretical and methodological issues. *British Journal of Sociology*, 44, 501–518.

O'Connor, J. S., Orloff, A. S., & Shaver, S. (1999). *States, markets, and families: Gender, liberalism and social policy in Australia, Canada, Great Britain, and the United States.* New York: Cambridge University Press.

Omi, M., & Winant, H. (1990). *Racial formation in the United States: From the 1960s to the 1990s.* New York: Routledge.

Orloff, A. (1993). Gender and the social rights of citizenship: The comparative analysis of gender relations and welfare states. *American Sociological Review*, 58, 303–328.

Orloff, A. (1996). Gender and the welfare state. *Annual Review of Sociology*, 22, 51–78.

Padavic, I., & Reskin, B. F. (2002). *Women and men at work.* Thousand Oaks, CA: Pine Forge Press.

Pager, D., Western, B., & Bonikowski, B. (2009). Discrimination in a low-wage labor market: A field experiment. *American Sociological Review*, 74(5), 777–799.

Peattie, L., & Rein, M. (1983). *Women's claims: A study in political economy.* Oxford, UK: Oxford University Press.

Petchesky, R. P. (1984). *Abortion and woman's choice: The state, sexuality, and reproductive freedom.* New York: Longman.

Piven, F. F. (1990). Ideology and the state: Women, power and the welfare state. In L. Gordon (Ed.), *Women, the state, and welfare* (pp. 250–264). Madison: University of Wisconsin Press.

Poulantzas, N. (1978). *State, power, and socialism*. London: Verso.

Prechel, H. (1990). Steel and the state: Industry politics and business policy formation, 1940–1989. *American Sociological Review, 55,* 648–668.

Prechel, H. (2000). *Big business and the state: Historical transitions and corporate transformations 1880s–1990s*. Albany: State University of New York Press.

Pringle, R., & Watson, S. (1992). Women's interests and the poststructuralist state. In M. Barret & A. Phillips (Eds.), *Destabilizing theory* (pp. 53–73). Stanford, CA: Stanford University Press.

Quadagno, J. (1992). Social movements and state transformation: Labor unions and racial conflict in the war on poverty. *American Sociological Review, 57,* 616–634.

Quadagno, J. (1994). *The color of welfare: How racism undermined the war on poverty*. New York: Oxford University Press.

Quadagno, J. (2000). Another face of inequality: Racial and ethnic exclusion in the welfare state. *Social Politics, 7*(2), 229–237.

Radelet, M. L. (1981). Racial characteristics and the death penalty. *American Sociological Review, 46,* 918–927.

Raymond, J. (1979). *The transexual empire*. Boston: Beacon Press.

Reese, E. (2005). *Backlash against welfare mothers: Past and present*. Berkeley: University of California Press.

Reich, M. (1981). *Racial inequality*. Princeton, NJ: Princeton University Press.

Reskin, B. F., & Hartmann, H. I. (Eds). (1986). *Women's work, men's work: Sex segregation on the job*. New York: National Academy Press.

Reskin, B. F., & Roos, P. A. (1990). *Job queues, gender queues: Explaining women's inroads into male occupations*. Philadelphia: Temple University Press.

Rich, A. (1995). *Of woman born: Motherhood as experience and institution*. New York: W. W. Norton & Company.

Rose, P. I. (1997). *Tempest-lost: Race, immigration, and the dilemmas of diversity*. Oxford, UK: Oxford University Press.

Rothman, B. K. (1982). *In labor: Women and power in the birthplace*. New York: W. W. Norton & Company.

Ruggie, M. (1984). *The state and working women*. Princeton, NJ: Princeton University Press.

Sadist, M. (2006). *B.D.S.M. for dummies*. Raleigh, NC: Lulu Press.

Sainsbury, D. (Ed.). (1994). *Gendering welfare states*. Thousand Oaks, CA: Sage.

Sainsbury, D. (1996). *Gender, equality, and welfare states*. New York: Cambridge University Press.

Sapiro, V. (1990). The gender bias of American social policy. In L. Gordon (Ed.), *Women, the state, and welfare* (pp. 36–54). Madison: University of Wisconsin Press.

Schur, E. M. (1984). *Labeling women deviant: Gender, stigma, and social control*. New York: Random House.

Sharma, S., & Kumar, S. (2003). The military backbone of globalisation. *Race and Class, 44*(3), 23–40.

Shaver, S. (1993). Body rights, social rights, and the liberal welfare state. *Critical Social Policy, 13,* 66–93.

Sklar, K. K. (1993). The historical foundations of women's power in the creation of the American welfare state. In S. Koven & S. Michel (Eds.), *Mothers of the new world: Maternalistic policies and the origins of the welfare state* (pp. 43–93). New York: Routledge.

Skocpol, T. (1988). The limits of the New Deal system and the roots of the contemporary welfare dilemmas. In M. Weir, A. S. Orloff, & T. Skocpol (Eds.), *The politics of social policy in the United States* (pp. 293–311). Princeton, NJ: Princeton University Press.

Skocpol, T. (1992). *Protecting soldiers and mothers: The political origins of social policy in the United States.* Cambridge, MA: Harvard University Press.

Smith, D. E. (1990). *Texts, facts, and femininity: Exploring the relations of ruling.* New York: Routledge.

Smith, D. E. (1999). *Writing the social: Critique, theory, and investigations.* Toronto: University of Toronto Press.

Smith, R. M. (2001). Citizenship and the politics of people-building. *Citizenship Studies, 5*(1), 73–96.

Sorrels, B. D. (1983). *The nonsexist communicator: Solving the problems of gender and awkwardness in modern English.* Englewood Cliffs, NJ: Prentice Hall.

Squires, G. (1994). *Capital and communities in black and white.* Albany: State University of New York Press.

Stevens, J. (1999). *Reproducing the state.* Princeton, NJ: Princeton University Press.

Sutton, T. (1992, May–June). Bustin' loose: Why big breasts are back. *Utne Reader,* pp. 60–61.

Taguieff, P.-A. (2001). *The force of prejudice: On racism and its doubles* (H. Melehy, Trans.). Minneapolis: University of Minnesota Press.

Takaki, R. (1982). Reflections on racial patterns in America: An historical perspective. In W. A. VanHorne & T. V. Tonnesen (Eds.), *Ethnicity and public policy* (Vol. 1, pp. 1–23). Milwaukee: University of Wisconsin System American Ethnic Studies Coordinating Committee/Urban Corridor Consortium.

Taylor, V. (1989). Social movement continuity: The women's movement in abeyance. *American Sociological Review, 54,* 761–775.

Thernstrom, S., & Thernstrom, A. (1997). *America in black and white: One nation, indivisible; race in modern America.* New York: Simon & Schuster.

Tomaskovic-Devey, D. (1993). *Gender and racial inequality at work.* Ithaca, NY: ILR Press.

Tuchman, G., Daniels, A. K., & Benet, J. (Eds.). (1978). *Hearth and home: Images of women in the mass media.* New York: Oxford University Press.

Turner, M. A., Fix, M., & Struyk, R. J. (1991). *Opportunities denied, opportunities diminished: Racial discrimination in hiring.* Washington, DC: Urban Institute Press.

Uggen, C., & Manza, J. (2002). Democratic contraction? Political consequences of felon disenfranchisement in the United States. *American Sociological Review, 67*(6), 777–803.

U.S. Census Bureau. (2009). *Statistical abstracts, 2009.* Retrieved from http://www.census.gov/compendia/statab

U.S. Department of Labor. (1991). *A report on the glass ceiling initiative.* Washington, DC: U.S. Government Printing Office.

van Dijk, T. A. (1993). *Elite discourse and racism.* Newbury Park, CA: Sage.

Wallach, L., & Sforza, M. (1999, January 25). NAFTA at 5. *The Nation,* p. 7.

Warner, M. (1999). *The trouble with normal: Sex, politics, and the ethics of queer life.* Cambridge, MA: Harvard University Press.

War Times. (2010). Retrieved from http://www.war-times.org

Weinstein, J. (1968). *The corporate ideal in the liberal state, 1900–1918.* Boston: Beacon Press.

Wilson, C. A. (1996). *Racism: From slavery to advanced capitalism.* Thousand Oaks, CA: Sage.

Wilson, W. J. (1987). *The truly disadvantaged.* Chicago: University of Chicago Press.

Wilson, W. J. (1996). *When work disappears: The world of the new urban poor.* New York: Knopf.

Winant, H. (1994). *Racial conditions: Politics, theory, comparisons.* Minneapolis: University of Minnesota Press.

Winant, H. (2000). Race and race theory. *Annual Review of Sociology, 26,* 169–185.

Wolf, N. (1991). *The beauty myth.* New York: Morrow.

Yanow, D. (2003). *Constructing "race" and "ethnicity" in America: Category-making in public policy and administration.* Armonk, NY: M. E. Sharpe.

Yuval-Davis, N. (1997). *Gender and nation.* Thousand Oaks, CA: Sage.

Zolberg, A. R. (1990). Reforming the back door: The Immigration Reform and Control Act of 1986 in historical perspective. In V. Yans-McLaughlin (Ed.), *Immigration reconsidered: History, sociology, and politics* (pp. 315–339). Oxford, UK: Oxford University Press.

Zylan, Y. (2000). Maternalism redefined: Gender, the state, and the politics of day care, 1945–1962. *Gender & Society, 14*(5), 608–629.

Index

Page numbers followed by f *or* t *indicate figures or tables*

About the Authors

Davita Silfen Glasberg is a professor and department head in the Department of Sociology at the University of Connecticut, and former director of the University of Connecticut Human Rights Minor Program. She has taught both undergraduate and graduate courses and authored or coauthored five books and dozens of journal articles on issues of power and oppression, finance capital and the state, and inequality and diversity. She is currently working as coeditor (with William T. Armaline and Bandana Purkayastha) on an edited collection of articles on human rights in the United States, as well as coauthoring (with Angie Beeman and Colleen Casey) a study of predatory lending and patterns of racialized inequality. Her special interests are human rights, political sociology, political economy, and systems of inequality and oppression.

Deric Shannon is a PhD candidate in sociology at the University of Connecticut. He is a coeditor of *Contemporary Anarchist Studies*, the first anthology of anarchist scholarly work, as well as the author of numerous books, chapters, and journal articles, typically on radical political thought. He is an assistant editor of the academic journal *Theory in Action* and serves on the Board of Directors for the Transformative Studies Institute. He is the director of Transformative Radio (http://www.transformativeradio.org), a radical web radio station featuring lectures and interviews for those interested in social justice, tangible resistance, and radical change. His current research interests include culture and social change, sexualities and queer studies, and radical political traditions.